MAGIC IN MEDIEVAL ROMANCE
FROM CHRÉTIEN DE TROYES TO GEOFFREY CHAUCER

IN THIS SERIES

Bonnie Millar, *The* Siege of Jerusalem *in its physical, literary and historical contexts*

Anne Marie D'Arcy, *Wisdom and the Grail: The image of the vessel in the* Queste del Saint Graal *and Malory's* Tale of the Sankgreall

Michelle Sweeney, *Magic in medieval romance from Chrétien de Troyes to Geoffrey Chaucer*

Magic in Medieval Romance
from Chrétien de Troyes
to Geoffrey Chaucer

MICHELLE SWEENEY

FOUR COURTS PRESS

Set in 10.5 on 12.5 point Ehrhardt for
FOUR COURTS PRESS LTD
Fumbally Lane, Dublin 8, Ireland
E-mail: info@four-courts-press.ie
http//:www.four-courts-press.ie
and in North America for
FOUR COURTS PRESS
c/o ISBS, 5804 N.E. Hassalo Street, Portland, OR 97213.

© Michelle Sweeney 2000

A catalogue record for this title
is available from the British Library.

ISBN 1–85182–536–3

All rights reserved. No part of this publication
may be reproduced, stored in or introduced into
a retrieval system, or transmitted, in any form or by
any means (electronic, mechanical, photocopying,
recording or otherwise), without the prior
written permission of both the copyright
owner and publisher of this book.

Printed in Great Britain
by MPG Books, Bodmin, Cornwall

*My thanks to my parents
and my husband Shane
for their patience;
and my warmest appreciation
for all the advice from
my in-house medievalist and close colleagues
at Trinity College, Dublin
and University College, Dublin*

Contents

INTRODUCTION: CREATING MEANING FROM MAGIC ... 11

    The function of magic in medieval romance ... 11
    A new type of text: medieval romance ... 14
    Elements of the new genre: looking beyond Celtic inspiration ... 16
    How the romances use magic: creating continuity ... 18
    Methodology and genre studies ... 20
    Magic and romance criticism ... 22
    Gendered magic ... 26
    Definitions of magic ... 28
    From Rome to the shores of the barbarians: a brief history of magic ... 35
    Who controls the magicians?: disentangling Church and State ... 40
    Magic and the everyman ... 42
    The function of magic in the romances ... 45
    Romance magic and the individual ... 48
    Romance magic, fate, fortune and medieval Christianity ... 49
    Conclusion ... 52

I THE ORIGINS OF ROMANCE ... 54

    The magical link between fact and fiction ... 54
    Historical texts and the formation of romance ... 55
    "Truth" in the Romances and Lais ... 58

Were the romances conceived on Anglo-Norman soil?	59
Historical sources for the Matière de Bretagne	61
The place of magic in the birth of a secular history	66
Magic as a literary tool	70
Influences beyond the historical	73

2 BREAKING THE CELTIC SPELL — 76

The function of the magical and the marvellous in French romance	76
The use of magic in the French romances	77
New methods of looking at magic in the romances of Chrétien	79
Complex applications of magic	87

3 REVISING ROMANCE — 115

Attacking the heart of the matter: introduction to insular romance	115
The world of insular romance	121

4 MAGICAL ADAPTATIONS — 124

The search for the perfect world	124
Sir Tristrem	125
Ywain and Gawain	131
Syr Launfal	138

CONCLUSION: ROMANCE ENDINGS — 146

Magic in the hands of men	146
Influence on Chaucer: where did clerical magic originate?	147

Contents

Fourteenth-century magic and its relationship to religion, philosophy and scholarship	152
The science of magic and fate	156
A woman in a man's world: magic and the individual	158
Old magic and new magic	159
Magic and society	167
The function of magic in romance	168
BIBLIOGRAPHY	171
INDEX	193

INTRODUCTION

Creating meaning from magic

THE FUNCTION OF MAGIC IN MEDIEVAL ROMANCE

There is little argument about the fact that medieval romances were written first and foremost to be enjoyed and that they have a siren-like ability to lure an audience into imaginative participation with the text. These two points, however, may be the only ones upon which modern critics can agree when it comes to discussing these diverse texts. Currently, critical opinions concerning romance range from classifying it as pure entertainment to designating it a genre invested in sophisticated analysis of contemporary social issues. This study will argue that romances, through the use of magic, explore issues of interest and concern to their audiences. Some of the most popular issues to be found consistently under debate in the romances are ideas of love, the nature of free will, how communities are structured, and the claims of loyalty; and one of the most popular motifs consistently to appear in the romances is magic. This introduction draws together strands from historical, theological and sociological disciplines to create the backdrop necessary for understanding the function of magic in the medieval romances. This process demonstrates that romances encourage a rapport with the audience and engage not only its imagination but also its intellect. The influence of magic in many areas of medieval society, plus its appeal to the imagination, it will be argued, render it a virtually irresistible tool for authors interested in exploring social and spiritual issues.

In studying various works of Chrétien de Troyes, Marie de France and Chaucer, along with the early English redactions of *Sir Tristrem*, *Ywain and Gawain* and *Syr Launfal*, this work assures a balanced discussion of the place of magic in the medieval romances. Such a wide range of romances exists that it seemed sensible to select a combination which would help to overcome some of the inherent difficulties in a study which spans centuries. For example, both *Sir Tristrem* and Chrétien's *Cligés* engage Thomas of Britain's *Tristran* in ways that reflect the differing techniques and concerns of French and insular authors. *Ywain and Gawain* is a natural choice as it is one of only two Middle English romances which, in all certainty, was adapted from Chrétien's *Yvain*.[1] *Syr Launfal* represents the end product of

[1] *Ywain and Gawain*, ed. Maldwyn Mills (London: Everyman, 1992) xi.

Middle English adaptations made to the Anglo-Norman *Lanval* of Marie de France. The *Franklin's Tale* was chosen as the concluding text, owing to the fact that Chaucer claims that it is based on a Breton *lai*; Wimsatt describes it as "probably one of Chaucer's last significant reflections of French court poetry" – which makes its place as the concluding text in a study of the relationships between French and English romances all the more appropriate.[2] These texts demonstrate a consistent approach to magic and a concern for the political and social realities of the day. This is true regardless of the fact that those realities changed significantly from France to England, from the twelfth to the fourteenth century, and from author to author. In coming to terms with the romances it is not always possible to give a complete background to historical events or a comprehensive assessment of all the factors which were involved in the writing of these texts. Detailed footnotes and a bibliography, however, have been included to help direct the reader to resources which may offer a more complete picture of the issues under discussion.

This introduction outlines firstly the methodologies employed in this study; secondly, the status of magic in romance criticism; and, thirdly, the place of magic in the world of medieval romance and society. It argues that medieval authors deliberately employed magic in their romances in order to encourage their audiences toward a multi-level interpretative engagement with the texts.

Marie de France provides the guiding principle to this research. She writes:

> Custume fu as anciëns,
> Ceo testimoine Preciëns,
> Es livres ke jadis feseient,
> Assez oscurement diseient
> Pur ceus ki a venir esteient
> E ki aprendre les deveient,
> K'i peüssent gloser la lettre
> E de lur sen le surplus metre.
>
> (*Prologue*, 9–16)

---

2 James A. Wimsatt, *Chaucer and His French Contemporaries: Natural Music in the Fourteenth Century* (Toronto: University of Toronto Press, 1991) 172.

> The custom among the ancients –
> as Priscian testifies –
> was to speak quite obscurely
> in the books they wrote,
> so that those who were to come after
> and study them
> might gloss the letter
> and supply its significance from their own wisdom.[3]

Marie designs her *lais* along these guidelines, which means that she intends her works to provoke contemplation and analysis. The premise of this book is that a sophisticated use of magic was one of the authorial tools which she, and her contemporaries, used to create morally ambiguous situations which encouraged analysis by the audience. The success or failure of a character against a magical trial, for example, provides evidence concerning his or her moral status. A magical trial also serves to reveal the position of a character on issues important to the community, such as when to maintain loyalty to a king over loyalty to a lover. In creating romances that employ magic in this way, the author exposes the audience to situations which stimulate its imagination and powers of analysis.

Romance authors were also able to encourage the exploration of human motivation by using magic to create or expose complex scenarios that could not be readily resolved by any one set of established moral guidelines. This technique enabled a broader discussion of social issues than would have been allowed in situations constrained, for example, by the boundaries of Christian dogmatism. Magic could enrich the romances in this manner owing to its complicated and controversial place in the medieval world. Magic as a topic of interest and concern for theologians, lawyers, kings, courtiers and the common man, achieves the rare status of a concept which impacts across medieval class, education and gender barriers.

To understand the function of magic in medieval romance, it is necessary to appreciate its function in the medieval world. Magic is coupled to some of the most important works of the medieval age, such as the theological texts of Augustine and Aquinas, the histories of Geoffrey of Monmouth and Wace, as well as playing a significant role in medicine and the nascent studies of science. Romance writers capitalised upon the

---

3 *The Lais of Marie de France*, ed. Jean Rychner (Paris: Champion, 1966) 11; *The Lais of Marie de France*, ed. and trans. Robert Hanning and Joan Ferrante (Durham: Labyrinth Press, 1978) 28. These texts will be the source texts cited for material from the *Lais* of Marie de France, unless otherwise noted.

associations between magic and these fields of study to create a more serious framework for their texts. The romances could then operate beyond the level of simple entertainment and provide the interested audience with social commentary, moral analysis, and material for discussion on a wide variety of issues.

A NEW TYPE OF TEXT: MEDIEVAL ROMANCE

The virtue of interpretation had long been appreciated in monastic circles, and for those interested in medieval exegesis, the works of Hervé de Bourgdieu, Drogo of Paris, and Berengar of Tours spell out that skilful interpretation of the sacred text was considered the highest form of learning.[4] The idea of applying the skill of interpretation to secular stories, however, was a new development. Eugene Vinaver in *The Rise of Romance* argues that twelfth-century secular writers would have been keen to demonstrate their possession of such sought-after skills and excelled in "the practice of a craft unknown to earlier writers in the vernacular".[5] This was made possible by a shift in the centres of learning from monasteries to universities which allowed a wider range of students to acquire skills which had been previously associated with monastic learning.[6] It is possible to gauge the importance placed on learning rhetoric and grammar in the twelfth-century schools by examining the commentaries of such writers as John of Salisbury. Donald Howard in his work *The Three Temptations* suggests that this type of education would have inspired the translation of universal themes (for example humanity and its relationship to the cosmos or to God) into concrete and specific topics, such as the interaction between two lovers. He suggests that Chrétien's use of *san* (authorial intent) and *matière* (source materials) to create *conjointure* (the art of interweaving divergent source materials) proves his awareness of such writing techniques.[7] The word *romanz*, which Chrétien also used to describe his works, has a long

[4] For a more detailed discussion of exegesis see Eugene Vinaver, *The Rise of Romance* (Oxford: Clarendon, 1971) 17, 26–7. [5] Vinaver, *Romance*, 17. [6] For a discussion of the university curricula in Paris and Oxford see: Jacques Le Goff, *Intellectuals in the Middle Ages*, trans. Teresa Fagan (London: Blackwell, 1993) 6–64, esp. 20–24. See also R.W. Southern, *The Making of the Middle Ages* (New Haven: Yale University Press, 1953) 182–3. [7] Donald Howard, *The Three Temptations* (Princeton: Princeton University Press, 1966) 233. *San* can also be spelled *sans*, *sen*, and *sens*. For a more comprehensive discussion of these terms see Douglas Kelly, *The Art of Medieval French Romance* (Madison: University of Wisconsin Press, 1992) 114–25; and Douglas Kelly, "Chrétien de Troyes: Narrator and His Art", in *Romances of Chrétien de Troyes*

history in the French tradition; for example in the Carolingian Renaissance its earlier form, *romaine*, was used to distinguish writings "in the vernacular" as from writings in Latin (*latine*). The use of such terms also suggests an interest in writing, but, more particularly, writing in the language of the common people. Howard's theory may or may not be correct, but certainly an interest in the skill of writing, in tandem with the desire to communicate significant content concerning secular issues to a popular audience, came to fruition in the twelfth century with the creation of what Chrétien calls a *bele conjointure*.

The work of George Duby argues that the romances were constructed and encouraged by the nobility, not only as a discussion of secular issues, but as a source of influence upon secular concerns in the changing world of twelfth-century French society. His study exemplifies some of the very direct connections that the romance form had with the concern for government and maintaining the feudal structure. He states:

> I have no hesitation contradicting those commentators who saw in courtly love a female invention. It was a man's game and amongst all the writings which encouraged individuals to give themselves over to it, there are few which are not deeply misogynistic ... I am convinced that princely patronage deliberately encouraged the institution that secular liturgies exemplified in Lancelot and Gawain. It was a way of tightening the grip of the sovereign's power over the social class [young knights] which at the time was perhaps the most useful reform of the state.[8]

Romances were originally composed to entertain a courtly audience and reinforce a belief in its own superiority. In teaching young men to desire, but not to act upon that desire, the courtly code privileges the knight who can best submit himself to the desires of others. It also translates his burgeoning sense of self into a sense of fidelity to his lord. In political terms, these knights make the best subjects, and, as Duby argues, "thus disciplined by courtly love, male desire would appear to have been used for political ends".[9]

By appreciating the fact that the romances are clearly a component part of the world of literature, but that the world of literature does not

---

Symposium (Kentucky: French Forum Publishers, 1985) 14, 21. These definitions will also be discussed in further detail on page 76 above. 8 George Duby, *Love and Marriage in the Middle Ages*, trans. Janet Dunnet (Chicago: University of Chicago Press, 1988) 58; second half of this quote is located on pages 60–1. 9 Ibid., 63.

exist in isolation, one can fruitfully explore the nature of the influence of literature upon its audience. It is also possible to investigate, as Duby has done, the impact of political concerns and spiritual issues upon the subject matter of the texts themselves.

ELEMENTS OF THE NEW GENRE: LOOKING BEYOND CELTIC INSPIRATION

Determining an agreed set of generic qualities for the romances has been a source of difficulty for modern critics. When considered in all its various forms, however, magic is one of the few properties that appear in romances with relative consistency throughout the medieval period. Despite the regular presence of the magical, critical discussion of its potential functions in romances has only just begun to develop in new directions. The two most influential and commonplace critical justifications thus far for the presence of magic in the romances concern its origins in Celtic sources and its usefulness for basic plot management by the author.[10]

The Celtic connection, despite the enormous amount of research carried out, has done little to encourage the idea of the romances as sophisticated texts. For example, R.S. Loomis' justification for studying magic in the romances of Chrétien was that "by discovering accidents of transmission [magic from Celtic sources] we could relieve Chrétien of responsibility for the faults in construction and the lapses in coherence to which otherwise he would have to plead guilty".[11] It may well be that critics such as Loomis, who exhaustively strove to prove that the place of magic in the romances was owing solely to its Celtic antecedents, influenced the direction of research away from other, more complex, views.[12]

---

10 R.S. Loomis, *Arthurian Tradition and Chrétien de Troyes* (New York: Columbia University Press, 1949) 6; R.S. Loomis, *Celtic Myth and Arthurian Romance* (New York: Columbia University Press, 1926) 69–84; R.S. Loomis, *The Grail: From Celtic Myth to Christian Symbolism* (New York: Columbia University Press, 1963). Gottfried von Strassburg, *Tristan with the 'Tristran' of Thomas*, ed. and trans. A.T. Hatto (London: Penguin Classics, 1960) 8, 21; Beroul, *The Romance of Tristan*, ed. and trans. Alan S. Fedrick (London: Penguin Classics, 1970) 12. See also R.S. Loomis, ed., *Arthurian Literature in the Middle Ages* (Oxford: Clarendon, 1959); Claude Luttrell, *The Creation of the First Arthurian Romance* (London: Edward Arnold, 1974).
11 Loomis, *Chrétien de Troyes*, 6. These comments concern Chrétien's works but it is clear from Loomis' extensive writing on Celtic myth that he felt that the process of translation reduced their symbolic power and their impact on subsequent narratives.
12 See any of Loomis' texts, but especially, *Celtic Myth and Chrétien de Troyes* for examples of just such an agenda. There is room for much work to be done in terms

Eugene Vinaver does contest Loomis' conclusions, but, in his own work on "interlacement", suggests instead, and rather disappointingly, that the appropriate response to magic is one where "we must refrain from asking unnecessary questions [which magic raises] and understand the whole in terms of the dichotomy of *conte* and of *conjointure*, neither of which should be diminished or obscured by the presence of the other".[13] Vinaver assumes that there is little authorial design in the use of magic, as he claims that "incidents occur and magical objects appear at random, no matter where they come from or what their original significance may have been".[14] It is difficult to accept the validity of such reasoning since Chrétien and succeeding romance writers stress the interaction between the worlds of meaning and magic, text and subtext.

Lynette Muir in *Literature and Society in Medieval France* leaves aside the "Celtic antecedent" theory of magic and provides two very practical explanations for the appearance of magic in, for example, the romances of Chrétien: namely, function and ornament.[15] She argues that magic functions to facilitate the demands of an unwieldy plot. Lunete's production of a magic invisibility ring, for instance in *Le Chevalier au Lion* (*Yvain*), simply serves to allow the hero to stay alive long enough to meet his future wife. Muir describes the sword-bridge in *La Charrette* as ornamental and does not see it as having meaningful impact upon the story.

What both these "Celtic" and "practical" points of view fail to take into account is that magical encounters often reveal important information about the characters involved. The audience is encouraged to question why a character succeeds or fails in magical endeavours. The understanding of how magic functions in the romances becomes particularly valuable, to take Muir's example, in appreciating Chrétien's goal in *La Charrette*. The uncertainty of Lancelot's moral position is publicised when he ominously fails to complete without injury any of the magical trials he undertakes. The plot progresses, but, as the magical encounters reveal, Lancelot never evidences any emotional growth or maturity in his moral outlook. Lancelot's inner conflict over the desire to maintain his reputation versus his desperate

of re-evaluating the role of magic in Celtic literature. This study, however, is not the appropriate forum; therefore, there will be only occasional attempts to redress the imbalance that Loomis and fellow critics have created in the appreciation of the complexity of Chrétien's Celtic sources.   13 Vinaver, *Romance*, 44, 34–46. *Conjointure* as defined by Vinaver means 'to link' or 'to make a whole out of several parts'. It is not a substitute for *conte* (meaning); it is, instead, a means of making meaning from several different sources.   14 Vinaver, *Romance*, 41.   15 Lynette R. Muir, *Literature and Society in Medieval France: The Mirror and the Image, 1100–1500* (London: Macmillan, 1985) 83–5.

desire for Guenevere is never satisfactorily resolved, leaving the audience to question his actions with regard to Meleagant. The fact that Lancelot requires magical rings to see reality, and that he never unravels the moral quandary he is in over his love for Guenevere, leaves the audience puzzling over the ending of this story.

Examining the use of magic by the romance authors from a different perspective would clearly be fruitful; thus this study seeks to provide an alternative approach to both the "Celtic" and "practical" theories of the place of magic in the texts under discussion. In exploring the *Historia regum Britannae* of Geoffrey of Monmouth and the *Roman de Brut* of his adapter Wace, one can see a potential source of influence for an approach to magic derived from the classical tradition. The discussion of Monmouth's influence upon the works of Chrétien in Chapter 1, will set the stage for appreciating how the romance writers redirected the powerful Celtic symbols which they had acquired from earlier traditions.

This argument for a deliberate reformulation of the use of magic by the romance authors from what was its function in the Celtic tradition, is reinforced by an appreciation for the second flaw common to both the "practical" and the strictly "Celtic antecedent" arguments for the place of magic in the romances. This is the failure to appreciate that medieval writers intentionally employed magic as a literary tool. The remarkable consistency with which romance authors from the twelfth through the fourteenth centuries used magic in all its forms to achieve certain goals in their texts is evidence for a general appreciation of its usefulness in designing the romances.

HOW THE ROMANCES USE MAGIC: CREATING CONTINUITY

The same forms of magic appear throughout several generations of texts – for example, rings, potions, swords, and certain types of illusions. The fact that these magical tokens are incorporated by a variety of authors spanning different countries, languages and centuries suggests that the larger population would have had a general understanding of how these tokens were expected to operate. Borrowing from a pool of well-known and accepted magical artillery saved romance writers the need for lengthy explanations. It was also tremendously provocative to leave the creator of these magical devices unidentified: this increases both the suspense surrounding their use, and the anxiety of the audience regarding their origins. If the audience did not know who had created these magical tokens, then there was always room for doubt about the safety of their use. This nebulous aura surrounding the magical tokens also allowed the romance author to suggest or hint at the darker sides which might exist in a character. For example in *Le Chevalier au Lion*, when Yvain uses the magical ring to hide from his attackers at the castle of the marvellous spring, the fact that he seems to have the power of a demon is suggestive of the demon-like emotions which drove him to kill the lord of the castle without mercy. Yvain is clearly not a demon, nor is he given the ring by a demon, but the episode reveals to the audience the depth of learning and maturity that Yvain still needs to achieve.

The fundamental principle that is most important to this study is that magic is used to achieve a similar purpose across the range of texts under discussion, that is, evaluation of the characters' values, identities or moral beliefs. This is achieved through the establishment of a marvellous or magical test which reveals to the audience certain aspects of the personality of a given character. For example, if Lancelot could cross the Sword Bridge whole and intact, then the audience would be right to consider him one of the best knights in the court of Arthur. If he were bleeding from a hundred slashes, the audience would be right to suspect that Lancelot has been compromised either morally or spiritually. In *La Charrette*, Lancelot's adultery has compromised both his moral and social status, a situation that is reflected in his mixed success at magical or marvellous endeavours. In the *Franklin's Tale*, the use of magic and *illusioun* by Aurelius to deceive Dorigen into committing adultery reveals the flaws in his character and the twisted nature of his love.

Magic used as a literary tool enables an imaginative link between the world of the audience and the text under discussion. If an audience could not identify with the values of the hero, then that hero's struggle to negotiate a place in the romance world would be of no interest. This imaginative link functions by allowing the author to create a desensitized space in which the discussion of difficult or provocative topics is achieved without alienating the audience. Used as a literary device, magic also enables the romance author to encourage associations between the text and a series of complex ideas stemming from the place of magic in medieval society. The unity of interests which Christianity and shared political/social structures brought to both continental and insular cultures, meant that the presence of magic in a French twelfth-century romance could be used to generate a discussion of free will, and that the use of magic in a fourteenth-century romance could still be appreciated by an English audience as a means of exploring the same issue. That is not to suggest that there were not many changes both in technique and sophistication in the romances; there were, but the romances did not evolve so far from their founding principles and structures that they were no longer recognisable to later medieval audiences.

METHODOLOGY AND GENRE STUDIES

The basis of this book is founded upon at least two theoretical points open to dispute: the first is the existence of an interactive audience; the second is the idea of genre.

Paul Strohm argues that: "The medieval sense that the requirements of an audience might influence literary creation deserves consideration . . . Such a theory would assign to the audience, and to the author's sense of the audience, a role not simply founded in passive consumption but on active participation, in determining textual meaning and influencing the form of texts."[16] If the concept of audience is only treated within the realm of sociolinguistics, then it is possible to argue, as Bakhtin and Voloshinov do, that every utterance is two-sided.[17] Assessment of a speech act, however, is not sufficient to explore the full potential of a literary work; hence it is more productive to appreciate the literature as an artistic work, a specialised form of communication. Strohm assesses the situation: "The text is not transmitted from the author to the reader, but it is constructed between them as a kind of ideological bridge." The literary work is mediated then through the immense volume of "existing generic possibilities (for the writer) and generic expectations (for the audience)".[18]

It is important to this study to establish that most medieval romance authors had a sense of romance as a genre or as a body of texts which were interrelated.[19] This is not a radical theory and proof for it can be gathered from the texts themselves. In *Ywain and Gawain*, for example, the author declares that one of the young heroines is reading a "real romaunce" (3089), and Thomas Chestre states that his tale is "Jn romaunce as we rede" (742). Chaucer's use of the *Miller's Tale* and the *Reeve's Tale* to mock the principles upon which romances were built is further evidence that some general conception of romance was appreciated by the fourteenth-century audience, or a satire of such ideals would not have been very

---

16 Paul Strohm, *Social Chaucer* (Cambridge, Mass.: University of Harvard Press, 1989) 49.   17 M.M. Bakhtin and P.M. Medvedev, *The Formal Method in Literary Scholarship*, ed. Albert J. Wehrle (Cambridge: Harvard University Press, 1985) 18; V. N. Voloshinov, *Marxism and the Philosophy of Language*, trans. L. Matejka (New York: Seminar Press, 1973) 86.   18 Strohm, *Social Chaucer*, 50.   19 See Jameson for a discussion of the importance of the concept of genre in romance: Fredrick Jameson, "Magical Narratives: Romance as Genre", *New Literary History* 7 (1975): 153–63.

effective. There are also many examples of authors reacting to rival texts with disdain, which suggests a keen competition for popularity among audiences and superiority in their chosen field. An example of this type of inter-romance style of commentary can be seen in Chrétien's *Cligés*: Fenice declares repeatedly that she would rather be torn limb from limb than be considered in the same breath as Iseut and Tristan. Examples of such self-conscious statements by medieval writers demonstrate that there existed some tangible conception of the makeup and content of a romance. In the opinion of modern criticism, however, there is as yet no generally agreed definition of what comprises a romance. Crane articulates the problems in studying the romance genre. In this instance, she addresses the situation with particular regard to *lais* and Chaucerian fiction and argues that "Chaucer and his contemporaries did attribute generic meaning to the term *romaunce*. In the fourteenth century, the term could designate works written in French and sometimes any written source, or secular works that were not rigorously historical, or a generic category of narrative fictions concerning the deeds of chivalric heroes."[20] Crane further argues that if *lais* were excluded from consideration that that would "falsify" their place in the history of the romance genre.[21] William Calin in his study of the French tradition and its place in English literature, suggests that those *lais* which are even moderately long can be considered "a version of the Arthurian romance in miniature".[22]

A very straightforward criterion distinguishes a romance from other forms of literature in this study to ensure that the issue of genre does not overwhelm the investigation of the romances in the succeeding chapters. This criterion is that at least one of these traditionally accepted romance genre elements should appear in the text under discussion: the challenge, magic, the marvellous, wonders, questions of fate, the quest motif, the wayside ordeal, the winning of the lover. These are common romance elements found to varying extents in Marie de France, Chrétien, Gottfried von Strassburg, and most English works. The establishment of such a

20 Susan Crane, *Gender and Romance in Chaucer's Canterbury Tales* (Princeton: University of Princeton Press, 1994) 9. See also Paul Strohm, "The Origin and Meaning of Middle English Romaunce", *Genre* 10 (1977): 1–28.   21 Crane, *Gender and Romance*, 9; see also Pamela Gradon who feels that it is "doubtful whether the romance can be indeed regarded as a genre at all" and that it would, instead, be "preferable to talk of a romance mode." Pamela Gradon, *Form and Style in Early English Literature* (London: Methuen, 1971) 269–70. For a concurring opinion, see W.R.J. Barron, *English Medieval Romance* (London: Longman, 1987) 4.   22 William Calin, *The French Tradition and the Literature of Medieval England* (Toronto: University of Toronto Press, 1994) 22.

conservative criterion for identification of a romance should help to ensure general approval of the methodology employed in this study. The absence or presence of these motifs and their differing treatments will provide avenues of exploration into the intentions of the author in the text and the reception of it by the audience.

It is much more difficult to develop a sense of the audiences that these romances would have had, as there is little evidence to suggest any one continuous body, of kings, noble men and women, the middle-class, intellectuals, etc., or any particular combination of the above. In some romances, the poet states the name of the patron, or alludes to his or her potential audience, which is a rare clue for the modern critic about the composition of that particular audience, but then there is the difficulty that one is never sure in what way such information is meant to influence the material; for example, the Countess of Champagne, Chrétien tells his audience, provided him with the *matiere* and *san* for *La Charrette*, but it is difficult to know if he includes this information to act as a disclaimer or vote of thanks for her patronage. It is particularly awkward in regard to the span of romances studied in this book, as the time period is so extensive and the ground covered so vast, that what few generalisations one could make about audiences so diverse would probably not be very enlightening.

A brief appraisal of the current status of magic in romance criticism, however, will facilitate the study of the function of magic in the romances under discussion. This appraisal will address both the insights offered by modern fantasy theories and current debate about the importance of magic in aiding interpretation of the romances.

MAGIC AND ROMANCE CRITICISM

Many modern critics, such as Brewer, suggest that the presence of magic undermines the literary value of the romances, a view which may owe its current formulation to such texts as Auerbach's *Mimesis*.[23] In this work, Auerbach states pejoratively that the romances of the Middle Ages are not mimetic but "an escape into the fable and fairy tale".[24] His understanding of "fairy" is that it functions merely to provide an escape from reality. He criticises the romances for their "unfavourable" impact on the development of "a literary art which should apprehend reality in its full breadth and

---

23 Derek Brewer, *Tradition and Innovation in Chaucer* (London: Macmillan Press, 1982) 140.   24 Erec Auerbach, *Mimesis: The Representation of Reality in Western Literature*, trans. Willard B. Trask (Princeton: Princeton University Press, 1968) 138, 123-42.

is, according to twentieth-century critics, only interested in action. Tristrem seems to leave himself vulnerable, as if no longer in charge of his fate. These passive moments leave every sort of interpretation of his behaviour open to the audience, and his "will-lessness" is more symbolically meaningful than Thomas's efforts to present the emotional confusion of *his* Tristran.

The *Tristrem* poet, unlike his predecessors, seeks to undermine the magically-induced, passionate love from which Thomas's characters are suffering. He mocks this passionate love in two ways: first, he reduces the lovers' trysts to simple physical "playing", and then he allows Tristrem's dog, Hodain, to taste the love drink:

> Þe coupe he licked þ at tide
> Þ o doun it sett bringwain;
> Þ ai loued al in lide
> And þ er of were þ ai fain ...
>
> Þai loued wiþ al her miȝt,
> And hodain dede al so.
>
> (*Tristrem*, 1675–8, 1693–4)

It has been argued that this passage is simply a far-fetched explanation of the faithfulness of Tristrem's dog.[15] In allowing, however, that the author intended a finer design for his plot, it is not difficult to interpret the function of this passage as one which undermines and critiques Thomas's vision of passion. In Thomas's text, this magically-induced passion rages so wildly between the characters that in the end the lovers are consumed by it. Whether they are or are not responsible for their actions, or indeed, whether they had any choice in their fate, is made a secondary issue by the spectacular nature of their deaths.

In the *Tristrem* text, however, the author deals with these issues in a very different way. This ending in which a silly dog is given access to the love philtre, demonstrates primarily, and memorably, the power of the potion itself. Bédier concludes, owing in part to this ending, that the *Tristrem* text offers only "tiny souvenirs of Thomas's monumental conceptions" which are that "*voleir* (will) opposes Tristran to his own love, and that social and even religious fault is an inescapable condition of this *fine amor*".[16] Bédier

---

[15] This interpretation of the dog's role is offered by T.C. Rumble, "The Middle English *Sir Tristrem*: Toward a Reappraisal", *Critical Language* 11 (1959): 225.   [16] *Le Roman de Tristan par Thomas*, ed. Joseph Bédier, 2 vols S.A.T.F., 46 (Paris, 1902, 1905) as cited in Crane, *Insular Romances*, 190.

further claims that "a discussion of will has no place in an analysis of Tristrem's state of mind". It is not, however, that the *Tristrem* author is not interested in "free will"; he clearly is. It is only that he is not interested in debating the issues surrounding it in his text. Instead, he makes his point of view on passion and free will very clear by adding this memorable final scene to Thomas's original; once passionate love has arrived Tristrem does not have the willpower to resist it, nor does Ysonde; not even the dog has enough willpower to resist the effects of overwhelming passion.

This scene also serves to erase the half-developed claims of the previous authors that love existed between the two characters *before* the aid of the potion.[17] The characters are not responsible for their love, even subconsciously; just as the dog has been given a magical love potion, so too have these lovers. Therefore, the entire interpretative backdrop to Thomas's tale, which concerns the level of responsibility which the characters must shoulder for their adultery and betrayal of the king, is minimised. The *Tristrem* author would argue, it is reasonable to claim, that characters who are consumed by this kind of passion, much like Lancelot and Guenevere, are no longer thinking rationally, hence it is difficult to assign to them the consequences of rational actions.

In somewhat resolving these issues for the audience, the *Tristrem* author does not, however, minimise entirely the complexities of the text. The audience is left with the question of whether or not passion is a good thing, a virtue to be sought, or a catastrophe to be avoided at all costs. The presentation of this quandary is achieved by the repetitive addition of the epithet "*trewe*" to Tristrem's name, particularly in the final moments of the text. This focuses the modern reader's attention upon its importance to an English audience of the time (1728–36).[18] This epithet in many ways ironically encapsulates the heart of Tristrem's difficulties; he is known both for his faithfulness to Ysonde and at the same time for being *untrewe* to everyone and everything else. Magic made him true to love but could not make him have faith in the love of his partner, or be faithful to the oaths and obligations which he owed to his king.

This conclusion serves as an ironic jab at some of the serious issues dealt with by Thomas, such as fate, love, and loyalty. The *Tristrem* poet undermines the concept of fate by linking all who encounter the potion. By creating such a farce as that of the dog drinking the love potion, he undermines both the concept of loyalty, by reducing it to the love which a dog has for its master, and the idea of passionate love, by equating the experience of

17 *Ibid.*, 190. See the *Tantris* episode in Gottfried von Strassburg's *Tristan*.   18 Barnes, *Counsel*, 97–8. See also Crane, *Insular Romances*, 190–1.

effective. There are also many examples of authors reacting to rival texts with disdain, which suggests a keen competition for popularity among audiences and superiority in their chosen field. An example of this type of inter-romance style of commentary can be seen in Chrétien's *Cligés*: Fenice declares repeatedly that she would rather be torn limb from limb than be considered in the same breath as Iseut and Tristan. Examples of such self-conscious statements by medieval writers demonstrate that there existed some tangible conception of the makeup and content of a romance. In the opinion of modern criticism, however, there is as yet no generally agreed definition of what comprises a romance. Crane articulates the problems in studying the romance genre. In this instance, she addresses the situation with particular regard to *lais* and Chaucerian fiction and argues that "Chaucer and his contemporaries did attribute generic meaning to the term *romaunce*. In the fourteenth century, the term could designate works written in French and sometimes any written source, or secular works that were not rigorously historical, or a generic category of narrative fictions concerning the deeds of chivalric heroes."[20] Crane further argues that if *lais* were excluded from consideration that that would "falsify" their place in the history of the romance genre.[21] William Calin in his study of the French tradition and its place in English literature, suggests that those *lais* which are even moderately long can be considered "a version of the Arthurian romance in miniature".[22]

A very straightforward criterion distinguishes a romance from other forms of literature in this study to ensure that the issue of genre does not overwhelm the investigation of the romances in the succeeding chapters. This criterion is that at least one of these traditionally accepted romance genre elements should appear in the text under discussion: the challenge, magic, the marvellous, wonders, questions of fate, the quest motif, the wayside ordeal, the winning of the lover. These are common romance elements found to varying extents in Marie de France, Chrétien, Gottfried von Strassburg, and most English works. The establishment of such a

---

[20] Susan Crane, *Gender and Romance in Chaucer's Canterbury Tales* (Princeton: University of Princeton Press, 1994) 9. See also Paul Strohm, "The Origin and Meaning of Middle English Romaunce", *Genre* 10 (1977): 1–28. [21] Crane, *Gender and Romance*, 9; see also Pamela Gradon who feels that it is "doubtful whether the romance can be indeed regarded as a genre at all" and that it would, instead, be "preferable to talk of a romance mode." Pamela Gradon, *Form and Style in Early English Literature* (London: Methuen, 1971) 269–70. For a concurring opinion, see W.R.J. Barron, *English Medieval Romance* (London: Longman, 1987) 4. [22] William Calin, *The French Tradition and the Literature of Medieval England* (Toronto: University of Toronto Press, 1994) 22.

conservative criterion for identification of a romance should help to ensure general approval of the methodology employed in this study. The absence or presence of these motifs and their differing treatments will provide avenues of exploration into the intentions of the author in the text and the reception of it by the audience.

It is much more difficult to develop a sense of the audiences that these romances would have had, as there is little evidence to suggest any one continuous body, of kings, noble men and women, the middle-class, intellectuals, etc., or any particular combination of the above. In some romances, the poet states the name of the patron, or alludes to his or her potential audience, which is a rare clue for the modern critic about the composition of that particular audience, but then there is the difficulty that one is never sure in what way such information is meant to influence the material; for example, the Countess of Champagne, Chrétien tells his audience, provided him with the *matiere* and *san* for *La Charrette*, but it is difficult to know if he includes this information to act as a disclaimer or vote of thanks for her patronage. It is particularly awkward in regard to the span of romances studied in this book, as the time period is so extensive and the ground covered so vast, that what few generalisations one could make about audiences so diverse would probably not be very enlightening.

A brief appraisal of the current status of magic in romance criticism, however, will facilitate the study of the function of magic in the romances under discussion. This appraisal will address both the insights offered by modern fantasy theories and current debate about the importance of magic in aiding interpretation of the romances.

MAGIC AND ROMANCE CRITICISM

Many modern critics, such as Brewer, suggest that the presence of magic undermines the literary value of the romances, a view which may owe its current formulation to such texts as Auerbach's *Mimesis*.[23] In this work, Auerbach states pejoratively that the romances of the Middle Ages are not mimetic but "an escape into the fable and fairy tale".[24] His understanding of "fairy" is that it functions merely to provide an escape from reality. He criticises the romances for their "unfavourable" impact on the development of "a literary art which should apprehend reality in its full breadth and

---

23 Derek Brewer, *Tradition and Innovation in Chaucer* (London: Macmillan Press, 1982) 140. 24 Erec Auerbach, *Mimesis: The Representation of Reality in Western Literature*, trans. Willard B. Trask (Princeton: Princeton University Press, 1968) 138, 123–42.

depth".[25] He does not take into account that an author's use of magic and fantasy provides a safe space within the text, a world far away or long ago, enabling the exploration of issues which might otherwise prove difficult or destructive in a society. Equally, he does not take into account that fiction often reveals truths which reality obscures. Erec Rabkin, however, argues that the fantastic is a means of allowing authors to explore the human condition, or is used "to reveal the truth of the human heart."[26] Rosemary Jackson, in *Fantasy: The Literature of Subversion*, also argues that the value of fantastic literature does not reside in escapism but in its ability to subvert authority and express values outside tacitly accepted norms. Jackson believes that the fantastic expresses subversive desires according to the two functions of express: "it can *tell of*, manifest or show desire, or it can expel desire, . . . when this desire is a disturbing element which threatens cultural order and continuity".[27] In support of the idea of examining these modern theories with an eye to their insight into the medieval fantastic, Jacques Le Goff argues in *The Medieval Imagination* that the medieval marvellous was also a form of "resistance to official ideology of Christianity . . . [Therefore] the marvelous becomes the focal point of a form of cultural resistance."[28] Le Goff proposes that what is most disturbing about medieval marvels is "precisely the fact that they merge so easily with the everyday life that no one bothers to question their reality".[29]

Magic does not require rational explanation and thereby provides the author with a great deal of freedom. An author released from the constraints of cause and effect is also free from the restraints of logical narrative and sensible plot design. Kelly argues that what holds true for the fantastic also holds true for the medieval use of the marvellous and the magical, thereby drawing a direct connection between modern theory and medieval texts. He states: "Mutatis mutandis, the problem of the fantastic holds for the *merveilleux* as well. This is in part a matter of definition; no doubt, if one cannot find the actual word [fantastic] one can discover elements of the modern notion of the fantastic in the medieval marvelous."[30]

The concept of fantasy would have been familiar to medieval thinkers; fantasy – *fantasie, fantastica* – as cited by the MED is used by such authors as St Augustine, Lydgate, and Chaucer, to describe that which has only a

[25] Ibid., 142. [26] Eric S. Rabkin, *The Fantastic in Literature* (Princeton: Princeton University Press, 1976) 27, 4–5. [27] Rosemary Jackson, *Fantasy: The Literature of Subversion* (London: Methuen, 1981) 3–4 (Jackson's italics). For further discussion see Tobin Siebers, "The Uses of Fantasy", *Michigan Quarterly Review* 21: 3 (1981–82): 520–4. [28] Jacques Le Goff, *The Medieval Imagination*, trans. A. Goldhammer (Chicago: University of Chicago Press, 1985) 32. [29] Ibid., 33. [30] Kelly, *Art*, 150.

seeming "reality, ... or permanence; to ponder; to plan or devise a course of action; ... to create; the seat of the imagination."[31] The modern reader may see the natural links between the medieval and the modern concepts of fantasy and the fantastic, a connection which Manlove in *The Elusiveness of Fantasy* describes as "fictions, evoking wonder, and containing a substantial and irreducible element of supernatural worlds, beings or objects with which the mortal characters in the story or the readers become on at least partly familiar terms".[32]

Having the romances defined as fantasy stories enables the modern reader to assess from different points of view how medieval authors structured these stories and to what ends. Romance authors used a fantasising technique to distance their contemporary audiences from reality, while they were, in fact, simultaneously engaging them with their political, moral, or social agendas. Chrétien, for example, adopts the quasi-historical characters of Arthur, Lancelot, and Kay, etc., and claims of ancient sources, in order to confer legitimacy on his own tales and to capitalize on interest in such noble, yet explosively passionate, stories. The same is true for Marie de France, the English adapters of these authors, and Chaucer. The curious status of the Arthurian material, located somewhere between fact and fiction, lends itself to exactly such an authorial manoeuvre. The events at Camelot are distant enough and mythologized enough to be more fantastic than real, yet Arthur is one of the ill-starred historical figures of Geoffrey of Monmouth's *Historia regum Britanniae*. This bridge between the fantasy world and the real one allows the author to introduce issues which have consequences for the real world under the guise of only dealing with topics which are pertinent to the world of fantasy.

The romances are not a sophisticated rendition of myth for entertainment, but a highly self-conscious form of fiction. They are stories constructed for edification *and* enjoyment, which is why they absorbed Christian guidelines and were able to extend beyond the restrictions of the parable or hagiographic genres. It is also essential to note that romance authors incorporated the strongest available imagery and

---

31 *Fantasie, Middle English Dictionary* (*MED*), 1971 edn. *Fantasie; fantastica; fantastik; Fantasie:* "1. (a) One of the mental 'faculties', or 'bodily wits', variously classified in scholastic psychology and literary tradition as to its supposed location in the brain and its functions, whether the imagined apprehension and recall of sensory data, the formation of delusive images or ideas; musings about the past or speculation about the future, the devising of works of art etc.; the imagination, and the supposed seat of this faculty". 32 Colin N. Manlove, "The Elusiveness of Fantasy", in *The Shape of the Fantastic*, ed. Olena Saciuk (New York: Greenwood Press, 1986) 53.

language in order to give depth and poignancy to their works. Magical and religious vocabularies, the most powerful means of expression, were obvious contenders for influence over both language and plot structures. Romances borrow from the world of myth and Christian ideology, but depend upon the power of secular attractions. While considering the discussion of secular heroes or heroines the audience may dream of love and still be taught the reality of loving. Without the presence of reality somewhere in the text, one cannot make sense of the romances. The world of a romance is a highly sophisticated blend of fantasy and reality: things do not need to be explained, yet investigation may occur of the difficult but familiar issues of everyday life, such as loyalty bonds, class cultures, economic tensions, religious doubts, and the meaning of love and honour.

The majority of modern critics, however, have yet to appreciate the role of magic or fantasy within the romances, a fact easily illustrated by negative commentaries to be found concerning the entire array of medieval romances. For example, in what seemed a promising article, "Magic, Fate and Providence in Medieval Narrative and *Sir Gawain and the Green Knight*", T.A. McAlindon consigns magic to a role subsidiary to that of religion. He claims that magic is "less a vision of deeper reality than a passport to imaginative and moral freedom".[33] A.T. Hatto in his introduction to Gottfried von Strassburg's *Tristan*, is equally critical of the role of magic. He dismisses the love-philtre as "pure fairy-tale, set in motion by Gottfried with as much realistic psychology as it will bear. For whole stretches one feels one is reading a novel and then the old tale reasserts itself. At times we find him shaking his head over the story's love of the irrational."[34] Alan Fedrick claims in his introduction to Beroul's *Tristan* that magic functions to thrill men "who knew no better than to believe what they saw and heard".[35] A.C. Spearing argues in *Medieval to Renaissance in English Poetry* that "we must recognise in Chaucer, wherever we look, a contempt for romance of all kinds".[36] Derek Brewer and J.A. Burrow also assert in various ways that Chaucer has little time for marvels, illogical plots, or romances in general.[37]

---

[33] T.A. McAlindon, "Magic and Medieval Narrative in *Sir Gawain and the Green Knight*", *Review of English Studies* 16 (1965): 122, 124.   [34] *Tristan*, ed. Hatto, 21.   [35] *Tristan*, ed. Fedrick, 12.   [36] A.C. Spearing, *Medieval to Renaissance in English Poetry* (Cambridge: Cambridge University Press, 1985) 36. All Chaucer quotations are from Larry Benson, gen. ed., *The Riverside Chaucer*, 3rd ed. (Boston: Houghton, 1987).   [37] Derek Brewer, *Symbolic Stories: Traditional Narratives of the Family Drama in English Literature* (Cambridge: D.S Brewer; Totowa, N.J.: Rowman & Littlefield. 1980) 92–3, 99; Robert Worth Frank, Jr., *Chaucer and the Legend of Good Women* (Cambridge, Mass: Harvard Univ. Press, 1972) 111–33; J.A. Burrow, "The Canterbury Tales, 1: Romance", in Piero Boitani and Jill Mann, ed., *The Cambridge*

Even more distressing are the comments of Lee Ramsey in *Chivalric Literature* concerning the general status of romance:

> The rhetoric of the romances is often poor, the philosophic content meager, and the characters simple and obvious. The emotional effects sought after are likewise obvious, often crudely so.[38]

When faced with such a sobering convergence of negative opinions concerning magic or, indeed, concerning the romances themselves, it seems necessary to analyse the nature of medieval attitudes towards magic to establish the appropriate approach to understanding its value in the romances.

GENDERED MAGIC

It is important to identify exactly what is meant by the term 'magic' both in this study and, as far as it is possible, in the medieval world. Kieckhefer defines medieval magic in his sociological study as: "those phenomena which intellectuals would have recognised as either demonic or natural magic. That which makes an action magical is the type of power it invokes: if it relies on divine action or the manifest powers of nature it is not magical, while if it uses demonic aid or occult powers in nature it is magical."[39] This definition, however, is not sufficient for the use of magic in the romances, as it is often the case that tokens are described as magical, marvellous, or wondrous, but they are not accredited to the divine, the occult, or the powers of the demonic.

Technically, magic should have a magician, a demon, or a witch to instigate the formulas necessary to create power. However, what is frequently the case in the twelfth- and thirteenth-century romances is that the originator of a magical event or the creator of magical tokens does not feature in the story. Furthermore, it is usually only a minor participant who produces the necessary token before disappearing into a vast realm of secondary characters. It may be the case that an owner is ascribed to a magical ring or healing potion, but rarely is he or she classified as its creator. This is true even in such cases as Laudine, the wife of Yvain, and Lunete, her lady-in-waiting, in that they provide him with a magical ring when he needs it, but

---

Chaucer Companion (Cambridge: Cambridge University Press, 1986) 109. For criticism of romance see Spearing, *Medieval to Renaissance*, 38–9.   **38** Lee Ramsey, *Chivalric Romance: Popular Literature in Medieval England* (Bloomington: University of Indiana, 1983) 7, 5-6.   **39** Richard Kieckhefer, *Magic in the Middle Ages* (Cambridge: Cambridge University Press, 1989) 14.

do not actively participate as main characters in the intricacies of the plot of *Le Chevalier au Lion*. It is not always female characters who introduce magic into the romances, but it is certainly predominately the case that the women seem to have access to magical philtres created by Morgan or have ladies in waiting who are witches from Thessaly. In the texts, however, it often seems that the magic itself is more important than the identity of the character who is actually offering it. For example, it is probably not so vital to the import of the text that Fenice knows a witch from Thessaly; what is important is that she has access to a means of realising her will and controlling the use of her body. In the *Franklin's Tale* magic seems to have the opposite effect; it acts as the means by which Dorigen loses control over her body. Indeed, its presence in the tale seems to neutralise Dorigen's femaleness in that Arveragus demands that she honour her word, which he claims is the "hyeste thyng that man may kepe"(1479). Despite his demands, honour remains in the province of the male world, which is a point that the Franklin makes very strongly in his conclusion. Even from these two brief examples it is clearly deeply significant that magic is related to control over the female body in these texts.[40] The link between magic and power over an individual is tied in many ways to the link between control over female sexuality and the need to ensure the pure bloodlines of dynastic houses. The complexity surrounding such relationships offers one explanation as to why women were most often accused of being the purveyors of magic.[41] In other words, there was tremendous anxiety surrounding the idea that a woman could use the *seemingly* magical power of her sexuality to control men. In fact, it is the romances and other such forms of literature with their preoccupation with women and magic, which contributed to the hysteria concerning female power over men, the birthing process, and the sexual perversions attributed to heretics in the later medieval period.[42]

[40] See *Feminist Approaches to the Body in Medieval Literature*, ed. L. Lomperis and Sarah Standbury, (Philadelphia: University of Philadelphia Press, 1993). Ruth Evans and Lesley Johnson, ed., *Feminist Readings in Medieval Literature* (London: Routledge, 1994). [41] H.R. Bloch, *Medieval Misogyny* (Chicago: University of Chicago Press, 1999) 5–11, 93–4, 183–97. See also *A History of Women: Silences in the Middle Ages*, ed. Christiane Klapisch-Zuber (Cambridge, Mass.: Harvard University Press, 1992) 43–70, 323–35, 267–318. [42] Claudia Opitz, "Life in the Late Middle Ages", in *A History of Women: Silences of the Middle Ages*, ed. Christiane Klapisch-Zuber, 267–318, (esp. 297–311). See also Joann McNamara and Suzanne Wemple "The Power of Women through Family", in *Women and Power in the Middle Ages*, ed. Mary Erler and Mary Kowaleski (Athens: University of Georgia Press, 1988) 11, 83–101.

There has been a tremendous amount of work carried out under the auspices of gender studies in connection to the role of women and their status in the romances as magic bearers. Such critics as Susan Crane and Elaine Tuttle Hansen have comprehensively approached the issue of magic from a gendered perspective.[43] In order to avoid the revisiting of a road already much travelled, this study will not concentrate specifically upon female magic in the romances. It will focus, instead, upon the hero or heroine with regard to his or her experience of magic in the text, and the other avenues of exploration which the function of magic in the romances makes accessible.

It is also possible, however, to see that the deeper issue behind the anxiety of who controls magic, women or men, is one concerning who has power in society. In devising a means of controlling one member of a community, the poet has a powerful metaphor for a discussion of who has power over the entire society. It also brings into play the issue of free will and divine providence. If magic can offer a means of controlling individual action or influencing future events, then the poet has introduced a potent medium for exploring the nature of such issues in both the tale and the larger world. This is especially true of magic; it was declared superstitious nonsense by such scientists as Roger Bacon and yet accepted as the work of demons by Augustine and Aquinas.[44] This place somewhere in between fact and fiction offers romance poets a tremendous amount of freedom in its use. This makes magic in all its nuances very difficult to define and suggests that it is important to keep in perspective all the various functions of the magic in the text.

DEFINITIONS OF MAGIC

A vocabulary of magic is shared by a wide range of romance texts despite their being written in different languages and over a considerable span of time. The word *magic* can be seen in Old French in the forms *magique* and *merveilleux*; in Middle English the words are *magik*, *magyk*, and *merveille*; in

---

[43] For an in-depth discussion of gender and magic see Susan Crane, *Gender and Romance;* Elaine Tuttle Hansen, *Chaucer and the Fictions of Gender* (Berkeley: University of California Press, 1992); Anne Laskaya, *Chaucer's Approaches to Gender in the Canterbury Tales* (Cambridge: D.S. Brewer, 1995); Judith Butler, *Gender Trouble: Feminism and the Subversion of Identity* (New York and London: Routledge, 1990); Carolyn Dinshaw, *Chaucer's Sexual Poetics* (Madison: University of Wisconsin, 1989); Joan Ferrante, "Male Fantasy and Female Reality in Courtly Literature", *Women's Studies* 11 (1984): 67–97; Roberta Krueger, *Women Readers and the Ideology of Gender in Old French Verse Romance* (Cambridge: Cambridge University Press, 1993).   [44] This subject will be discussed in depth in succeeding sections of this Introduction.

Old English *wundor* or *wundor-cræft* derives from the Old High German *wunder*. These similarities spring from the fact that the cultures under discussion were heavily influenced in their understanding of magic by the Church, the Graeco-Roman world, the traditional culture of the Germanic peoples, and the Celtic tribes.[45] What should be stressed is that, based on the studies of Thorndike and Flint, it is clear that magic is frequently a part of the "real world" for medieval society.[46] It is difficult to provide precise definitions of these terms, or the terms associated with magic, as their use in the medieval world was not precise. Kieckhefer argues, however, that "certain forms of magic were so widespread that they formed a 'common tradition' found among both the clergy and laity, among both nobles and commoners, among both men and women, and (with certain qualifications) among townspeople and country people, in later medieval Europe. This is not to say that such magic was always and everywhere the same, but its basic forms were essentially similar wherever it occurred."[47]

Throughout this study, the term *magic* will be used for the phenomena which intellectuals would have recognised as natural or supernatural occurrences which demonstrate the influence of man over nature or mankind. The *Second Oxford English Dictionary* (*SOED*) provides this definition of *magic*:[48]

> *Magic sb.*1.a. The pretended art of influencing the course of events, and of producing marvellous physical phenomena, by processes supposed to owe their efficacy to their power of compelling the intervention of spiritual beings, or of bringing into operation some occult controlling principle in nature; sorcery, witchcraft.... 3. *Transf.* The art of producing (by legerdemain, optical illusion, or devices suggested by knowledge of physical science) surprising phenomena resembling the pretended results of 'magic' conjuring.
>
> *The magic which made use of evil or doubtful spirits was of course always regarded as sinful; but natural magic, i.e. that which did not involve recourse to spirits, was in the Middle Ages usually recognised as*

---

45 Kieckhefer, *Magic*, 17.   **46** Lynn Thorndike, *The Place of Magic in the Intellectual History of Europe* (New York: Columbia University Press, 1905) and *The History of Magic and Experimental Science*, 8 vols. (New York: Macmillan and Columbia University Press, 1923–58). Valerie Flint, *The Rise of Magic in Early Medieval Europe* (Princeton: Princeton University Press, 1991).   **47** Kieckhefer, *Magic*, 17.   **48** Owing to the tremendous variation in spellings, I will try to maintain a consistency in the choice of words and names. Magic, for instance, is found within the various texts to be spelled as, *magyk magik, magike* etc.

a legitimate department of study and practice so long as it was not used for maleficent ends.[49]

The *Middle English Dictionary (MED)* defines *magic* as: "*Magik* [O.F. *magique*] (a) The knowledge of hidden natural forces (e.g. magnetism, stellar influence), and the art of using these in calculating future events, curing disease, etc; ~ natural; (b) sorcery, enchantment."[50] These definitions take into account the complex and fluid nature of the terminology. Magic is beyond the scope of ordinary men, but it is within the power of men aided by demons who, Finlayson says, "most theologians agree, work their marvels largely through their superior knowledge of natural forces. This is worth stressing – marvels are not contraventions of natural law but created by the release of hidden powers of nature."[51] In this study, not all instances of magic will be classified as demon-related, but it should be noted that in the medieval world there were also, clearly, varying opinions as to the source of magic's power.

Magic, natural magic, or white magic are terms used most often to describe actions or events considered to be acceptable within the realm of God's Providence. If an action depends completely on divine intervention then it is not magical but miraculous. *Miracle* is defined by the *MED* as: "*Miracle* [L. *miráculum*; O.F. *miracle*]: 1.a. (a) A wondrous phenomenon or event; an extraordinary or remarkable feat; a marvel; 1b. (a) A miracle performed by God, Christ, angels, saints, the Cross, etc.".[52] This differs significantly from the Christian definition which identifies a miracle as primarily an act inspired by God. The *SOED* defines it as "a wondrous event occurring within human experience, which cannot have been brought about by human power or by the operation of any natural agency".[53] This flexibility between definitions allowed magic to be associated with divine and supernatural methods of assessing moral virtue and good character. A relationship between magic and the divine does not only exist in the romances. Aquinas believed that there were magicians who worked miracles through demons; for example, he distinguishes between good and bad magicians when he says, "Good Christians, so far as they work miracles by Divine justice, are said to work miracles 'by public justice'; but bad Christians 'by the signs of public justice,' as invoking the name of Christ, or by making use of other sacred signs."[54] *Necromancy*, however, is most often

---

49 *Magic*, SOED, 1989 edn.   50 *Magik*, MED, 1975 edn.   51 John Finlayson, "The Marvellous in Middle English Romance," *Chaucer Review* 33: 4 (1999): 370.   52 *Miracle*, MED, 1977 edn.   53 *Miracle*, SOED, 1989 edn.   54 Thomas Aquinas, *Quaestio* III, art. 3 as cited in Thorndike, *History of Magic*, II: 602.

the term employed to denote actions explicitly reliant on the conjuring of demons and invocations to the Devil.[55] *Nigromaunci* as defined by the *MED* means: "Sorcery, witchcraft, black magic, occult art".[56] Although, clearly, this definition fits within the scope of *magic*, there were (and are) very negative stigma attached to this term which usually associate it with evil deeds and devilish intentions.

In coming to terms with the use of magic in the romances, it is important to appreciate the idea of the marvellous, as the terms *magical* and *marvellous* were often used interchangeably in the texts. It is arguable that romance writers did this deliberately owing to the need for an acceptable place for magic in their works. In softening the lines between magic and the marvellous, the potentially negative aspects of magic were downplayed. The *MED* defines *marvellous* as: "Merveille [O.F. *merveilleux*] 1a. (a) A thing, act, or event that causes astonishment or surprise; a wonderful feat; an unnatural occurrence or circumstance; a wonder of nature or art; a monster or monstrosity; (b) *don* (*maken, wirchen*) merveill(s, to perform a wonderful feat or feats, work a wonder. *Merveillŏus* [O.F. *merveillos*] 2. (a) Miraculous; (b) supernatural, magical."[57] The terms *wonder* functioned in a similar manner to *marvellous*, in that its use softened any potentially negative connotations to the word *magic*. Wonder is defined in the *OED* as: "*Wonder* [O.E. *wundor, wundor-cræft*: marvellous skill or power; L. *mirable*: wonderful, marvellous, miracle] 1. A marvellous object; a marvel a prodigy (*Beowulf* 840). 2. A deed performed or an event brought about by miraculous or supernatural powers . . . 5. Evil or shameful action; (*O.E. Chronicles*, Laud MS, 1137) . . . 7. The emotion excited by the perception of something novel and unexpected, or inexplicable; astonishment mingled with perplexity or bewildered curiosity (*St Dunstan*, 1290)."[58]

The power of magic was made more evocative when romance authors blurred the already nebulous dividing lines between these terms. This procedure allowed them to create suspense and suspicion around the motives and actions of the character under discussion. Intentionality could then also be brought into play in the romances; if a character intended good works then the magic at his/her disposal would be white magic; if s/he intended evil ends, then he or she was by default a necromancer. Chrétien, for example, has Erec in *Erec and Enide*, identified as a demon when he miraculously rises from the dead; or again, the "invisible" Yvain is likewise identified to great effect by his attackers at the castle of the marvellous spring. Mistakes can be made, as in the case of Yvain, but the use of magic

---

55 Ibid., II: 152–3. 56 *Nigromaunci*, MED, 1979 edn. 57 *Merveille*, MED, 1975 edn. 58 *Wonder*, OED, 1989 edn.

must *not* necessarily be taken by the audience to implicate the hero or heroine in black or demonic practices. If this were not the case, the romances would not be able to involve their characters so casually in events from which they could not be morally redeemed. However one defines these terms, it is clear that it is difficult to depart from the world of good and evil, right and wrong. This creates natural links between questions of morality, ideas of God, the nature of power in the world (natural, man-made, demonic, and that of God) and magic.

In studying the magical and the marvellous in the medieval world, it becomes clear that a certain amount of laxity was also tolerated in terms of defining phenomena, a situation that the romance authors used to their full advantage. Gervase of Tilbury prefaces his *Otia imperialia* with an interpretation of *mirabilia* which provides insight into the medieval acceptance of the unknown: "Mirabilia vero dicimus quae nostrae cognotioni non subjacent etiam cum sint naturalia (we call marvels those phenomena that surpass our understanding even though they be natural)".[59] The medieval audience accepted that marvels existed and that events could be natural but still inexplicable.[60] Kelly cites as an example of this William of Newburg's attitude towards wonders: "Mira vero hujusmondi, dicimus non tantum propter raritem [sic], sed etiam quia occultam habent rationem (wonders of this kind are so called in truth not only because of their rarity, but also because they have hidden rationale)".[61] "Hidden rationale" can be interpreted by the modern reader as the work of man, God, or nature, and does not necessarily have to be the work of a demon. Marvels were not created by Christian, demonic, or completely natural powers, thereby allowing certain flexibility in their use.

Based upon a study of communally held beliefs, Funk and Wagnells' *Standard Dictionary of Folklore* provides a list of magical powers: "divination, invulnerability and superlative strength, transformation of self and others, ability to fly, power to become invisible or cause others to become so, ability to impart animation to inanimate objects, to produce at will anything required, knowledge of drugs to produce love, fertility, death etc., and invariably power over others though charms and spells".[62] To readers of medieval romance this list seems more like a catalogue of the magical motifs

---

[59] Gervase of Tilbury, "Otia imperialia", ed. Leibnitz, 881–1005, as cited in Le Goff, *Medieval Imagination*, 34.   [60] Kelly, *Art*, 156.   [61] William of Newburg, "Writings", in Benoit Lacroix, "*L'historien au moyen âge*", Conference Albert-le-Grand, 1966. Montreal: Institut d'Études Médiévales (Paris: Vrin, 1966) as cited in Kelly, *Art*, 156.
[62] Funk and Wagnells, *Standard Dictionary of Folklore, Mythology and Legend*, ed. Maria Leach (San Francisco: Harper Collins, 1984) 1178–80, esp. 1179.

found in one's favourite texts. However, what is most interesting about Wagnells' research is that it actively seeks to illustrate the precipice upon which magic delicately balances between good and evil. It achieves this by offering a wide range of terms for differing degrees of good, evil, and mixed magical practitioners, for example, witches, shamans, necromancers, *licwiglunga*, magi, demons, astrologists, alchemists, legerdemains, diviners, etc. It is not surprising that the use of magic in the romances elicits such a variety of responses, as it is clear that many viewpoints on the types of magic in operation existed in medieval society.

It should not be assumed that magic was solely the domain of the credulous and the superstitious in the medieval world. The research of Claire Fanger suggests that some types of magic required the skills of learning and research and were therefore most often in practice among the cognoscenti. This allows the use of magic to be further subdivided between *intellectual magic* (that which is discussed and used by scholars and scientists), and a less learned variation referred to as *practical magic* (the use of magic by wise women and healers to effect charms, hexes, and less complex rituals). It is interesting that Fanger defines magic by the nature of its intended effects, as opposed to its methods, and sees demonic magic not as evil but as a rather spiteful "and petty-minded sort – causing disease, harm, or deformity in another person; manipulating the emotions of others to induce love or hatred between two people, or to get a person of the opposite sex to submit to the operator's desires".[63] What is especially useful for this study is that she contributes to the evidence for the intermingling between magical practices and religious, scientific, and medicinal practices in the medieval world.

Evidence for such an intermingling is also available directly from medieval sources. Isidore of Seville, for example, was concerned to condemn magic as evil practice, yet he believed that "no harm" came from knowing that "certain stones possess astonishing powers, that the dog-star afflicts bodies with disease, and that the appearance of a comet signifies pestilence, famine or war."[64] In the twelfth century John of Salisbury in *Policraticus* condemned the magic arts as being "more harmful than the illusions of the stage".[65] Michael Scot also denounced magic and necromancy but at the same time asserted that the magician was wise in both the secrets of nature

---

[63] Claire Fanger, *Conjuring Spirits: Texts and Traditions of Medieval Ritual Magic* (London: Sutton, 1998) vii-viii. This approach to defining the medieval idea of magic is considered by Kieckhefer to have been made popular only after a series of sixteenth-century religious debates, and then again, by late nineteenth and early twentieth century anthropological writings. See Kieckhefer, *Magic*, 14–5. [64] Thorndike, *Place of Magic*, 14. [65] Thorndike, *History of Magic*, II: 158.

and the ability to predict the future.[66] The thirteenth-century scientist Roger Bacon was dubious about the existence of magic. In his *Opus majus*, and in the *Letter on the secret works of art, and nature and the results of magic*, he states:

> Beyond these there is a more damnable practice, when men despising the Rules of Philosophy, irrationally call up wicked Spirits, supposing them of Energy to satisfy their desires. In which there is a very vast error . . .[67]

If Bacon was a sceptic when it came to magic he was, however, a believer in dragons; he states that it is certain that "Ethiopian sages have come to Italy, Spain, France, England and these Christian lands where there are good flying dragons, and by an occult art that they possess, excite the dragons from their caves."[68] This is a perfect example of how magic functioned simultaneously in the realms of science, religion, superstition, fantasy, etc., in the medieval world. It seems virtually impossible to a modern audience that a belief in dragons could be any more acceptable than a belief in magic. In the medieval world, however, it was still the case that popes and peasants alike believed in magic. Such well-known historians as Tilbury and Cambrensis, for example, report stories of *incubi*; equally informative are the records which remain of numerous witch trials, particularly in France, which provide "a powerful testimony" to the reality of magic.[69] Such realities suggest that the medieval world had different criteria for evaluating "truth" and it is clear that the line between truth and fiction is one which was still very flexible in its conception.

What was also surprisingly flexible, was the distinction between magic and the miraculous which can be seen from the various ways in which intellectual magic was applied. The philosopher, clerk, scientist, doctor or theologian who used natural magic often wanted holy inspiration as well as the improvement of his/her faculties. This is the type of "good magician" which Aquinas described; s/he is one who is interested in acquiring worldly knowledge and positive influence in his or her community. *The Sworn Book of Honorius*, the *Ars notoria*, and its revision, the *Liber visionum Marie*, instruct the user that the help of the angels, prayer, meditation, and fasting

---

66 Ibid., II: 319. **67** *Friar Bacon, his Discovery of the Miracles of Art, Nature and Magick*, trans. T.M. (London, 1659): sect. 3–4 as cited in Finlayson, "Marvellous in Middle English Romance (1999)", 367. See also Roger Bacon, *Opus majus*, trans. R.B. Burke, 2 vols. (Philadelphia, 1928) 2: 587. **68** Thorndike, *History of Magic*, II: 657. **69** J.A. MacCulloch, *Faith and Fable* (London, 1932) 28 as cited in Finlayson, "Marvellous in Middle English Romance (1999)", 370.

are required to achieve magical success.[70] The line between Christian inspiration and magical invocation seems difficult to distinguish even for a medieval audience, a fact illustrated by the controversy concerning the above mentioned texts; they claimed to be holy, offering nothing but benefit to mankind and operating strictly by the will of God, but that did not prevent theologians condemning them any less than texts which endorsed demonic magic. This demonstrates what a difficult path the romances would have had to negotiate to make the place of magic in their texts acceptable. In coming to terms with the function of magic in the romances, it is necessary to appreciate not only its relationship to fiction and Christianity but also its place in the medieval world.

FROM ROME TO THE SHORES OF THE BARBARIANS: A BRIEF HISTORY OF MAGIC

In the works of such authors as Pliny the Elder or Seneca, marvels of nature are reported not as true by fact or scientific evidence, but as true by way of common belief. No sooner has Pliny dismissed magic in his text on natural history than he hesitates and suggests that there is "no one who is not afraid of spells and incantations".[71] This type of artful dodge is one that allows the writer to discuss the interesting topics of astrology, astronomy, and medicinal cures, which involved prayers, incantations and magical tokens, without dwelling on the logistics of how such powers functioned.

Valerie Flint in *The Rise of Magic in Early Medieval Europe* argues that there was always a strong belief in magic among the poor and uneducated, but that it experienced an upsurge in popularity among the intellectuals and theologians of the early Middle Ages. She argues that the Church, from its origin, appropriated magic to answer people's questions about the inexplicable happenings in their everyday lives.[72] Once the link between Christianity and magic was established, it became easier for the Church to reconcile various types of magic to its own purposes. Magic adopted by the Church was then described as miraculous; all other types of magic were referred to as demonically inspired. The miraculous power of Jesus, for example, may be associated with that of a white warlock who exorcised devils, raised the

---

70 *Ars Notoria*: London, British Library, Harley 181, Sloane 513, Sloane 1712; *Liber visionum*: London, British Library, Additional 18027; *Sworn Book*: British Library, Sloane ms.313.   71 Pliny, *Natural History*, trans. D.E. Eichholz, 10 vols (Cambridge Mass.: Harvard University Press, 1962) xxxvii. 15, X: 211.   72 Flint, *Rise of Magic*, 9–12, 173–99.

dead, and cured sickness.[73] This kind of power over evil also often manifested itself in the stories of saints' lives: St Francis, St Anthony, and St Stephen, for example, were famous for having vanquished hundreds of devils and demons throughout the various attacks made on their virtue. To many modern readers it may seem blasphemous to interpret celestial intervention as magical and yet the groundwork for such interpretation was laid by the poets and preachers themselves in the constant blurring of the distinctions between supernatural power and divine aid. Magic and Church ritual were intertwined on even the most basic level of social perception.

In the fourth century, however, the source of magical powers did come under fierce debate when it was widely proclaimed that the decline of the Roman Empire was owing to the abandonment of the pagan gods for the Christian God. Augustine wrote his seminal text *De civitate Dei* in response to this claim. He declared that the pagan religions of Rome were all grounded in necromancy.[74] Equally influential and foremost of the early treatises arguing the existence of demons was his *De divinatione daemonum*. Augustine defines demons as "a species of beings, superior to men, living forever ... endowed with supernatural powers of perception; and as fallen angels, the sworn enemies of the true happiness of the human race".[75]

Augustine did not believe in there being categories of good and bad magic.[76] He even went against folk tradition and the common practice of his contemporaries by declaring that the Devil was the source of all magic. It stands to reason that he also made a strong argument for the differentiation between magical acts and miracles. Anthropologists, such as Olof Pettersson, and historians, such as A.H.M. Jones, would argue, however, that at the time it was impossible to "objectively or scientifically disassociate 'magic' from 'religion' and on the same count, to differentiate between 'magic' and 'miracle'".[77] Augustine, in contrast, believed that the magician relied upon spells and incantations and was in league with the devil or enslaved by demons, while the Christian miracle worker only made use of faith and

---

[73] For examples of Jesus exhibiting such "magical powers" see Matthew 8:28–34, 10:32–34; Mark 5:1–17 and the story of Lazarus. [74] Augustine, *Concerning the city of God against the pagans*, trans. Henry Bettenson (London: Penguin, 1984) viii. [75] Peter Brown, *Augustine of Hippo: A Biography* (London: Faber and Faber, 1967) 311. [76] Augustine, *The City of God*, Fathers of the Church (New York), XIV, 131–32 as cited in Kieckhefer, *Magic*, 26–9. [77] A.H.M. Jones, *The Later Roman Empire*, 3 vols (Norman: University of Oklahoma Press, 1964) II: 90 and Olof Pettersson, "Magic and Religion", *Ethnos* XXII (1957) 109–99 as cited in Eugene D. Dukes, *Magic and Witchcraft in the Dark Ages* (Lanham, New York: University Press of America, 1996) 166–7. For a more comprehensive discussion see C.G. Loomis, *White Magic* (Cambridge: Medieval Academy of America, 1948).

prayers.[78] The aim of Augustine was to eradicate abhorrent magical practices. Ironically, in his efforts to diminish the power of pagan deities, he succeeded in giving credence to magic as important to Christianity. His conviction that demons and devils were dangerous secured belief and thereby social acceptance of their existence in the general Christian community.[79]

With the decline of Roman influence and the upsurge of Germanic and Celtic cultures in Western Europe, accommodation of certain elements in pagan culture became the common practice of the Christian missionaries. Pope Gregory the Great (590–604) preached tolerance to his missionaries in England and ordered that pagan temples should not be demolished but reconsecrated. This policy also applied to pagan holidays, festivals and some ritual practices.

In the traditions of the Angles, Saxons and Jutes, magical power allowed the gods to demonstrate their control over mankind. Magical tools could be used to create charms or perform wondrous deeds. According to myth, the god Woden mastered the runic alphabet and used its characters to create healing charms. In any discussion of magic in this period it is important to note that Christianity was fighting to make a place for itself; hence its individuality was most effectively defined by striking out against those pagan ideas which it could not absorb. For example, the pagan practice of worshipping many gods was reconfigured and undermined by developing the practice of praying to angels or saints who, as less powerful figures, allowed supreme power to be bestowed upon the one God. There could be no confusion then between pagan rituals and Christian practice nor any misapprehension about whose god was most powerful. This set the stage for Christians to associate black magic with heathenism and potential evil, while renaming as miraculous the white magic which reinforced the power of their God.

Keith Thomas argues:

> The claim to supernatural power was an essential element in the Anglo-Saxon Church's fight against paganism, and missionaries did not fail to stress the superiority of Christian prayers to heathen charms. The medieval Church thus found itself saddled with the tradition that the working of miracles was the most efficacious means of demonstrating its monopoly of the truth ... They related the miraculous achievements of holy men, and stressed how they could prophesy the future, control the weather, provide protection against fire and flood, magically transport heavy objects, and bring relief to the sick.[80]

78 Dukes, *Magic and Witchcraft*, 125–9. 79 Flint, *Rise of Magic*, 147. 80 Keith Thomas, *Religion and the Decline of Magic* (New York: Charles Scribner's Sons, 1971).

Magic was too valuable to the Church to suffer elimination since it did much to illustrate the puissance of bishop-saints or to empower a local priest with the ability to overcome devils and demons.[81]

Through the ever-growing influence of the Church, non-Christian magic slowly came to be vilified as a practice that destroyed communities and undermined the very fabric of a society. The Catholic Church sought to identify itself with the good of the community through influencing its courts and kings. It aligned itself and its beliefs with the sources of influence and control in society. It wanted non-Christian magical practices identified with the advancement of the individual and selfish personal gain. This paved the way for magic to be identified with heretics, marginalised groups, and difficult individuals, all of whom could be troublesome to the establishment.

It became the function of Church *and* State to eradicate demon-inspired witchcraft from medieval society. There are several sets of extant laws which provide sources for legal evidence concerning the status of magic in the early medieval world. For example, the laws of Edward and Guthrum state that: "If witches or diviners, perjurers or foul, defiled notorious adulteresses, be found anywhere in the land, let them be driven from the country and the people cleansed, or let them totally perish within the country, unless they desist."[82] In 690, Theodore of Canterbury proscribed the penalty of a year's penance for women who destroyed people through witchcraft, magic arts or evil spells. As the pagan practices slowly died out in Britain, the success of the Church at equating magic with heresy became apparent. In 901, Edward banished "diviners, death-workers and adulteresses" from the land. King Ethelstan, in 940, decreed the death penalty for witchcraft and deathdeeds wherever the guilt was obvious and death the result (guilt proved by ordeal merited only imprisonment). In 959, Edgar declared an edict against "enchantments, necromancies and divination".[83]

It is only through records and stories concerning such figures that the modern reader can begin to appreciate the interconnected nature of Anglo-Saxon, Frankish, and Christian cultures. As early as the travels of the Northumbrian Alcuin, records demonstrate that there was a tremendous

---

26. Many of these stories were retold in *The Golden Legend*, a popular compilation by a thirteenth-century archbishop of Genoa, which was to be translated by Caxton in 1483 and reissued in England at least seven times before the Reformation. For further information see B. Colgrace, "Bede's Miracle Stories", in *Bede: His Life, Times and Writings*, ed. A. Hamilton Thompson (Oxford: Clarendon, 1935) 20–35. 81 Flint, *Rise of Magic*, 127–8, 129–87. For further discussion see, John Ballaz Novak, "Magic as a Theme in *Sir Gawain and the Green Knight*", Dissertation, New York: University of Syracuse, 1979. 82 Ronald Holmes, *Witchcraft in British History* (London: Frederick Muller, 1974) 37. 83 Ibid., 38.

Creating meaning from magic

amount of interaction between these communities. Alcuin was a graduate of the school at York and was both friend and adviser to Charlemagne. There are other historical figures who embody the traditions of France, Normandy, England, and Norway, such as King Egbert, a pupil of Charlemagne who early in the ninth century was king of England. King Canute in 1016 was reigning head of a Nordic Empire consisting of Denmark, Norway, Normandy, and England. Shared traditions can also be seen in the fact that the basis of English coronations still resides in the combination of early English and West Frankish rituals.[84] The case of Edward the Confessor further illustrates the intimacy of the relationship between Normandy and Anglo-Saxon England; before becoming king of England he spent his youth in exile in Normandy. Clearly, the changing ideas of Christianity, Germanic culture, Celtic traditions, and social laws were being shared among these people long before the official date of the Norman Invasion in 1066.

It is also clear that post 1066, magic continued to play an important role in medieval culture. In the laws of William the Conqueror several edicts exist against the death of animals or men by magic, and against foreseeing the future to cause harm or ill wishing.[85] Such edicts were composed with an eye to preventing social evils and an interest in preserving the common good against illicit advancement of nefarious individuals. The first known witch-trial in England was during the reign of King John (1199– 1216); a Jew named Gideon stood accused of sorcery by a merchant's wife. He established his innocence by undergoing an ordeal by red-hot irons.[86]

In the reign of Henry II, according to John of Salisbury's *Policraticus*, there were declarations against "those who practised the evil arts of magic and divinations [and they] were ordered to be excluded from the court: for all these operations or rather sorceries arise from the pestilential familiarity of demons and men".[87] Marvels played a significant role in legitimising the right of royal houses to rule. Royal dynasties attempted to trace their roots to mythical pasts, in the hope that such histories would cast a supernatural aura of power upon families struggling to reign. In the early thirteenth century, Cambrensis recorded that the Plantagenets were descended from a female demon.[88] Philip Augustus attempted to use this propagandist myth of marvellous origin against the Plantagenets, in the hopes of doing away with the

---

[84] P.H. Sawyer, *From Roman Britain to Norman England* (London: Routledge, 1978, 2nd ed. 1998) 186–7. [85] Holmes, *Witchcraft*, 37–40. [86] Ibid., 51. [87] Ibid., 39. [88] Bradford Broughton, *The Legends of King Richard I, Coeur de Lion: A Study of Sources and Variations to the Year 1600* (Paris: The Hague, 1966), as cited in Le Goff, *Medieval Imagination*, 33.

children of this demon.[89] In associating ruling classes with mythical origins, the line between the never-never land of the romances and reality in the medieval period becomes ever finer. Kings and courts used the power of mythical sources as propaganda for their own legitimacy and greatness only because it was effective to do so. The medieval population was thereby encouraged to ignore the line between myth and history, fact and fiction.

At the same time that kings and courts were making much of magic's myth-making qualities, they were defending themselves from attack by magical means. The cases of Thomas Southwell, canon of St Peter's Chapel, Westminster, and Roger Bolingbroke are examples; both were found to be associated with Eleanor Cobham, wife of the duke of Gloucester, in a plot to take the life of King Henry VI by magical means. Eleanor was banished for life to the Isle of Man, Southwell died in the Tower, and Bolingbroke was tied to a hurdle and dragged through the streets of London before being hanged and quartered.[90] Thorndike cites a catalogue of magical intrigues in *A History of Magic and Experimental Sciences* in which she describes the reign of Louis X (1314–16) as short but terrible.[91] Enguerrand de Marigny, Pierre de Latilly, and Francesco Gaetani were each accused of plotting at one time or another the magical destruction of the King.[92] Charles IV (1322–28) proceeded to try Countess Matilda of Artois for magically poisoning his predecessor. Edward II matched his French cousin's methods in 1324, when over twenty persons were tried for having attempted to bring about the death of the English king and his favourites by magic.

WHO CONTROLS THE MAGICIANS?: DISENTANGLING CHURCH AND STATE

It was the Church that set in motion the fiercest retaliation against the forces of magic. In 1200, Pope Innocent III began the first Inquisition, a process that would deal harshly, not only with heretics (real or imagined), but also with witches. In fact, it was one of the most effective means that the Church had yet devised for dealing with magic. It was through the trial of the "magical" society of Templars by the pope and the king of France, Philip IV, that the Inquisition gained much of its notoriety. This

---

[89] Broughton, *The Legends of King Richard I, Coeur de Lion*, as cited in Le Goff, *Medieval Imagination*, 33. [90] Holmes, *Witchcraft*, 44. [91] Thorndike, *History of Magic*, III: 21–3. See also Henry Charles Lea, *A History of the Inquisition of the Middle Ages*, 3 vols (Philadelphia: Lea Brothers, 1883); and Kieckhefer, *Magic*, 187–8. [92] Holmes, *Witchcraft*, 44.

secret society was feared both by the Church and by politicians, hence their unification against it. Backed by a king's authority, the Inquisition acted without consideration for justice or morality. The knights were tortured until they "confessed". There were a number of sins to which the knights did/had to confess: 1) formal renunciation of Christ; 2) killing of children and the use of their bodies for magical purposes; 3) worship of idols or animals; 4) acts of desecration of the Cross; and 5) the use of the obscene kiss.[93]

Once the Templars were crushed, the Inquisition was in need of more victims to sate its hunger, hence it focussed upon the ignorant and superstitious. The Bulls of Pope John XXII issued in 1318 and 1320 accused heretics of using divination and sorcery. This was a fairly general accusation, which was then "improved" upon by Nicholas Jaquarius in 1458, when he claimed that all witches belonged to the same secret sect. Pope Innocent VIII demonstrated support for this type of thinking by issuing his Bull *Summis desiderantes* in 1484 which declared that:

> ... many persons of both sexes, unmindful of their own salvation and straying from the Catholic Faith, have abandoned themselves completely to devils, incubi and succubi, and by their incantations, spells, conjugations, and other accursed charms and crafts, enormities and horrid offences, have slain infants yet in the mother's womb.[94]

Four years after this declaration and with the full authority of the Church, *Malleus maleficarum* (*The Hammer of Witches*) was written by the Dominican Inquisitors Henry Krämer and James Sprenger, and issued as the definitive text-book for witch hunters. Although this is not the appropriate forum for a full discussion of this text, it may be mentioned in passing that the misogynistic attitudes of its authors are clear, and it must be wondered if their virulent campaign against female heretic-witches was owing to a hatred of women rather than to a fear of magic.

In England, the existence of, or fear concerning, heresy and the use of magic affected the culture in very different ways. John Wycliffe (1320–84), a Doctor of Theology at Oxford, accused the clergy of corruption and criticised the Church's interpretation of the Bible. The Lollards, as Wycliffe's followers came to be called, stressed that the Scripture was the ultimate authority even for matters of civil law and politics. Wycliffe urged that all classes should read or at least have access to the Bible; hence his interest in a translation of it. With the invention of the printing press in 1436, it became possible to mass-produce books, and early in the sixteenth century

[93] Ibid., 46. [94] Ibid., 48.

booksellers in England began to sell copies of the *Matthew Bible*.[95] Such developments broke the stranglehold the Church had formerly held on the interpretation of Christ's words and God's message. It also increased the desire of the Church to rid itself of such troublesome heretics. For example, such famous followers of Wycliffe as John Huss of Prague University were so threatening to the Church that under false promises of safe-passage the pope lured him to Rome, where he was burned at the stake. This caused such a succession of riots in Bohemia that the Church mounted several Crusades to try to bring it back under its sphere of influence, all of which failed until peace was achieved in 1456.

Back again in England, the Lollards successfully mounted an anti-magic campaign against the Church. Turning the tactics of subversion neatly upon the master, the Lollards declared that the use of images and relics by the Church for healing purposes represented the use of superstitious magic.

As the political future of Rome grew ever more uncertain, Church authorities struggled to stamp out heretics and dissenters through Bulls such as the above-mentioned *Summis desiderantes* issued by Pope Innocent VIII, in which dissenters were classified as witches, and heretics labelled helpers of Lucifer, the "Prince of Darkness". The metamorphosis of the Greek god, Phosphorous, once considered good and powerful, into the medieval incarnation of Lucifer, mirrors the evolution of the role of magic in the medieval world.

MAGIC AND THE EVERYMAN

From the study of medieval court and clerical politics, it is obvious that magic played a powerful role in the hands of the unscrupulous. These illustrious arenas were not the only areas influenced by magic, however, as there is evidence of a thriving culture of healers and wise women in the general community. A complex relationship between the mystical powers of God and the practicalities of magical cures had evolved to "solve" the problems and fears of everyday life, for example:

> The communicant who did not swallow the bread, but carried it away from the church in his mouth, was widely believed to be in

---

[95] A.J. Maas, "Lollards" and "Translations of the English Bible", *Catholic Enclyclopedia*, vol. XV, transcribed by Dennis McCarty, online edition, 1999, January 5, 2000 <http://www.newadvent.org/cathen/09333a.htm>.

Creating meaning from magic 43

> possession of an impressive source of magical power ... Medieval stories relate how the Host was profanely employed to put out fires, to cure swine fever, to fertilise fields and to encourage bees to make honey. The thief could also convert it into a love-charm or use it for some maleficent purpose. Some believed that a criminal who swallowed the Host could be immune from discovery ...[96]

Magic and the mysteries of the Church were on some level compatible, enabling the practitioner of magic to call upon God to strengthen his or her power. In 1528, as an example of such a practitioner, Margaret Hunt described her methods to the Commissary of London. She claimed that she firstly ascertained the names of the sick persons and then knelt and prayed to the Blessed Trinity to protect them from all their enemies. She then told them to say for nine consecutive nights five Paternosters, five Aves, and a Creed, followed by three more Paternosters, three Aves, and three Creeds.[97] These Christian rituals were incorporated into her magical rites, demonstrating the flexible nature of the relationship that existed between magic and faith in the medieval world.

The idea of magic permeated many areas of medieval life, even the intimate ones. The fear of magic, for example, acted as a weapon in the balance of power in medieval marriage. *Causa 33* in Gratian's *Decretum* is one in a series where he discusses male impotence as induced by female use of *maleficia*.[98] Edward Peters reports that several texts focused on such issues, and cites as an example Ivo's rewriting of Hincmar of Reim's ninth-century treatise *De divortio lotharii*:

> The canon *Si per sortiarias* states that if a man is rendered impotent by magic and his impotence cannot be ended by penitence, exorcisms, prayers, almsgiving, and the like then the marriage may be ended. This text, far more than any other, including the *Canon Episcopi* was of interest to canon lawyers because it touched the vital area of developing marriage law...[99]

---

96 Thomas, *Decline of Magic*, 34–5. 97 W.H. Hale, "A Series of Precedents and Proceedings in Criminal Cases, Extending from the year 1475 to 1640," in *Act-Books of Ecclesiastical Courts in the Diocese of London* (London, 1847) 107–8, as cited in Thomas, *Decline of Magic*, 178–9. 98 Edward Peters, *The Magician, the Witch and the Law* (Philadelphia: University of Pennsylvania Press, 1978) 74–5. 99 Ibid., 75; See also Edward Peters, *Witchcraft in Europe 1100–1700: A Documentary History* (Philadelphia: University of Philadelphia Press, 1972); and Peters, *Heresy and Authority in Medieval Europe* (Philadelphia: University of Pennsylvania Press, 1994); and Flint, *Rise of Magic*, 155, 292–6.

It is interesting that even in the area of carnal love the Christian Church had much to say about the power of magic. Examples of works concerned with the influence of magic in marriage and on the home life are the very early *Lives of Saints* by Aelfric, *The Confessions of Egbert*, and Saint Caesarius' sermons, in which magicians were condemned as potentially threatening to a person's chastity and virtue.[100] According to McNeil and Gamer's *Medieval Handbooks of Penance*, Egbert's *Confessions* is also of interest for its rule of three years penance to be adjudged to any wife who tampered with her husband's love.[101] Later works to discuss medicinal as well as magical love-potions include Burchard, the bishop of Worms' *Decretum*, Rabanus in his *Poenitentiale ad Deribaldum*, and the work of St Victor.[102] The early eleventh-century *Corrector* of the Bishop of Worms is virtually a treatise on popular magical beliefs and an essential handbook for priests who were responsible for disciplining the peasantry for their superstitions.[103]

The link between the intellectual circles and magic makes sense, as magic was a popular area of study with scholars. It was said in "The Common People" in *The Golden Groove* that "he is not adjudged any scholar at all, unless he can tell men's horoscopes, cast out devils or hath some skill in soothsaying".[104] Astrologers could be called upon to regulate the affairs of state and advise in such important decisions as when to marry or make a will.

Peters argues that the discussion of magic by such famous figures as William of Auvergne, Albertus, Aquinas, and Arnold of Villa Nova seems to have been provoked not only by general fear or awareness of magic, but by the fact, confirmed by Grosseteste and William of Auvergne, that magical books and texts were available in both Oxford and Paris.[105] This

---

100 Flint, *Rise of Magic*, 69–70, 232–3, 150–1. **101** *Medieval Handbooks of Penance: A Translation of the Principal Libri Poenitentiales*. ed. and trans. John McNeill and Helena M. Gamer (New York: Columbia University Press, 1938) 246. **102** Burchard of Worms, '*Decretum*', in *Patrologia Latina*, vol. 140 ed. J.P. Migne (Paris. 1878–90) 831–54, 943–1058. Burchard's *Decretum* can also be found in McNeill, *Handbooks of Penace*, 314–45. See also Flint, *Rise of Magic*, 41–2, 147, 231–6, 301–28. Rabanus, *Poenitentiale ad herihaldum* xxv, xxx in *Patrologia Latina*, vol. 110, ed. J.P. Migne (Paris, 1878–90) 467–94, 1090–110, as cited in Flint, *Rise of Magic*, 11, 41–2, 147, 231–6, 301–28. **103** C. Vogel, "Practiques superstitieuses au début du xie siècle d'après le *Corrector sive medicus* de Burchard évêque de Worms", *Etudes de civilisation médiévale ... offertes a E.-R. Labande* (n.d.) 751–61 as cited in McNeil, *Handbooks of Penance*, 33. **104** W. Vaughan, *The Golden Groove* (London, 1600), as cited in Thomas, *Decline of Magic*, 227. For a discussion of magical associations with the word *scholar* see J. Fletcher, *The Chances* vi (London, 1647) as cited in Thomas, *Decline of Magic*, 227. **105** Peters, *The Magician*, 111, 110–13, 66–7.

signifies that there was a great deal of interest in, and availability of, information concerning magic. *Picatrix* and *Liber juratus* are only two of the most eloquently constructed defences of magic produced in the thirteenth century. Magic was held by some to be able to affect the workings of a society at every level, whether through a love potion available from any wise witch for the lowliest peasant, or through the murder of a pope or a king. This demonstrates the potent force of secular beliefs even in sophisticated Christian societies.

This brief description of the evolution of magic from the hands of the gods to the power of the individual is only meant to serve the reader as the most basic introduction to a history of magic. It illustrates that the place of magic in secular and Christian culture is so firmly entrenched that it is difficult to separate out the various strands of its influence. This exploration of the complex relationship of magic to the medieval world should serve as a foundation for understanding how a Christian romance, like Christianity itself, was able to tolerate the use of magic.

This summary also demonstrates that magic had a place in medieval society which was not only located in the imagination. Despite the clear evidence for magical weapons and characters in the lore of Celtic and Germanic tribes, the modern reader can also see that with the addition of classical traditions and Christian dogma, new dimensions were added to the source material for the romances. Kieckhefer describes magic in the medieval world as "the crossing-point where religion converges with science, popular beliefs intersect with those of the educated classes, and the conventions of fiction meet with everyday life".[106] In acknowledging that the people who feared it or controlled it considered magic a powerful tool, the modern reader may develop a better sense of its place in the romances.

THE FUNCTION OF MAGIC IN THE ROMANCES

The function of magic (whether real or illusory) as identified by the Church in medieval society, was to confer power upon an individual in that society. This function necessarily links it to the issues of man's place in the community and matters of spiritual belief. This mirrors the place of magic in the romances; Jameson, for example, sees magic and "otherness" as the "raw materials" which the "medieval romance found ready to hand in its socio-economic environment."[107] Crane, in *Gender and Romance in Chaucer's Canterbury Tales*, defines magic in the romances

---

[106] Kieckhefer, *Magic*, 1-2. [107] Jameson, "Magical Narratives", 142.

as "the manifestation of powers that are not directly attributable to Christian faith, yet are so far beyond the ordinary course of nature as to be inexplicable according to its laws".[108]

Romances focus on the achievement of a balance between private needs and public obligations. By incorporating a strong magical presence into the romance, an author creates a medium that explores both the relevant political and social issues of the day, and timeless questions of faith, love, loyalty, fate, and destiny. While the romances evolve from the twelfth to the fourteenth century, these issues remain constant by means of an author's skilful appropriation of certain aspects of the core tale which are then reconfigured: for example, Chrétien's *Cligés* is written with knowledge of, and disagreement with, Thomas of Britain's *Tristran*; Marie de France's roughly contemporary *Chevrefoil* offers a third source of dissenting interpretation of *Tristan*, which in turn influences Gottfried's *Tristan* and the English redactor's version, *Sir Tristrem*.

These stories share many similarities, but the most striking is the clear concern for the power of magic. Changes result from emendations made to suit the tastes of the local audience or the particular aims of the author's agenda. Magic's links to medieval society in terms of personal, social and religious issues draw an audience into an examination of the romances in those areas: the character's sense of identity, his/her place in society, and relationship with God. Romance authors achieve this response by orchestrating situations in which characters discover weaknesses through interacting with magic. For example, a character's being at the mercy of magic, as in the case of Yvain's need for a magic potion to restore his mind, in *Le Chevalier au Lion*, indicates that he must come to terms with some weakness in one of the areas of the influence of magic, namely, personal values, social status or spiritual beliefs. When a character no longer needs magic, s/he has acquired the right balance between personal needs and the needs of the community. For romance heroes such as Perceval or Gawain – and for the audience also – this process leads to an understanding of true faith and the cost of its practice.

It is important to note, however, that there was more than likely an unwritten and perhaps unacknowledged code among the romance writers which limited the use of black magic in order to retain, in general, the Church's tolerance of the literature and, in particular, other forms of acceptable magic which appeared in the literature.[109] The regularity of the

---

[108] Crane, *Gender and Romance*, 132. Crane provides an interesting list of magicians in the romances. [109] See Morgan for a discussion of the Green Knight, in Gerald Morgan, *Sir Gawain and the Green Knight and the Idea of Righteousness* (Dublin: Irish

Creating meaning from magic 47

presence of magic in the romances and the consistency of its description was a successful formula, as is evident from the popularity of the genre. Clearly, despite all forms of protest, magical *aventures* flourished through to the fifteenth century and beyond.

While the romances discussed in the succeeding chapters focus on love and *aventure*, love's meaning and usage are defined differently by each author. The Arthurian romances of Chrétien and *Lais* of Marie de France concentrate on balancing conflicting loyalties and obligations: love generates one set of loyalties to a wife or lover which may come into direct opposition to previously established loyalties to court and king. The quests of the characters represent the process of finding resolutions to these conflicting obligations through being tested, most often by magical means and marvellous events. The romances of *Sir Tristrem*, *Ywain and Gawain*, and *Syr Launfal*, all adaptations of the French and Anglo-Norman texts, conceive of love within the context of maintaining *trowth*, defined as maintaining one's faith, or truth, in the public, personal, and spiritual senses of the word.[110] This translates into loyalty and being true, not merely to one's own expectations, but also to those of family and community. In these texts, love is a personal obligation (as opposed to a passion for another person) which comes into conflict with pre-established social duties. Chaucer's *Franklin's Tale* also focuses on a complex redefinition of *trowth*. The ability to be true to oneself, or to maintain love, depends upon the ability of the hero or heroine to keep faith. In this tale, magic is used to create situations where what should not occur does indeed occur, and the wild promises which were made to keep a lover at a distance or to preserve the honour of a husband, are required to be kept.

The interdependent nature of many of the romances indicates a prior widespread appreciation for magic, a conclusion enabled by their authors' obvious assumptions. The place of magic in the text is rarely explained; the audience is assumed to be familiar with magical characters such as Morgan Le Fay, or locations such as the isle of Avalon, and the existence of magical swords, rings, beds, bridges and girdles. If the romance is to achieve maximum impact, the audience must already be conversant with magical motifs.

Academic Press, 1991) 60–80.   [110] For a more complete definition see Chapter 3, below.

ROMANCE MAGIC AND THE INDIVIDUAL

The source of magic in the romances is rarely, if ever, attributed to a demonic origin and there are virtually no examples of black magic or necromancy in the romances under discussion. Therefore, the type of magic which most often appears in the romances is the product of knowledge which an individual has concerning the "secrets" of nature.[111] It is difficult to define the power with which magic provides a character as it varies depending on the object or event under discussion. The most common types of magic used by individuals in the romances are: rings which protect the wearer, make one invisible, or help one to see spells; swords which provide superhuman strength; potions which restore natural functions, slow down natural functions, cause true love, or bemuse the recipient; and, the use of astrology and astronomy to foretell the future or alter it. Stevens suggests that magic can give individuals "superhuman powers".[112] Humans can through magic, in theory if not in practice, exercise control over nature with the assistance of forces more powerful than those humans wield alone. To control nature is of course already an infringement upon the powers of God, but where the real sensitivity lies is in the idea that magic allows one person to control other members of the community. Based upon these conceptions of magic in the medieval world, a medieval poet could use magic to precipitate a discussion concerning free will and fate in his or her text. An example of this would be Chaucer's creation of Dorigen's "black rock" scene in the *Franklin's Tale*. Aurelius' access to magic seems to give him "unnatural" control over her fate. In the provocative romance, *Sir Gawain and the Green Knight*, Gawain accepts a magical girdle due to the fact that he thinks it will give him power over his own fate. In Chrétien's *Cligés*, Fenice seems to control her own fate through magic, in that she prevents the consummation of her marriage to the emperor. In the *lai Yonec*, Marie presents a particularly complex approach to magic, human will, and Christianity, in that her heroine ensures that magic is condoned by God, before she allows herself to commit adultery with a lover, whose magical transformation into a bird she has made possible through her prayers and desire. In this situation, magic has come to represent the supernatural power that God can confer upon an individual to allow justice to be done, or vengeance to be had, as in the case in this *lai*.

---

[111] Scot as cited in Thorndike, *History of Magic*, II: 319. For further discussion see page 33 above. [112] J.E. Stevens, *Medieval Romances: Themes and Approaches* (London: Hutchinson University Library, 1973) 97.

It is clear from the vision of medieval life which has been recreated by historians that magic played an important role in secular life. This role was mirrored in the romances: a person who had access to magic, or some form of power that was interpreted to be magical, had a special place in the community. In the romances, if a character can operate magic, s/he is securely placed in society. Examples of such characters in the romances would be Morgan in *Sir Gawain and the Green Knight*, the Clerk in the *Franklin's Tale*, or the character of Morgan as she appears in the romances of Chrétien. This position is very different from that of the majority of characters, which is one of being a carrier of magic tokens or the victim of magic itself. Such characters are Dorigen, and eventually Aurelius, in the *Franklin's Tale*, Gawain in *Sir Gawain and the Green Knight*, Lancelot in *La Charrette*, and the host of secondary characters with which the romances are peppered, who guard, deliver, and retrieve magical tokens. The use of magic, or perhaps more accurately, the need of magic by these characters often illustrates to the romance audience their vulnerability in terms of sense-of-self or social standing. Once a character can conquer the need for magic or pass a marvellous test unscathed, it signals in the romance that he or she has emerged from the learning process. The character has achieved a secure social standing or has come to terms with the personal conflict which had been inhibiting growth and maturity. In the romances, magic does not provide clear answers for the characters, only a wide range of natural and supernatural possibilities, which to negotiate successfully requires thought and interpretation.

ROMANCE MAGIC, FATE, FORTUNE AND MEDIEVAL CHRISTIANITY

In acknowledging how magic in the romances reflects the concerns of the community, it becomes equally important to study how magic is used to reflect the concerns of medieval Christianity. R. W. Southern argues in *The Making of the Middle Ages* that the literary transition from epic to romance mirrors the transformation of the intellectual, spiritual, and social life of the twelfth century. Exemplified by the writings of St Anselm and St Bernard, changes are seen in the shifting of emphasis from communal exercise in endurance, such as was displayed in the *Chanson de Roland*, to a view of life as individual seeking and journeying, as in the romances Chrétien.[113] Southern argues that the spiritual emphasis on self-knowledge found

---

113 Southern, *Making of the Middle Ages*, 244.

expression on the secular plane in the *aventures* of the heart discussed in so many of the romance stories.

That there is a link between Christianity and magic in literature is not a new idea, but the way in which the two function in the romances bears consideration. Klassen argues in his study of extant manuscripts dealing with magic that it is most often Christian thinkers who discuss magic in their texts. Such discussions are to be found in, for example, the works of Thomas Aquinas, Peter Abano, Giovanni da Fotana, Nichole Oresme and James the Carthusian.[114] Equally, many extant texts which discuss magic were discovered along with religious manuscripts or were owned by monks.[115] What can be deduced from this is that the symbiotic relationship of the Church and magic, apparent in the Christian guidelines preserved by magical romances, is a product of generations of mutual tolerance and need for each other's resources. Christian theories concerning fate and free will were just two of the key questions with links to magic under debate by the seminal thinkers of the age.[116]

In the romances the Christian God who recognises magic is a Boethian one: He may interfere in the course of everyday life, but does not have to, leaving man's will an important role to play in the outcome of events.[117] In the romances, a character is expected to be in control of his or her own actions and when that freedom is taken away by magic, it allows the author to explore what could potentially happen without morally impugning the character under discussion. The romances represent the movement from scholastic debate to the imaginative enactment of the potential ramifications of the loss of free will. One of the main points of discussion in the *Tristan* tale, for example, is whether Tristan has free will. Is it his choice to love the queen and consequently betray King Mark? What are the consequences of his actions? Whether the magic potion absolves him of all responsibility for his actions is also under intense debate. The exploration of such "contemporary issues" through the paradigm of romance allows for the examination of potentially explosive outcomes, without serious repercussions for the audience.

The question of fate is also frequently considered in the romances. Heroes and heroines alike bemoan as the vagaries of fortune what seem to be the results of their own choices. It is also true that fate is most often cursed for allowing love to strike in the most inappropriate places. This

---

114 Fanger, *Conjuring Spirits*, 15.   115 Ibid., 17–18.   116 Karin Aijmer, "The Semantic Development of the Will", in *Historical Semantics, Historical Word Formation*, ed. Jacek Fisiak (New York: Mouton, 1985) 1–21.   117 Hugo Bekker, *Gottfried von Strassburg's Tristan: A Journey through the Realm of Eros* (Columbia: Camden House, 1987) 59.

Creating meaning from magic

is, of course, the type of situation which the romances love to exploit. Does a character choose to love someone, or do the arrows of love strike the unwitting hero or heroine? Are characters fated to love one another? What role does free will play in matters of magic or the heart? One of the most widely considered texts concerned with fate in the medieval period was Boethius' *De consolatione philosophiae*. This text argues that the individual's fate and fortune are ordered according to a larger plan, an agenda which an individual is incapable of seeing:

> Each future thing is understood by a kind of mind which bends it back and recalls it to the presence of its own manner of knowledge; it does not change, as you think, with alternate knowledge of now this and now that, but with one glance anticipates and embraces your changes in its constancy.[118]

Hugo Bekker describes Boethius' plan very straightforwardly in his work *Journey through the Realm of Eros*:

1. God's immutable plan is Divine Providence;
2. Divine Order which unfolds itself in things mutable is Fate;
3. Man's freedom to act is defined as Human Will;
4. What seems irrational or arbitrary in Fate, is Chances of Fortune.[119]

This synopsis allows the modern reader to get a better understanding of the use of fate and fortune in the romances. H.R. Patch argues that medieval Christians from Boethius to Dante maintained the pagan tradition of the goddess Fortuna side by side with a belief in God's omnipotence.[120] If it is possible for the medieval audience to reconcile pagan gods and Divine will, it comes as less of a surprise that magic, fate, fortune, and even pagan deities were tolerated in a Christian romance. Arcite and Palamon, from the *Knight's Tale*, and Dorigen and Aurelius from the *Franklin's Tale*, are only four of the most famous examples of characters who simultaneously pray to the gods, curse fate, and believe in the Wheel of Fortune. The function of magic in a romance concerned with fate and fortune is most often to seem to provide or

---

[118] Boethius, *De consolatione philosophae*, ed. Adrianvs A. Forti Scvto, S.T.D. (London: Burns, Oates & Washbourne, 1925) 163; Boethius, *Consolation of Philosophy*, ed. and trans., V.E. Watts (London: Penguin Classics, 1969) 168. [119] Bekker, *Journey*, 59. See also F.P. Pickering, "Notes on Fate and Fortune", in *Medieval German Studies*, vol. 36 (London: University of London, Germanic Studies, 1965): 1–15. [120] H.R. Patch, *The Goddess Fortuna in Medieval Literature* (Cambridge, Mass.: Harvard University Press, 1927. 2nd edn. London: F. Cass, 1967) 18–20.

remove from the character control over his or her life. The resulting situation often leads to the character – and the audience – examining not only the nature of the world in which they live, but also the dynamics of its power structures. This entails an assessment of the relationship between men in the community, and the relationship of God to the community.

Romance authors did not limit their relationship to the Church to discussions of fate and fortune. In borrowing heavily from the mythology of the Church, Chrétien and Chaucer, for example, co-opted the power of religious language to give their texts depth and resonance. The traditions of the Church and the saints presented a tremendous resource for ritual and symbolism. In using the rituals and language of repentance for the discussion of love, authors cemented the relationship between love and spiritual experience in their romances.[121] In *Le Conte du Graal*, Perceval's discovery of his true self, for example, is established by the religious rituals of confession in conjunction with the search for self-knowledge entailed by a magical quest. The research of Mary Flowers Braswell in *The Medieval Sinner* supports the claim that the Church often employed the idea of testing faith as a means of counteracting exactly the kind of spiritual problems which characters such as Erec, Yvain, and Dorigen suffered: pressing doubts, pride, and moments of unexamined (untried) faith.[122] It is not surprising that the romances inverted that structure to suit the exploration of secular problems. Magic as opposed to miracles, allowed the characters to come to terms with social and personal issues. For example, in *Yvain*, it is a potion provided originally by Morgan that cures the hero of his madness and allows him to begin the journey to a new identity in the Arthurian community.

CONCLUSION

The power of magic in the medieval romances, as well as in the medieval world in general, may best be measured by the enthusiasm of the reformers

---

[121] For other examples of secular writers borrowing from religious practices and language see Gower, *Confessio Amantis*, ed. Russell A. Peck (London and Toronto: University of Toronto Press, 1980) VIII, 2894–97. For one of the most comprehensive surveys of the superstitions surrounding the sacraments see C.G. Loomis, *White Magic: An Introduction to the Folklore of Christian Legend* (Cambridge, Mass.: Harvard University Press, 1948). [122] Mary Flowers Braswell, *The Medieval Sinner: Characterisation and Confession in the Literature of the English Middle Ages* (Rutherford: Fairleigh Dickinson University Press, 1994) 95–100, 33–5. See also A. Hopkins, *The Sinful Knights* (Oxford: Clarendon, 1990) 20–3, 66–9.

Creating meaning from magic 53

to extinguish it. As the medieval world moved towards the Reformation, the power of magic within the Church was a central point of contention among the reformers. John Bale in the sixteenth century complained that the Mass had become a remedy for the diseases of man and beast. The Mass was employed by "witches ... sorcerers, charmers, enchanters, dreamers, soothsayers, necromancers, conjurers, cross-digers, devil-raisers, miracle-doers, dog-leeches and bawds".[123] The corpus of these parasitic beliefs, which attached themselves to the Mass and most Christian sacraments, was given a material significance that the Church never formally acknowledged. "By the eve of the Reformation," claims Thomas, "these rituals had become crucial 'rites of passage', designed to ease an individual's transition from one social state to another, to emphasise his new status and to secure divine blessing for it."[124] The medieval use of magic for social, literary, and religious goals culminated in a Reformation movement intent on stamping it out in all its forms in the fifteenth and sixteenth centuries.

The strength of the influence of magic on medieval society requires that the modern reader should approach the romances with a keen eye to its function in them. This brief overview only sets the stage for what is a long and complicated history of magic in the medieval world. To fail to acknowledge its influence is to diminish and oversimplify a phenomenon which medieval authors saw as a means of interrogating their own community's sense of self and purpose. If one ignores the function of magic in the romances, then a fruitful source of controversy and exploration of social, theological, and moral issues is lost.

---

[123] *Select Works of John Bale*, ed. H. Christmas (Cambridge, 1849) 236 as cited in Thomas, *Decline of Magic*, 35. [124] Thomas, *Decline of Magic*, 36.

The origins of romance

THE MAGICAL LINK BETWEEN FACT AND FICTION

An examination of the first romances and earliest extant *lais* reveals that they were interested in exploring the themes of love, social status, and self-knowledge. It is clear that magic was also associated with these topics in medieval culture. Therefore, it is not surprising that romance authors made much of the sophisticated connections that could be linked to the presence of magic in their works. There is no question that early romance writers had access to magical and marvellous themes from their Celtic sources, but what is interesting is the use to which they put these materials. It is clear that they used the magical and marvellous as themes to explore moral and social issues of justice and free will, which is to say, in ways which were quite foreign to Celtic traditions. Chrétien de Troyes and Marie de France employed magic and the marvellous to function as a means of providing provocative information which engaged the audience with the political and social issues under discussion in the community. The use of magic and the marvellous as a bridge between the world of the imagination and the reality of medieval politics, religion, and science means that its use could open up a text beyond the boundaries of the imagination and link it to the realms of other types of discourse. In coming to an understanding of this use of magic in romance, it is valuable to attempt to discover where its roots are located.

This chapter focuses most fully upon the relationship between Chrétien and Geoffrey of Monmouth, as it will argue that the historical techniques of Monmouth influenced Chrétien's use of magic in ways which transformed it into something quite different from the use of magic by earlier Celtic sources. A discussion concerning the ways in which Celtic craftsmen employed magic will not be addressed in any detail owing to the considerable amount of research that already exists on that subject. Loomis' research, for example, details in an exceptionally methodical way virtually every Celtic motif in the works of Chrétien and many other romances. It seems inadvisable, therefore, to try to recreate such a study in what could only be a brief and unsatisfactory manner.[1] Instead, this chapter explores

---

[1] See Bibliography for an extensive list of Loomis' works; the links between romance

some of the influences upon the originator of Arthurian romance and seeks to address what materials other than Celtic could have affected Chrétien's style and technique.

HISTORICAL TEXTS AND THE FORMATION OF ROMANCE

Rooted in the clerical disciplines of the medieval world was a strong interest in magic and in forms of writing. It is not surprising, therefore, that early authors of fiction, who often shared the education of clerics, could call upon the techniques of historians, theologians and rhetoricians to develop the inclusion of magic as a method of developing new forms of literature. In an analysis of *Historia regum Britanniae* by Geoffrey of Monmouth and its French counterpart the *Roman de Brut* by Wace, one is able to trace possible precursors to the use of magic by Chrétien in the romances. For example, all three authors use the results of magical trials to illuminate different aspects of the personalities of their characters. If the hero or heroine is struggling to establish an identity or change status within the community, s/he must typically endure a series of magical trials that reveal the progress of his or her maturation. This preoccupation with identity in the romances and in these histories of Britain, reflects what Robert Hanning argues is a new level of concern in the twelfth century for establishing a sense of the individual.[2] Geoffrey's version of history has many hallmarks of a romance, such as the appearance of marvels and magicians; in addition, love is held to be an adequate motivator for immoral acts.[3] This "Arthurian romance" illustrates how social issues, Christian concerns, and what will become identified as romance concerns, operate concurrently within the historical format which Geoffrey adopts.

The romances of Chrétien are well known for their interest in the relationship between fiction and historical truth. This preoccupation could be placed in context if the romances were found to owe their origins, in part, to historical writing. However, it is also clear that the romances invested in issues that were beyond the realm of history, such as the development of the individual identity and appreciation of the complexities of social structures.

---

magic and Celtic magic will be discussed in greater detail in the following chapter.
2 Robert Hanning, *The Individual in the Twelfth Century* (New Haven and London: Yale University Press, 1977). 3 Geoffrey of Monmouth, *Historia regum Britanniae*, ed. Acton Griscom (New York: Longman's Green, 1929); Geoffrey of Monmouth, *The History of the Kings of Britain*, trans. Lewis Thorpe (London: Penguin Classics, 1966).

These themes are reflected in the events of Perceval's story as he fails to ask the right questions when the Fisher King is testing his suitability. This experience reveals to the audience that he is still too immature to appreciate fully the marvellous/magical/spiritual gifts on offer. Such a situation must encourage the audience to consider the relationship between the spiritual nature of a knight's journey and the quest as a rite of passage into manhood. Perceval learns how to be a man through learning how to be a knight, and by making a place for himself in the Arthurian community.

The formative role of magic in the formation of the Catholic Church, as well as its provocative position in any debate concerning free will, leave the audience pondering what exactly it is that Perceval has to learn: how to be a better Christian, or how to be a better man?[4] Regardless of which interpretation is the correct one, the relationship of magic to spiritual and social topics in the medieval world enables the romance author to encourage a much more serious discussion of contemporary issues than if the text were simply a rendering of Celtic myth.

When comparing a series of texts by Chrétien to the *Lais* of Marie de France, it is possible to establish a pattern of how and why these authors employed magic. That pattern is predicated upon a common appreciation for the place of magic both in medieval society and in medieval literature. Such an appreciation is derived from exposure to other literary traditions which incorporate magic, and exposure to a fund of common folk knowledge concerning magic. After investigating even just a sampling of the source materials which Chrétien and Marie used, it is possible to conclude that they were influenced by a resurgence of twelfth-century interest in historical writing, classical ideas, and rhetorical techniques.[5] It is clear that both authors were familiar with Anglo-Norman literature and historical texts. This is not surprising as there is a wealth of evidence to suggest that insular and continental societies shared many cultural links through the influence of Christianity, common ruling dynasties, and the experience of historical events such as the invasion by the Normans in 1066. This pool of mutual resources makes logical the comparison of French, Anglo-Norman, and Middle English texts.

---

4 See pages 24–47 above for a detailed discussion of the relationship of magic to religion.   5 A discussion of the influences upon these authors is to follow, but in brief, see the works of Ovid, Wace's *Brut*, *Piramus et Tisbé*, *Roman d'Éneas*, *Roman de Thébes*, *Romulus*, derived from the Latin version of Aesop, the *Roman de Renard* material, and it can be argued, Virgil's *Aeneid*. For a critical discussion of these influences, see *Lais*, ed. Hanning and Ferrante, 1–27, and David Staines, *The Complete Romances of Chrétien de Troyes* (Bloomington: Indiana University Press, 1993) ix–xxviii.

In examining a selection of the possible sources for Chrétien's Arthurian romances, Owen argues convincingly for a relationship between the romances and the *Mabinogion*.[6] They share many comparable features, leading to the argument that both writers shared a similar source, which was probably Anglo-Norman. Currently popular with romance critics is the theory that the Welsh *Gereint* stands as a possible source for *Erec* (*c*.1170), and that *Owein* is most likely the source for Chrétien's *Yvain* (*c*. 1177). Conversely, Chrétien's *Conte de Graal* (*c*.1182) may have influenced the Welsh *Prouder*. The problem with this theory, however, is the fact that the earliest extant form of these Welsh tales dates nearly a century after the death of Chrétien.[7]

A variety of separate traditions also influenced Chrétien's romances. It is arguable that *Cligés* (*c*. 1176) demonstrates familiarity with Thomas' Anglo-Norman *Le Roman de Tristan* (1155–70), and Wace's *Roman de Brut* (1155). Debate exists about whether or not the *Chanson de Roland* could also have influenced this text. The *Chanson* is taken to be an Anglo-Norman text; it has been dated as early as 1060, but is generally considered to have been written in the latter half of the twelfth century. The scriptural account of the Passion and Resurrection of Christ also more than likely influenced the description of Fenice's revival. Sources for *La Charrette* (*c*.1177) are Caradoc of Llancarvan's *Vita sancti Gildae* (certainly composed before 1160, and probably before 1136), and Christ's *Harrowing of Hell* from the popular *Gospel of Nicodemus*.[8] Frappier has explored the influence of Virgil as a source for Chrétien; and C.B. Lewis has written at length about classical mythology as a source for *Yvain*, in particular, but also a wider variety of Chrétien's works.[9]

It is particularly helpful to examine the *Lais* of Marie de France as a back-drop to Chrétien, since her use of marvels is in many ways complementary. It is most likely that Marie was of French birth but wrote at or for the English court of Henry II. She claims that her *lais* are based upon

---

[6] Chrétien de Troyes, *Christian von Troyes. Sämtliche Werke*, ed. Wendelin Foerster, 5 vols. Paris: Halle, 1884–99, 1932; Chrétien de Troyes, *Arthurian Romances*, ed. and trans. D.D.R. Owen (London: J.M. Dent, 1987) xiv. These are the source texts which will be employed for the works of Chrétien in this study, unless otherwise noted. [7] Owen, *Arthurian Romances*, xiv. [8] Ibid., xiv [9] J. Frappier, "Virgile source de Chrétien de Troyes?" *Romance Philology* XIII (1959–60): 50–8; C.B. Lewis. *Classical Mythology and Arthurian Romance: A Study of the Sources of Chretien de Troye's Yvain and Other Arthurian Romances* (Geneve: Slatkine Reprints, 1932); F.E. Guyer, "The Influence of Ovid on Crestien de Troyes", *Romanic Review* XII (1921): 97–134, 216–47. See also Guyer, "Some of the Latin Sources of *Yvain*", *Romanic Review* XIV (1923): 286–304.

Breton *lais*, but as there are no extant texts of the latter, it is impossible to verify the extent of their influence on her writing. Owing to gender, Marie probably did not have the extensive training in grammar, rhetoric, dialectic and logic that characterised the clerics and civil service graduates of twelfth-century schools. Marie's use of classical Latin, French, and English materials, however, illustrates that she was a highly-trained literary craftsperson. Some of her sources that can be traced are Wace's *Brut*, *Piramus et Tisbé* (1155–60), and *Éneas* (c.1160).[10] It is clear from *Chevrefoil* that Marie was aware of the Tristan legends. She drew upon Celtic tales, Ovid, a version of Romulus derived from the Latin version of Aesop, and the *Roman de Renard* material.[11] Marie's particular interest in the spiritual and the marvellous is evident in the *Lais*, but more fully so in her final work, *L'Espurgatoire Seint Patriz*.

"TRUTH" IN THE ROMANCES AND LAIS

The Anglo-Norman *Lai d'Haveloc* (1137) was considered to be historically "true" well into the fourteenth century. Peter Langtoft and Robert Mannyng discuss it in their fourteenth-century chronicles, and both Camden and Leland cite references to it in their histories.[12] This material also provided the source for the Middle English *Lay of Haveloc the Dane*.[13] It would be fruitful to compare this phenomenon to the Arthurian material written about in the romances, which also came from such historical sources as Geoffrey of Monmouth. What is of particular importance to this study is that the *lai* and romance were considered capable of fulfilling serious functions, such as the transmission of historical events. Information was not automatically dismissed owing to the fact that it was contained in one of these genre forms. If the audience learned from the experiences of Arthur, or magically-derived prophecies, for example, whether the facts were true might have been considered of secondary importance. This possibility is one which twelfth-century historians were clearly interested in, evidenced by the debates concerning the relationship of fact to fiction, and whether the "true" purpose of history was as educational tool, or as source of factual information.

---

10 *Lais*, ed. Hanning and Ferrante, 7.   11 Ibid., 8–9.   12 *The Birth of Romance. An Anthology*, ed. and trans. Judith Weiss (London: Everyman, 1992) xxv.   13 For details of all references to the Haveloc story in chronicles and histories, see *Havelok the Dane*, ed. Skeat, xliii–lii, ed. second rev. K. Sisam (Oxford, 1915, second rept. 1967); *Havelok the Dane*, ed. G.V. Smithers (Oxford: Clarendon, 1987).

The origins of romance

The link here between the use of magic by the author and general acceptance of the marvellous and magical by the population at large, once again becomes important, as it was this type of information which, when presented in either romance or historical formats, caused consternation among twelfth-century intellectuals. All of the sources thus far examined suggest that romance authors borrowed and adapted substantial amounts of material (both fiction and non-fiction) from insular origins.[14] Therefore, it is necessary to examine how insular authors treat magic and history in their texts to gain some understanding of its influence upon the romance redactors.

WERE THE ROMANCES CONCEIVED ON ANGLO-NORMAN SOIL?

The oldest extant examples of romance are Anglo-Norman: the *Roman de Horn* of Mestre Thomas, the *Roman de Tristan* of Thomas, and the *Roman de Toute Chevalerie* of Thomas of Kent. *The Romance of Horn* is probably native to Britain, a conclusion arrived at through the presence in it of Scandinavian and Germanic names which were not common to Normandy. Hence transmission was not via the Conquest, but rather linked to the history of Viking raids in Britain from the eighth to tenth centuries.[15] According to the study of the poem by M.K. Pope, the language of the writer suggests that Thomas was probably an Anglo-Norman clerk of French parentage.[16] He had a middling command of English and was familiar, if only vaguely, with English and Irish topography. Pope also suggests that the formative years of Mestre Thomas were most likely the last years of the reign of Henry I, and the tumultuous reign of Stephen.[17]

Formed independently of the Continental Old French tales of Alexander, Thomas of Kent's *Le Roman de Toute Chevalerie* evolved directly from Late Latin and Anglo-Latin sources.[18] *Chevalerie* then served as the principal source for the Middle English *Kyng Alisaunder*.[19]

Written in the literary French of the Angevin courts, *Le Roman de Tristan* contains discernible traces of an Anglo-Norman dialect, but

---

14 David Howlett, *The English Origins of Old French Literature* (Dublin: Four Courts Press, 1996) 120–1. **15** *Birth of Romance*, ed. Weiss, x. **16** *The Romance of Horn by Thomas*, ed. M. K. Pope, rev. T.B.W. Reid, Anglo-Norman Text Society XII–XIII (Oxford, 1964), vol. II, 122–3. **17** Ibid., 124. **18** *The Anglo-Norman 'Alexander'* ('*Le Roman de Toute Chevalerie*') by Thomas of Kent, ed. B. Foster & I. Short, Anglo-Norman Text Society XXIX–XXXI (London 1976 for 1971–3), 119–21. **19** *Kyng Alisaunder*, ed. G. V. Smithers, Early English Text Society Original Series CCXXVII, CCXXXVII (London, 1952, 1957).

unfortunately, that does not provide much information about Thomas. It can be inferred from his story that he was a court poet for a circle which had many associations with London and the Angevins. Hatto argues that this romance was written under the patronage of Eleanor of Aquitaine and was designed to be congenial to a queen who was known to preside over literary "courts of love".[20] The elements which Thomas introduced to the story, such as King Mark's voluntary separation from Ysolt, seem to parallel the events of Eleanor's life. It was public knowledge that King Louis VII of France had proved unequal to the role of Eleanor's husband. It had also been suggested that after her divorce she remarried Count Henry of Anjou perhaps a touch too swiftly. Her marriage transformed the political stage of Western Europe and led to the Hundred Years' War.

The idea that Thomas, the popular and widely acclaimed romance writer, uses fiction to explore the delicacies of such facts gives weight to the argument that subsequent romance writers followed suit and discussed equally controversial social and political matters. It is unfortunate that Chrétien's version of *Tristan* is no longer extant, as it would have been interesting to compare the two perspectives on marital and adulterous love.

It is clear that Chrétien did not originate the idea of using the romances to discuss difficult social issues. It is also clear that he did not originate the link between heroic figures and magical powers, as it is evident in earlier literary traditions encompassing such works as *Beowulf* and the sagas.[21] Magical strength and survival against marvellous dangers are two of the most common motifs to appear in this type of literature and usually serve to demonstrate the power and greatness of a hero and heroine. These secular works, much like Geoffrey's *Historia regum Britanniae*, seek to depict heroes who can function in a Christian world but who are not intended to be canonised as saints.[22] However, what Chrétien does accomplish in his *bele conjointure* is the creation of a relationship between Arthurian myths, history, the magical, and the discussion of socially relevant issues.[23] To find precedents for this combination it is necessary to explore the twelfth-century's rebirth of interest in the classical, and the revitalisation of the studies of history, philosophy and theology.

A logical place to begin exploring the influences on Chrétien would seem to be the source material for the *Matière de Bretagne*. The most popular source of Arthurian material available to Chrétien was the history of

---

20 *Tristan*, ed. Hatto, 355–63.   21 For examples, see Beowulf's slaying of Grendel and the Dragon.   22 It could also be fruitfully argued that Chrétien borrowed heavily from the genre of hagiography but that proposition will be further explored in a separate study.   23 See pages 14–15 and 76 above for a discussion of this term.

Geoffrey of Monmouth made accessible by the *Roman de Brut* authored by Wace. Research concerning the literary techniques of these two historians, as will be demonstrated in this study, suggests a possible influence for Chrétien's use of magic as a means of testing characters to assess the state of their moral and social standing in the community.

HISTORICAL SOURCES FOR THE MATIÈRE DE BRETAGNE

For material concerning Arthur there are several generally agreed-upon sources. One of the oldest is the *Anglo-Saxon Chronicle* (891), often linked to King Alfred the Great. The much later *Gesta regum Anglorum* (1125), authored by William of Malmesbury, provides a compelling source of historical information mixed with instances of the marvellous and the magical. Five editions of the *Historia Anglorum* (1129–54) authored by Henry of Huntingdon do not appear to have been as popular as the *Historia* of Geoffrey and therefore would probably not have travelled as far nor have been as widely read. Most controversial of all of these histories, however, and the text to have the greatest effect on the Arthurian material, is the *Historia regum Britanniae*.

Sources employed by Geoffrey are thought to be Gildas' *De excidio et conquestu Britanniae*, a Celtic Latin text from the sixth century, and Caradoc of Llancarvan's *Vita Gildae*, a twelfth-century text.[24] Also identified as influential is the *Historia Brittonum*, often ascribed to Nennius (in a later rendition of the ninth-century compilation), as well as the works of Livy, Virgil, and potentially one of the Welsh Triads, namely the *Tysilio*.[25]

In a discussion of how French authors obtained materials concerning Arthur, the generally agreed avenues of transmission are Geffrei Gaimar's translations of the *Historia regum Britanniae* as *L'Estoire des Bretuns*, and the *Anglo-Saxon Chronicle* as *L'Estoire d' Engleis*. The Norman Jerseyman Wace, already discussed as a prime source for the romances of Chrétien, included in his *Brut* the first appearance of the Round Table. His primary source was the *Historia regum Britanniae*, and his secondary sources include the *Historia Brittonum* and the *Gesta regum Anglorum*. The first Anglo-Norman adaptation of this history is the *Brut* (1190) and the first Middle English text is Laʒamon's *Brut* (1190), the principal source of which is deemed to be Wace.

---

[24] Caradoc of Llancarvan, *Two Lives of Gildas*, ed. and trans. Hugh Williams (Wales: Llanerch, 1990). [25] Robert H. Fletcher, *The Arthurian Material in the Chronicles* (New York: Burt Franklin, 1960) 8–9, 80–115. For discussion of Livy and Virgil see Per Nykrog, "Rise of Literary Fiction" in *Renaissance and Renewal in the Twelfth Century*, ed. R. Benson (Oxford: Clarendon, 1982) 596.

Having assessed the impact of all of these historical materials, it is not unreasonable to suggest that Geoffrey's *Historia*, through Wace's adaptation, provided Chrétien not only with information concerning Arthur, but also with a compelling example of how to write fiction as a means of arriving at a discussion of serious social issues. Geoffrey envisioned his *Historia regum Britanniae* as an historical text; one would suspect, however, that his departures from the traditional sources of British history were deliberate, and designed to engender debate over the nature and design of his text.

William of Newburgh (1198) offers this attack on the text of Geoffrey: "[it is] disguised under the honourable name of history, thanks to his Latinity, the fables about Arthur which he took from the ancient fictions of the Britons and increased out of his own head . . . whether from an inordinate love of lying or for the sake of pleasing the Britons, of whom the majority are said to be brutishly stupid . . ."[26]

William of Malmesbury, a contemporary of Geoffrey, also questions the status of his text by saying that this is the Arthur "concerning whom idle tales of the Bretons rave wildly even today, – a man certainly worthy to be celebrated, not in foolish dreams of deceitful fables, but in truthful histories".[27]

In trying to establish what William meant by "truthful histories" it is only possible to define them by what they were not, i.e. they were neither "idle tales" nor "fables". It is interesting that, despite establishing these criteria for twelfth-century historical works, in his own *Gesta regum Anglorum* William took care to describe the occult practices of Pope Sylvester II and a catalogue of marvels which included magicians' trips to hidden worlds.[28] As both a Christian and a respectable historian, Malmesbury's own treatment of marvels illustrates that in the twelfth century there was still vigorous debate concerning distinctions between the magical, the miraculous, and lies told by the unscrupulous.

Geoffrey's fellow historians accused him of hovering too close to the line between history and fiction, and in truth it is possible to see the reasons for some of their misgivings, since he does use questionable methods,

---

26 Newburgh, *"Prooemium"*, in *History of England*. See quote as cited in Fletcher, *The Arthurian Material in the Chronicles*, 101–2. See Howlett, *Chronicles of Stephen*, vols I and II (Rolls Series, 1884–1885). 27 *Gesta regum Anglorum*, ed. Bishop Stubbs, 2 vols (Rolls Series, 1887–1889) as cited in Rodney Thompson, *William of Malmesbury* (London: Boydell, 1987) 11. 28 See Gerbert the magician, the witch of Berkeley and the two clerks of Nantes, in *Gesta*, i, 194–203; *Gesta*, ii, 167ff, 294–5 as cited in Thompson, *William of Malmesbury*, 11. For a further discussion of Malmesbury see Robert Hanning, *The Vision of History in Early Britain from Gildas to Geoffrey of Monmouth* (New York: Columbia University Press, 1966) 130.

questionable sources, and even goes so far as to explore love, as opposed to God's will, as an acceptable motivating force behind the actions of his historical figures.[29] However, despite the obvious appeal for creative writers, one must also acknowledge that there did exist other, more cynical, reasons for Geoffrey's choice of subject matter. Arthurian material provided historical legitimacy for the new Norman kings sitting uncomfortably on the throne of Edward the Confessor.[30] King Henry II and his successors were impatient to establish their rights to England and most likely sponsored this historical endeavour.[31] Geoffrey's *Historia* flattered the Normans, sanctioned their right to the crown, and traced the nation's historical roots to the most famous of all mythologies, that of Troy.

The romantic transformation of Geoffrey's history by Wace, achieved without having to make significant alterations to the text, best illuminates how close Geoffrey's text was, not to fable, but to the origins of a new type of literature: romance. Complete with marvels and love stories, Geoffrey's work perhaps best exemplifies the first step in a process of creating a form of writing which complements at one and the same time the goals of history and the concerns of literature, a form which Chrétien would come to describe as *bele conjointure*.

To arrive at a better sense of the relationship between history and fiction in the twelfth century, this example from the *Brut* illustrates the type of complexities which these authors had to negotiate:

> Que pur amur de sa largesce,
> Que pur poür de sa prüesce,
> En cele grant pais ke jo di,
> Ne sai si vus l'avez oï,
> Furent les merveilles pruvees
> E les aventures truvees
> Ki d'Artur sunt tant recuntees

---

29 Hanning, *Vision of History*, 175. Geoffrey's pre-romance heroes are Assyracus and Androgeus. 30 See Bloch for a discussion of how literature was used by the crown and by nobility. Marc Bloch, *Feudal Society*, trans. L.A. Manyon, 2 vols. (Chicago: Phoenix Books, University of Chicago Press, 1961) 1, 25–6. See also Southern, *Making of the Middle Ages*, 93–5 for a discussion of Edward's miraculous / magical healing power. It was a new power which successive kings attempted to claim as proof of divine distinction. 31 Rosamund McKitterick, *The Uses of Literacy in Early Medieval Europe* (London: Cambridge University Press, 1990) 258–334. See McKitterick for a discussion of the many ways in which literature and literacy were used to further political and social ends. See also Brian Stock, *The Implications of Literacy* (Princeton: Princeton University Press, 1983).

> Ke a fable sunt aturnees:
> Ne tut mençunge, ne tut veir,
> Ne tut folie ne tut saveir.
>
> (*Brut*, 9785–94)

In this time of great peace I speak of – I do not know if you have heard of it – the wondrous events appeared and the adventures were sought out which, whether for love of his generosity, or for fear of his bravery, are so often told about Arthur that they have become the stuff of fiction: not all lies, not all truth, neither total folly nor total wisdom.[32]

This is the text, with its treatment of history and magic, fact and fiction, upon which Chrétien certainly based some of his knowledge of Arthur.[33] It is interesting that at no other point in the *Brut* does Wace discuss the role of fiction in relation to history, so it is not beyond the pale to suggest that general discussions of Arthur may have been closely aligned to the controversies concerning the nature of history and the nature of fiction.

To underline what his text is not, Wace further highlights his dismay over what others are doing to the Arthurian material:

> Tant unt li cunteür cunté
> E li fableür tant flablé
> Pur lur cuntes enbeleter,
> Que tut unt fait fable sembler.[34]
>
> (*Brut*, 9795–8)

The raconteurs have told so many yarns, the story-tellers so many stories, to embellish their tales, that they have made it all appear fiction.[35]

This complex attitude towards the authority of historical sources and the power of fiction, is closely mirrored by Chrétien's attitude toward historical sources and storytellers.[36] He states in *Erec et Enide*:

---

[32] Wace, *Wace's Roman de Brut: Text and Translation*, ed. and trans. Judith Weiss (Exeter: University of Exeter Press, 1999) 246–7. [33] Arguments against this point of view are eloquently expressed in Nykrog, "The Rise of Literary Fiction", 603–4. [34] *Brut*, ed. Weiss, 246. [35] Ibid., 246–7. [36] For an interesting discussion of Chrétien's serious intentions to recreate *Erec et Enide* into an important story, see D.W. Robertson, *Essays in Medieval Culture* (Princeton: Princeton University Press, 1980) 65–6.

> ... et tret d'un conte d'avanture
> une molt bele conjointure
> par qu'an puet prover et savoir
> que cil ne fet mie savoir
> qui s'escïence n'abandone
> tant con Dex la grasce l'an done:
> d'Erec, le fil Lac, est li contes,
> que devant rois et devant contes
> depecier et corronpre suelent
> cil qui de conter vivre vuelent.
>
> (*Erec et Enide*, 13–23)[37]

... and from a tale of adventure he [Chrétien] fashions a very elegant composition, giving manifest proof that there is no wisdom in not freely making one's knowledge available so far as God's grace allows. The tale, which the professional story-tellers habitually fragment and corrupt in the presence of kings and counts, is about Erec, son of Lac.[38]

To paraphrase Chrétien, the very first lines of the text serve to warn the audience to take proper care and not be misled when approaching this romance. He suggests that some things are despised which are much more valuable than people realise and therefore it is a good thing to try and improve them. For his part, the author has done this by taking a "*conte d'aventure*" and turning it into a "*molt bele conjointure*."[39] The introduction by Chrétien of *conjointure*, a term much discussed by romance critics, suggests that he is interested in taking a variety of sources and creating new meaning from their unification.[40] The historical texts of Geoffrey and Wace exhibit a link between individual behaviour and access to magical or marvellous powers, and, it can be argued, create for the romances a ready morality

---

[37] Chrétien de Troyes, *Erec et Enide, Les Romans de Chrétien de Troyes*, ed Mario Roques, vol. 1 (Paris: Librairie Ancienne. Honoré Champion, 1955) 1. All subsequent citations for Chrétien's romances will be taken from the C.F.M.A. texts as listed in the bibliography, unless otherwise noted. [38] Owen, *Arthurian Romances*, 1. All subsequent translations of Chrétien's romances will be taken from the Owen text unless otherwise noted. [39] Nykrog, "The Rise of Literary Fiction", 603. [40] See Introduction for discussion of this term. This would find support in the way in which Alanus de Insulis in *De planctu Naturae* used the related terms "conjunctura" and "integumentum, involucrum, pallium and cortex". For further discussion see Robertson, *Essays*, 3–20, 52–3.

system based upon primarily secular and social principles of behaviour. In building upon those historical methods, Chrétien develops a type of literature which gives secular events as much potential significance as spiritual ones.

The historical research of Flint, Thorndike and Thomas demonstrates that a variety of august intellectuals, who were neither simple nor credulous, concerned themselves with magic, marvels, and divination. It is not entirely surprising then, that Geoffrey incorporated such themes into his history of Britain. What is interesting is that Geoffrey takes the traditional Christian use of magic and bends it to his own design, a design which seems to stem from the weight of classical influences upon his outlook.[41] In taking classical ideals and merging them with a Christian-based narrative concerning the once-pagan British people, Geoffrey incorporates a wide range of traditions to create a story which tells his view of history.

THE PLACE OF MAGIC IN THE BIRTH OF A SECULAR HISTORY

Based on the methods of Eusebius and Orosius, Gildas and Bede interpreted the fall of Britain through the tools of scriptural exegesis.[42] Historians could interpret a miraculous event (a magical or marvellous event but defined by Christian writers as miraculous), as a sign that God demonstrated his support for a hero, heroine, or a particular country.[43] Periods of suffering or invasion demonstrated God's disfavour; for example, Bede linked the fall of the British to their sins, the greatest of which was the failure to proselytise the Saxons.[44] Geoffrey, however, deviates from seeing God's footprint in history in his *Historia*, and explores instead a new interpretation of historical events.[45] The new vision encompasses both the rise *and* fall of Britain.[46]

---

[41] For a more detailed study of magic in the classical world, see Kieckhefer, *Magic*, 19–36. [42] Carol Harding, *Merlin and Legendary Romance* (New York: Garland, 1988) 46. Harding argues that Eusebius and Augustine reaffirm that God does control history; fortune and blind chance do not fit into their views. Orosius combines Augustinian and Eusebian ideas to create his own "synthesis of national history and biblical narrative with its exegetical interpretations". See also P. de Labriolle, *The History and Literature of Christianity from Tertullian to Boethius*, trans. Herbert Wilson (New York: Knopf, 1924) and D.S. Wallace-Hadrill, *Eusebius of Caesarea* (London: A.R. Mowbray) 1960. [43] Gregory of Tours (538–594), *Historia Francorum*; this text is written in the style common to the insular Christian interpreters under discussion, only, clearly, from a continental perspective. [44] Hanning, *Vision of History*, 78. [45] Ibid., 121, 26, 36. For further discussion of Geoffrey's secular view of history, see Harding, *Merlin*, 45–8. For a dissenting point of view, see Myra Rosenhaus, "Britain between Myth and Reality", Dissertation, University of Indiana, 1982. [46] Hanning, *Vision of History*, 136–7.

Part of the foundation for this new historical vision was the twelfth-century resurgence of interest in the classical world. This intellectual trend encouraged new areas of study, for example the *Aeneid* or Boethius.[47] A complete discussion of classical history can not be attempted in this context but as a brief overview it can be said that the Greek histories of Herodotus and Thucydides represent a view of history which seeks out opportunity for human greatness in conflict with the forces of history.[48] Heroes seem to be obsessed with the desire to determine their own fates, rather than fall prey to predetermined ones. In some ways Roman historiography owes much to its Greek heritage, but the Roman fascination to discover order in history, transformed the Greek conception of it into a product which was unmistakably Roman in nature. Livy and Polybius set themselves the task of establishing order in history by trying to interpret as evidence the rise of Rome from principate to republic to empire.[49] It is perhaps the work of Virgil, however, which synthesises the goal of Roman history most effectively; he presents history on a mythic scale which is philosophically orientated.[50] The personal experiences of Aeneas have universal significance for man's eternal struggle to master his own passion and thereby build a lasting political structure. Virgil viewed human virtue as a historical force. It is important to note that in the twelfth century Virgil was considered to be the "maker of magical artefacts", and an "adept of the magical arts"; such a reputation, however, did not seem to effect his popularity.[51] Indeed, the reverence for Virgil as an ancient poet of great learning may have made the use of magic by other authors, of both literature and historical texts, more acceptable. Equally, the link between human virtue and magical forces may have emerged from such new attitudes towards classical authors and their techniques.

A keen pursuit of these interests could have contributed to a more classical vision of history by Geoffrey, in which for example, he sees history in terms of cyclical patterns that need to be identified and interpreted. Geoffrey envisioned that man could learn from events that had happened,

---

[47] Kieckhefer, *Magic*, 19–33; Hanning, *Vision of History*, 17–20.   [48] J.B. Bury, *Ancient Greek Historians* (New York: Dover, 1958) 17ff.; C.N. Cochrance, *Christianity and the Classical Culture* (London: Oxford University Press, 1940) 460–3. James Shotwell, *The Story of Ancient History*, 2nd ed. (New York: Columbia University Press, 1961) 191. Viktor Poschl, *The Art of Vergil* (Ann Arbor: University of Michigan Press, 1962) 134–8. M.L.W. Laistner, *The Great Roman Historians* (Berkeley: University of California Press, 1963) 1–38.   [49] Livy, *History of Rome (ab urbe condita libre)*, trans. B. Foster (New York: Putnam, 1959).   [50] Virgil, *Aeneid*, in *Works*, trans. H. Rushton Fairclough, 2 vols (Cambridge, Mass.: Harvard University Press, 1950).   [51] Kieckhefer, *Magic*, 113.

thereby enabling the prevention of future tragedies.[52] However, regardless of what lessons were there to be learned, the overriding force behind events is the hand of fortune. For example, in the *Historia* Geoffrey outlines the fortune and fate of kings whose thirst for power leads them to conquer too far afield from Britain. These over-reachers bring destruction down upon Britain and themselves. What is interesting, however, is that destruction removed from the personal realm is only another notch in the grand scheme which is the cycle of nations.[53] Maximianus, the unscrupulous politician who strips Britain and leaves her vulnerable to conquest in his efforts to colonise Brittany, serves as the perfect example of this process. Rome destroys Maximianus for the British, but this leads to a greater tyrant, Vortigern. The "wickedness" of Vortigern leads to powerful opposition, which takes the form of Merlin's prophecies and the foundation of his power-base in the politics of Britain. Subsequently, Merlin enables Uther's love for Ygerna to bear fruit, and Arthur, the great king, is born. These tales of individual wickedness and of greatness are the threads which comprise the overall pattern of the rise and fall of the Britains. This in turn will lead to the rise and fall of the Saxons, and open the door to the Normans in 1066.

Hanning explains that "against this near intoxication with the human greatness of national leaders [as seen in Geoffrey's text] must be set the cyclical view of history".[54] Hanning then identifies the place of fate and fortune in the text of Geoffrey: "for, if the heroic deeds of men emphasise human control of history, the view of history as an endless series of cycles emphasises the power of history over men. Operating through Fortune, the inexplicable and fickle force which raises man on her wheel and then throws him off, history tyrannises over man and mocks his efforts to control his fate and that of his nation."[55]

What is of particular significance to this discussion is the fact that Geoffrey neutralises the Christian features of Gildas, Bede, and parts of Nennius' history, through *eliminating* the St Germanus elements of the Vortigern story.[56] He then proceeds to construct a narrative based upon the secular aspects of Nennius' *Historia Brittonum*. By removing the Christian

---

[52] Wace corrects the flaws in Merlin's prophecies as presented in Geoffrey's *Historia*. Merlin in Geoffrey's work is shown to help only the two kings who learn from the lessons of history not to go a conquering, namely, Uther and Ambrosius.   [53] Hanning, *Vision of History*, 144–6.   [54] Ibid., 139.   [55] Ibid., 139.   [56] Vortigern believes the prophecies of the pagan magicians and St Germanus makes him look a fool. Geoffrey also eliminates the earlier story of St Alban the Martyr and the plagues, which in Gildas God sent before the coming of the Saxons.

heroes who were so very important to his sources, and by inserting details of Merlin, Geoffrey creates a magical or occult authority that helps *national* heroes to thrive. Geoffrey substitutes magical marvels for religious miracles.

Geoffrey's history still endorses the idea of a nation's success being reliant upon the moral qualities of its leader.[57] Now, however, it is not God alone who stands as the judge of a man's actions, but also the Fates and Goddess Fortuna. The story of Arthur may have been so compelling because it seemed to stand at the crossroads between literature and historical truth. It presents the tale of a man who brings his country to the greatest of heights only to have the wheel of fortune turn against him; at his peak he can conquer giants, when his place on the wheel of fortune shifts, nothing can save him.

This approach to the writing of history demonstrates Geoffrey's keen interest in discovering new methods for discussing why events happen. In the Christian framework, God authors all events, and discussing why or how they happen is often discouraged as an affront to the position of God as all-powerful and all-knowing. This is very limiting in terms of exploring the ways and means for human development. In attributing human motivation to the cause of historical events, Geoffrey creates the possibility for a discussion of men who choose to act in an honourable or dishonourable fashion. This provides an author with tremendous freedom to explore issues which relate to God, but also issues which are relevant to the individual and his or her community. One of the ways in which Geoffrey accomplishes this is by incorporating magic and marvellous events into his *Historia*. In using these means to assess the actions of a character, the author provides the audience with a good indicator of the hero's or heroine's moral standing and motivations. In using magic, Geoffrey also has the opportunity to explore the full range of human motivation. This enabled a text to develop along far more complex lines than a Christian history; in religiously-inspired texts a character is either good or evil. As the story of Uther in the *Historia* demonstrates, a character can be fundamentally good but driven to acts which compromise his moral standing, by such emotions as love, passion or lust.

---

[57] Hanning would argue that Geoffrey's text is virtually secular in its construction, but that is perhaps a bit extreme. See Hanning for the full details: "Geoffrey's carefully constructed historical account makes use of all the fall of Britain texts in ways which continually support the hypothesis that he intended to produce a thoroughly original and primarily secular account of the rise and fall of a nation." Hanning, *Vision of History*, 137.

MAGIC AS A LITERARY TOOL

Geoffrey of Monmouth and Wace both use magic to establish the influence and social standing of a character in the community. Wace provides an example of such a treatment of magic:

> En Avalon se fist porter
> Pur ses plaies mediciner.
> Encore i est, Bretun l'atendent,
> Si cum il dient e entendent;
> De la vendra, encor puet vivre.
> Maistre Wace, ki fist cest livre,
> Ne volt plus dire de sa fin
> Qu'en dist li prophetes Merlin;
> Merlin dist d'Arthur, si ot dreit,
> Que sa mort dutuse serreit.
> Li prophetes dist verité;
> Tut tens en ad l'um puis duté,
> E dutera, ço crei, tut dis,
> Se il est morz u il est vis.
> Porter se fist en Avalun,
> Pur veir, puis l'Incarnatiun
> Cinc cenz e quarante dous anz.
>
> (*Brut*, 13277–92)

He [Arthur] had himself carried to Avalon, for the treatment of his wounds. He is still there, awaited by the Britons, as they say and believe, and will return and may live again. Master Wace, who made this book, will say no more of his end than the prophet Merlin did. Merlin said of Arthur, rightly, that his death would be doubtful. The prophet spoke truly: ever since, people have always doubted it and always will, I think, doubt whether he is dead or alive. It is true that he had himself borne away to Avalon, five hundred and forty-two years after the Incarnation.[58]

This sophisticated presentation of historical plausibility and "marvellous facts" encourages the audience to believe in the magical greatness of Arthur. Wace implies that Arthur triumphs over mortal death and enjoys eternal existence. He is also concerned to mention that Arthur is still

---

58 *Brut*, ed. Weiss, 333–4.

important to the British community. Linked to how that community sees itself is the powerful idea of Arthur as a magical and marvellous king. Arthur's story is compelling on personal and national terms.

In the introduction to *Cligés*, it is possible to see the influence of Wace's "plausible historical tone and magical content" formula.[59] Chrétien is interested in establishing that his text has historical validity, a fact that can be seen in his claim that the truth of the story is not only written down but also very ancient and therefore more worthy of belief. Chrétien also adds a wish that, God granting, the fund of transcendent learning that has arrived in France should stay there, but somehow he doubts that that will be the case, as nothing seems permanent in his world. He notes that others had received such learning from God on loan, for example the Greeks and Romans, but that it did not last as "their glowing embers are dead" (44). To judge from these sentiments, it is plain that the description of Geoffrey's history by Hanning can also be applied to Chrétien's text:

> If the overt regulating factor in the succession of reigns in Britain is God's providence, there is nonetheless a covert, even unconscious recognition of a cyclic pattern in history, a pattern which remorselessly regulates the life and death of realms in a manner analogous to fortune's regulation of the lives and deaths of great men.[60]

The influence of historians on Chrétien, however, is not limited to encouraging the use of historical authority in his romances, nor even developing a secular use of magic; these authors also use magic as a means of establishing the motivation of a character. Magic functions as a barometer for the emotional development of the characters, both historical and fictional. This empowers the audience to assess how able the given character is to think rationally and act independently of the influence of the community. This is illustrated by the course of events in *Cligés*, where the strength of Fenice's will communicates itself to the audience by her ability to employ magical potions to achieve the desires of her heart. To maintain her purity, she uses magic to operate outside the normal parameters of the community and achieve what she thinks is right and proper. Geoffrey's description of the use of a magic potion by Uther, one which is given to him by Merlin,

---

[59] See Donald Maddox, *The Arthurian Romances of Chrétien de Troyes* (Cambridge: Cambridge University Press, 1991) 8–14. Maddox provides a very interesting discussion of the relationship between Wace, Monmouth, and *Cligés*. [60] Hanning, *Vision of History*, 136.

shares many uncomfortable parallels with the tactics of Fenice. Uther uses a potion to disguise himself as Gorlois, the duke of Cornwall, so that he can sleep with Gorlois' wife, Ygerna.[61] The husband is killed and Uther acquires the now pregnant widow as his wife. It is difficult to draw many distinctions between the use of magic to explore the motivations of either kings in a "factual" history, or empresses in a "fictional" romance. In both cases, love justifies the use of magic to obtain personal desires over the mores and rules of the community.

It is significant that the "happy endings" of both these narratives are undermined, leaving the audience puzzled as to the morality of the situations which have just been described; Uther, after years of being ill with an unidentified malady, dies by poison at the hands of his enemies; Cligés and Fenice live happily ever after, but each succeeding empress is kept locked in prison because each succeeding emperor fears betrayal. Indeed, both of these endings suggest that there may have been retribution for the acts of adultery, and perhaps, for the use of magic to achieve desires not sanctioned by society. An alternative reading of what these authors are implying is that love can inspire acts that are not necessarily good or moral. Magic and love are linked to demonstrate a potentially dark and volatile side of human nature. So powerful is this potential force that it can even change the course of history. Love and magic make possible human control over events, which is an idea so appealing and fraught with tension and excitement that it undermined Christian-focused historical readings of the fall of the Britain. It also made instantly popular both the *Historia* of Geoffrey and the romances of Chrétien.

The goal of this argument is not to establish Chrétien's sense of history, but to demonstrate that he could well have had alternative sources for his use of magic, which were not only based in oral traditions and their treatment of the Celtic marvellous. Chrétien created a sophisticated work which called upon the engagement of the audience to appreciate his intentions. The heart of the romances lies in a relationship to the audience without whose interpretative insight the tales would remain static and two-dimensional.

It is possible to hear echoes of Wace in Chrétien's description of his own romance form. He states that it is not fantasy, fiction, or lie; instead, it is a much more complicated mixture of information that requires the participation of the hearts of the audience in order to be understood properly. It is clear that Chrétien envisioned such an audience as necessary to appreciating his new romance. In *Yvain* he states:

---

61 Geoffrey, *Historia*, 205–8.

The origins of romance

> Et qui or me voldra entandre,
> cuer et oroilles me doit randre,
> car ne vuel pas parler de songe,
> ne de fable, ne de mançonge.
> Il m'avint plus a de set anz
> que je, seus come païsanz,
> aloie querant aventures,
> armez de totes armeüres.
>
> (*Yvain*, 169–76)

Whoever, then, should wish to understand me now must lend his heart and ears; for I have no intention to speak of a fantasy, a fiction or a lie such as many others have served up but shall instead tell you of what I have seen.[62]

It is clear that after having absorbed particular themes from such works as the *Historia*, Chrétien was also interested in building connections to other areas of intellectual interest, such as philosophy and theology. The romances would not evolve into pseudo-histories, but a congress of intellectual interests and ideas of the twelfth century.

INFLUENCES BEYOND THE HISTORICAL

The process of reading or listening that Chrétien is encouraging in *Cligés* finds its roots in the influences of Christian, Stoic and Chartrian concepts of humanity's awareness of its place in the natural order of things. These ideas were initially employed by the troubadour Marcabru to fashion *Fin' Amor*. This ideal of love unifies the concepts of physical and mental desire with spiritual (not necessarily Christian) aspiration. The tenets of the *Cortesia* system represent the sum total of outward expression of courtly virtues; *Jovens* is youthfulness of spirit, and *Jois* represents the quest for happiness in life; *Valors* is the expression of innate courtly virtue, and *Conoissena* is the power to discern good from bad, true from false, and the real from the illusory.[63]

Conoissena endures the digestive processes of both Christian theologians and romance authors; evidence for this claim is found in the romances' preoccupation with the need for self-knowledge, as well as the recognition and

---

[62] *Yvain*, ed. Roques, 5–6; Owen, *Arthurian Romances*, 283. [63] L.T. Topsfield, *Chrétien de Troyes: A Study of Arthurian Romances* (Cambridge: Cambridge University Press, 1981) 4–5, 50.

identification of the unknown. Chrétien inherits the dialectical methods of university education, as expressed by the twelfth-century *Arts of Rhetoric*, which teaches that "opposites are juxtaposed, compared, contrasted and analysed. For God to be recognised, Evil must be understood. To know wisdom, folly must be detected."[64] In Christian terms, it would be necessary to recognise evil and temptation to find the true path to God. In the romances, heroes have to learn the true path to moral and social acceptability. The "lyre of poetry," Alanus de Insulis says in *De planctu naturae* (c.1178–80), "sounds a false note on the superficial, literal shell of a poem, but, deeper within, it conveys to those who can hear it the secret of a higher understanding, so that when the externals of falsehood are cast away, anyone who could interpret the poem may discover the sweeter essence of the truth secreted inside it."[65]

It is clear that some element of the medieval audience was educated in the ways of discerning meaning and was, therefore, expected to practice that art on this new type of sophisticated literature, the romance. Many modern scholars, however, have failed to approach the romances with the necessary tools to discern different levels of possible meaning in the texts. In some cases it is simply the status of the romance as popular material that undermines its credibility as serious or meaningful literature. Having demonstrated that Chrétien based his romances on a collection of intellectual interests, and that the use of magic and the marvellous created a bridge between the imagination and medieval areas of academic study, it is surprising that so many critics still hold to the idea of the romance as crude fiction. Lee Ramsey, for example, argues that romance was "an ephemeral literature. When its day passed, it lost its effectiveness and came to seem dull or ridiculous ... The typical medieval romance shares characteristics common to other, later forms of popular literature. The most important of these characteristics is the emphasis on plot and action to the exclusion of everything else – rhetoric, idea, and character development included. The rhetoric of the romances is often poor, the philosophic content meagre, and the characters simple and obvious."[66] Ramsey suggests that the emotional effects sought after are likewise "obvious" and therefore of little interest or value. This type of criticism is often levelled at the romances owing to the prominent place of magical and marvellous motifs. The view that magic in these tales is unsophisticated and rather simplistic, a view often associated with "Celtic antecedent" theories, fatally undermines the ability of the critic

---

[64] Ibid., 18. See C.F. Faral, *Les Arts poétiques du XIIe et du XIIIe siècle* (Paris: Champion, 1962): 76–7. [65] Nikolaus M. Haring, ed., "Alanus de Insulis, *De planctu Naturae*," *Studi medievali* 19 (1978): 797–879 as cited and translated in Topsfield, *Arthurian Romances*, 2. [66] Ramsey, *Chivalric Romance*, 5.

The origins of romance

to see the romances in terms of their historical development toward a highly sophisticated genre. By moving away from the idea that Chrétien's use of magic had its only origins in Celtic oral culture, the modern critic can explore magic in the romances as the complex and sophisticated product of medieval interest in historiography, theology, and the uses of fiction.

Breaking the Celtic spell

THE FUNCTION OF THE MAGICAL AND THE MARVELLOUS IN FRENCH ROMANCE

Chrétien described his method of creating new stories from various sources as *conjointure*.[1] Kelly describes Chrétien's technique as "two levels of coherence in a given romance, the one determined by the *merveilleux* retained from the sources, the other by the integrity of authorial conception of the work".[2] Thus the reader restores "Chrétien's own balance of *matière* (source materials) and *san* (authorial intent) in appreciating the author's *conjointure*".[3] Essentially, Kelly would claim that Chrétien's skill is in carefully selecting and combining his source material into a more satisfying and meaningful arrangement. In accepting, however, that this is Chrétien's art, it is necessary to further assess the author's decision-making process: for instance, why is it that some of the instances of *merveilleux* which spring from Chrétien's Celtic sources are naturalised in his text, such as in the cases of the cart in *La Charrette* or the salve in *Yvain*, while others are preserved or even intensified in their magical powers, such as the magical rings of Lunete and Laudine, or the many potions used by Fenice in *Cligés*? The logic to this process seems to rest with what it is the author wants to achieve at that moment in the text; a magical test can allow the audience to judge the moral status of a character through the eyes of the community or it can expose the varied nature of the character's emotional development. The efficacy of this formula for understanding the function of magic in the texts of Marie de France and Gottfried von Strassburg, and in a host of the other early romances, illustrates that it can be applied fruitfully to more than just the works of Chrétien.[4] Examining the ways in which magic and the marvellous are used in these texts enables the modern reader to develop a sense of the function of magic as both medieval authors and audiences

---

[1] See pages 14–15 above for a discussion of this term. [2] Kelly, "Narrator and His Art", 14. See for further discussion, Jean Fourquet, "Le rapport entre l'oeuvre et la source chez Chrétien de Troyes et la problème des sources bretonnes", *Romance Philology* 9 (1955-6): 298–312. See also Kelly, *Art*, 15–31. [3] Kelly, "Narrator and His Art", 14, 21. [4] Owing to restrictions of space and to the aspiration for continuity, only Marie de France and Chrétien will be focused upon with any regularity in this chapter.

understood it. Approaching the use of magic in these texts from a different direction than possible Celtic sources, allows the modern reader to explore the influence on the romances of other areas connected to magic in the medieval world, such as classical learning, history, theology and philosophy.

By the twelfth century, for example, the Church had finally begun to bring the notion of knighthood, and therefore the noble idealisation of love, under its sway.[5] As the Church sided with kings, and not with the struggling classes of lower nobility and knights, the Church's pride of place in the romance genre was by no means certain or secure. This ambivalent relationship would explain why the romances discussed, and at various times seemed to legitimise, such concepts as adultery and the magical means to free will. Le Goff also suggests that they describe environments where "food was plentiful, sexual freedom existed, and no one did much work".[6] Chrétien's heroes are educated in how to make choices over their own fate and thus determine their own greatness. This was, of course, in direct contrast to an ideology which stressed man's unworthiness in the face of God's mercy and grace. Christianity's belief system sought to humble and limit an individual's feeling of self-worth and did not tolerate well the more ambitious, aggressive, worldly and self-aggrandizing tenets of the courtly code. The use of *merveilleux* in the French romances provided the authors with an alternative means of lending interest and "supernatural" authority to secular issues. In this way the romances were not reliant only upon Christian guidelines; this gave them the freedom to explore delicate and controversial issues from new directions and engage the imagination of the audience.

THE USE OF MAGIC IN THE FRENCH ROMANCES

Le Goff described the place of magic, or *merveilleux*, in the French romances by dividing its function into three categories: *mirabilis*, *magicus*, and *miraculous*. *Mirabilis* is "the equivalent to our notion of the marvellous, with its pre-Christian roots. *Magicus* was in theory a neutral term, for there was both black magic influenced by the devil, and white magic, which was considered legitimate ... There is also a specifically Christian supernatural, to

---

[5] Erich Köhler, "Il sistema sociologico del romanzo francese medievale", *Medioevo romanzo* 3 (1976): 341–4. Richard Glasser, "Abstractum agens und Allegorie im ältern Französisch", *Zeitschrift für romanische Philologie* 69 (1953): 41–57. [6] Le Goff, *Medieval Imagination*, 32.

which one might refer as the Christian marvellous: *miraculous*."[7] In practice, however, the power of magic can only be gauged by man's belief in it. In theory, it is man's only access to control over mankind, nature, and fate. It is the ultimate means of exercising free will.[8]

J.E. Stevens in *Medieval Romance*, defines the function of *merveilleux* by exploring and categorising the modern reader's experience of it in the romances:

1. The purely mysterious: unmotivated, unexplained and inexplicable: the Flaming Lance in *Lancelot*; the Marvellous Fountain with the Rain Making Stone in *Yvain* (and the English *Ywain and Gawain*);
2. The strictly magical: an event is magical, as I define it (according with anthropological definition), if it shows the marvellous controlled by man. Rings conferring invisibility or the power of tongues fit here, with magic ointments, swords, and so forth. The 'subtil clerk' of the *Franklin's Tale* is a 'magician'. Witches, wizards, warlocks, Merlin and Morgan le Fay, and their kind; and,
3. The miraculous: that is to say, the marvellous controlled by God. Miracles are God's magic, his supernatural interventions in the natural workings of the created world.[9]

Despite the usefulness of this definition, Stevens is a bit hasty to list magic under his umbrella term of *merveilleux*. Close reading demonstrates that there are specific instances in the French romances where the author is keen to separate magical moments from marvellous ones. For example, *nigromance*, *charme*, and *poisonez bevraje* are terms which are employed to specific effect in various romances.[10] These terms would have a negative impact upon the audience owing to their associations with necromancy. The more general term *merveilleux* with its suggestion of the miraculous or the marvellous seeks to generate some level of controversy, but not necessarily damn by association; these darker terms, however, and those like them, would instead suggest the work of a demon. Having clarified these contentions with his categories, however, it must be said that Stevens' distinctions provide the modern reader with a basic but efficient guide to the somewhat confusing term *merveilleux*.

7 Ibid., 30.   8 Peters, *Witchcraft in Europe*, 3, 4–14. See also Kieckhefer, *Magic*, 8–17; and Flint, *Rise of Magic*, 1–8.   9 Stevens, *Medieval Romances*, 97, 100–01.
10 For a definition of *nigromance* see page 31 above; *charme* is the equivalent of charm, and *poisonez bevraje* is the equivalent of magical potion or poisonous potion, depending upon the nature of its use in a particular context.

Breaking the Celtic spell

The way in which Chrétien uses *le merveilleux* in his romance instigates a debate concerning the development of self-knowledge.[11] Instances of magic in the texts of both Chrétien and Marie are inextricably tied to characters exercising their will and rational decision-making powers. For example, in the *lai Yonec*, the wife is locked in a the tower by her husband who prevents her from going to Mass; she prays for a lover and when one appears she sees the fact that her prayers have been answered as legitimising her desire to have a lover in the first place. Marie suggests that even God uses magic and adultery to teach the needy how to assert their will and to punish the unjust. As a second example of the function of magic, Chrétien reveals at the marvellous Sword Bridge encounter in *La Charrette*, that Lancelot needs to use a magical ring to assess reality. Normally characters require magical rings to create illusions or transform reality. This handicap suggests firstly that Lancelot maintains a different way of operating in "reality", and secondly, that his morality system might also be from the land of the fairies, which is where his surrogate mother called home. This would explain why he thinks he can maintain both his love for the Queen and his place of honour next to the King. The bringing into question of the morality of Lancelot's code of love serves to alert the audience to other possible problems in the text. It also reveals the extent to which Lancelot, while gripped by his obsession, cannot function by the accepted norms of his community. It is not surprising therefore that the people he meets are so resistant to accepting his code of practice. If Arthur's entire society functioned upon Lancelot's principles, all of Camelot would collapse.

NEW METHODS OF LOOKING AT MAGIC IN THE ROMANCES OF CHRÉTIEN

In rejecting Loomis' argument that the marvellous was simply an "accident of transmission", one must accept that Chrétien and Marie made choices about which material they incorporated into their texts.[12] It is clear that the study of Celtic motifs which Loomis undertook serves to illustrate many valuable connections between the romances and the Celtic world. Nykrog argues, however, that, while the method of isolating each narrative element and tracing its Celtic origins gives excellent results, "[it] does not contribute very much to the understanding of Chrétien's work

---

[11] Stevens, *Medieval Romance*, 81–3. [12] For the full citation see page 16 above.

in itself".[13] Careful examination of the tales reveals that there is a myriad of examples where the use of magic serves a specific function in the text, such as demonstrating a character's lack of faith or compromised social position. In exploring the intentions of the authors through the design of their texts, it is possible to appreciate the complexity both of the romances and of the functions assigned in them to magic and the marvellous.

Answering the questions of how and why magic and the marvellous are used highlights some of the most interesting conundrums in the text; for example, if Chrétien is obliged to use the Celtic Cart motif because of a transmission issue, why does he deliberately choose to naturalise its marvellous overtones? Conversely, why did Chrétien choose to expand upon the significance of other Celtic motifs, such as the Weeping Lance, and even go so far as to invest various items with Christian significance?

It is not enough simply to identify the origins of these motifs; what is crucial here is how Chrétien employed the magical and marvellous and to what ends. In *La Charrette*, for example, when Lancelot gets into a cart which is stated to have dubious functions, the audience knows that the "Greatest of Knights" has compromised his reputation. Owen argues that Chrétien has diminished the Celtic overtones in his description of the cart, but that it is still meant to faintly resemble its Celtic antecedent.[14] The Bed and the Lance motifs that also appear in this romance are commonplace throughout the Irish sagas, but Topsfield's research suggests that "mystical" carts (this cart is not mystical, but is, instead, shaded with ominous overtones), were important because they could carry heroes from one world to the next.[15] It may be that Chrétien's use of this dubious cart in *La Charrette* is meant to guide the audience toward the realization that the old Lancelot is dead and that he has been replaced by a knight who is obsessed with Guenevere; in this way the author would be symbolically incorporating some of the Celtic connections associated with carts into the body of his text. If this were Chrétien's plan, however, it seems as if the timing is a bit out of step, as Lancelot is already obsessed with Guenevere long before he gets into the cart. In that case, the all-important moment of transformation seems to have been lost from the

---

[13] Nykrog, "Rise of Literary Fiction", 603. [14] Owen, *Arthurian Romance*, xii; Loomis, *Celtic Myth*, 266–70; Loomis, *Chrétien de Troyes*. See also Jean Marx, *Legende* (Paris: Presses Universitaires de France, 1952) 284–7; V.J. Harward, *The Dwarfs of Arthurian Legend and Celtic Tradition* (Leiden: N.P. 1958) 124. [15] Topsfield, *Arthurian Romances*, 117. For more information on the Perilous Bed and the Bleeding Lance see Loomis, *Chrétien de Troyes*, 379–81, 205–10. Loomis, *Celtic Myth*, 266–70. See also Marx, *Legende*, 284–7.

text. It would seem to make practical sense then to search for other signs of significance attributed to the cart in the tale.

In the context of the romance, the function of the cart seems to be a test of Lancelot's love for his queen. Chrétien uses the cart to create for the audience a battle scene between reason and passion, which is the debate that he is interested in pursuing in this romance. The Cart episode demonstrates more clearly than perhaps any other moment in the text that Lancelot is in a no-win situation: he is damned for getting into the cart, and then damned for not getting in quickly enough. This is an apt parallel for the situation wherein he is damned for loving the queen and then damned for not loving her enough, depending upon whether he is judged according to Christian dogma or the codes of courtly lovers.

It is interesting that Chrétien does not suggest that it is owing to any sin against God (such as adultery or any sin of cupidity) that Lancelot is made to suffer.[16] Instead, he emphasizes that Lancelot's rational thought process is overcome by passion:

> Reisons qui ce dire li ose;
> mes Amors est el cuer anclose
> qui li comande et semont
> que tost an La Charrette mont.
> Amors levialt et il i saut,
> que de la honte ne li chaut
> puis qu'Amors le comande et vialt.
>
> (*La Charrette*, 371–7)

Reason, who dares tell him this, is not in the heart but the mouth; but Love, who bids and urges him to climb quickly into the cart, is enclosed within his heart. It being Love's wish, he jumps in regardless of the shame, since Love commands and wills it.[17]

In this context there is no need for an overtly magical test or indicator to convince the audience that Lancelot is not acting with *mesura*; the author states that Love wills Lancelot's leap into the cart, thereby absolving the thinking Lancelot from all responsibility for "wilfully" shaming himself.

---

16 See for further discussion of the cart: D.J. Shirt, "Chrétien de Troyes and the Cart", in *Studies in Medieval Literature and Languages in Memory of Frederick Whitehead* (Manchester: Manchester University Press, 1973) 363–99. 17 *Lancelot*, ed. Roques, 12; Owen, *Arthurian Romances*, 190.

The key to Lancelot's problem is that he is not taking responsibility for his own actions and that suggests that he is ruled by passion and immaturity. Lancelot even seems to ignore the issue of his adultery and disloyalty to Arthur, the seriousness of which is indicated by Keu's furious response to those same accusations (4878-922). Lancelot is "will-less", simply the slave of love.

It is important to note that the audience becomes the judge of Lancelot's vain efforts to maintain his heroic status while in the grip of his obsession with Guenevere. For example, the audience is made to witness Lancelot's humiliation when he has to ask to sleep in the Perilous Bed.[18] The enormous cost of Lancelot's cart experience becomes clear when he is told that such marvels are no longer available to the likes of him (486-502). Despite such active discouragement, Lancelot takes a chance and at midnight a flaming lance crashes through the rafters, wounds him and sets fire to the magnificent bed. Lancelot survives, but as in his future encounters, his wounds seem to undermine his right to the accolades that are normally associated with such marvellous trials. His right to high praise is further jeopardized when the next morning Lancelot sees Guenevere being driven past the castle. Lancelot is immediately enthralled, so much so that he almost falls from the window. It is assumed by Gawain that Lancelot hates his life so much that he wants to end it. It is clear that this near death is a result of his complete bemusement, but the reactions of the other characters to his behavior demonstrates how unacceptable his actions are, regardless of their origins.

Le Chevalier de La Charrette is a dramatic departure from Chrétien's previous works. One might imagine that the moral dilemma of the tale would hinge on the resolution of the moral quandary concerning the adultery between Lancelot and Guenevere. In *Yvain*, the culminating moment of the text is when the damsels in distress are set free. The apex of *Cligés* is when war is averted and the rightful heir becomes Emperor. In *Erec et Enide* a valiant knight is set free, which brings joy to the community; and, in *Le Conte du Graal*, there is the hope that the Wasteland could be made whole. In *La Charrette*, however, a knight is overcome by passion, and then left in a state of paralysis.

This tale, more than any other of Chrétien's romances, demonstrates the vagaries of *Fin' Amor*. *Fin' Amor* would have demanded complete obedience and submission to the lady who was the ideal of courtly virtues and source

---

18 See Loomis, *Chrétien de Troyes*, 204, for Celtic symbolism associated with the Perilous Bed. The Perilous Bed in the tale is one which is sumptuously dressed and available only to those who qualify as worthy in the eyes of the community.

of true joy to her lover. As in the poems of Ventadorn, such as *Can vei la lauzeta*, love might derange a knight and deprive him of self-control.[19] Such a possibility could account for the Cart episode in *La Charrette*, the disastrous consequences of which are made obvious by Lancelot's acquisition of a new name, Le Chevalier de la Charrette. Unlike the case in other romances, it is not a title which celebrates the knight's maturity or new place in Arthur's court; rather it places him beyond the pale of his community. The focus of this tale is not the universal struggle between good and evil, as represented by the endeavours of Lancelot to overcome the evil Meleagant; the heart and heat of this tale is Lancelot's adulterous love for Guenevere.

If Chrétien supported irrational love, or, in this case, adultery, it could be argued that he would also have altered the fate of the lovers. As it stands, however, they are still in the same situation as that of the infamous Tristan and Iseut. Should one now accept that love is a higher moral authority, capable of legitimately over-ruling reason? When Lancelot's position is taken at face value this would seem to be the case; if one looks beyond the surface, however, the character's need for magic and his mixed success against marvels, demonstrate that Lancelot is operating under questionable social standards and does not seem able to break free of his paralysis.

This is demonstrated by the course of Lancelot's actions in the story. Once Guenevere bemuses Lancelot, he seems incapable of decision-making or rational thought. For example, when Gawain and Lancelot meet a damsel who tells them of the only two passages to the land of Gorre, Lancelot abdicates his right to choose and is left to face the Sword Bridge because Gawain elects to attempt Guenevere's rescue via the Water Bridge. Once Lancelot is underway, he comes to a castle which Chrétien describes as the fairest this side of Thessaly (967–8), a remark which immediately alerts the audience to trouble. When Lancelot makes a minor attempt to make a "rational choice" by deciding to sleep with the Lady as payment for shelter, it is only possible to conclude that he is regressing (940–6). This decision would seem the least logical one which he could possibly have made, a truth which he only realises after becoming embroiled in a mock rape. Chrétien excuses Lancelot's poor judgement by reminding his audience that he is ruled not by reason but by love (1235–54).

The fact that Lancelot is having trouble thinking rationally explains some of the reasons why he does not seem to be learning from his adventures. It is interesting to compare how Yvain and Lancelot use magic.

---

19 Bernart von Ventadorn, *Seine Lieder*, ed. C. Apel (Halle: Niemeyer, 1915) as cited in Topsfield, *Arthurian Romances*, 68. See page 99 above for an example of this type of

Yvain's experiences at Laudine's castle demonstrate that he needs magic to escape punishment by the people of the keep. The magical properties of Yvain's ring are clear and he accepts it gratefully from Lunete. The need for a magical ring marks the process of Yvain's coming to terms with his need for a new identity, as the old Yvain literally disappears. Compare that adventure to Lancelot's; when a closed portcullis in a bailey under siege traps the lover, he looks for guidance to a magical ring given to him by his fairy family. It is interesting that he requires magic to see reality. His idealised love for Guenevere may well thrive in that same fairy world, which would put in perspective why it is that Lancelot's morality of love is failing to function very effectively in Arthur's world.

Chrétien's other heroes have all had to cross a final bridge between romance values and expectations and those of the real world before passing their final tests: Erec's "Joy", Yvain's *Pesme Aventure*, Fenice and Cligés' exposure to the community and then the prevention of war. All of these events introduced the characters to risks which the audience could appreciate and with which they could identify. In Lancelot's case his "honourable" adulterous love is beyond realistic expression. In order to avoid being censured, it must remain within the world of the romances. Chrétien presents this position by depicting Meleagant to be, not evil incarnate, but the representative of reality whose role is to expose the lovers as adulterers. In reality, the lovers are disloyal to their king as well as being sinners in the eyes of their community. When King Bademagu denounces Meleagant as foolish and dishonourable for his actions (6304–10), he responds incredulously: "Est ce songes, ou vos resvez, / qui dites que je sui desvez / por ce se je vos cont mon estre?" (6343–5).[20] Chrétien makes it clear that Meleagant is telling the truth about Guenevere's infidelity, he has simply accused the wrong knight, but the real problem is that he is speaking to a world which prefers illusion. Thus, the court approves of Lancelot's destruction of the voice which tries to force them to accept reality.

Lancelot has been dubbed Le Chevalier de la Charrette, a title which signifies that he is nothing more than Guenevere's creation. Not unlike Erec and Yvain at the beginning of their adventures, he requires a woman's love and ingenuity to give him purpose and identity; but he is nothing apart from his obsession with Guenevere. While the other characters evolve through learning to think and exercise free will, Lancelot resists freedom at all costs. His attempted suicide when he feels that Guenevere no longer loves him only reinforces this interpretation:

poetry.   20 "Is this a trance in which you dream when you say I am mad because I tell you of my very being?" *Lancelot*, ed. Roques, 193; Owen, *Arthurian Romances*, 270.

> Je ne sai li quex plus me het
> ou la Vie qui me desirre,
> ou Morz qui ne me vialt ocirre.
> ... Bien cuit que espoir ele sot
> que je montai sor la Charrette.
> Ne sai quel blasme ele me mete
> se cestui non. Cist m'a traï.
> S'ele por cestui m'a haï,
> Dex, cist forfez, por coi me nut?
> Onques Amors bien ne conut
> qui ce me torna a reproche;
> qu'an ne porroit dire de boche
> riens qui de par Amors venist,
> qui a reproche apartenist;
>
> (*La Charrette*, 4330–2, 4348–58)

I do not know who hates me more: Life, who wants to keep me, or Death who will not slay me... I think perhaps she knew I climbed into the cart. I don't know what she might have blamed me for except that. That was my undoing. If this was why she hated me, God! why did this misdeed count against me? A person who held me blameworthy for that never truly knew Love; for no one could name anything prompted by Love which would lend itself to reproach.[21]

It is clear that they have suffered imperfect communication, thereby allowing his two step hesitation to bring him to the point of suicide. Lancelot questions the validity of the love for which he has sacrificed everything. It is interesting that despite these questions, he still contemplates suicide owing to the fact that he cannot live without an identity, even if it is that of Guenevere's knight, Le Chevalier de la Charrette.

To further analyse the "paralysis" motif in medieval romance, Marie de France once again provides provocative material for comparison to *La Charrette*. In *Lanval*, Marie discusses how one man's needs are ignored by his society. It is the story of a brave knight forgotten by the court. King Arthur has not conferred upon Lanval the expected, and deserved, wife or bounty. In the midst of a deep depression, he meets a fairy whose beauty surpasses that of the first summer lily (107). The irony of the *lai* rests in the fact that when Lanval is provided with all the important status symbols of his culture, he only then learns to value love. In this way, Lanval and

---

[21] *Lancelot*, ed. Roques, 132–3; Owen, *Arthurian Romances*, 243.

Lancelot are very similar, since they both have the ability to do well at Arthur's court and yet their main preoccupation becomes love. They sacrifice all worldly fame and status for love. The characters are also similar in that they cannot discuss their love as it is forbidden either by the fairies or by society. The illusions surrounding their partners must be kept intact.

The conflict in *Lanval* comes to a head when the queen demands the knight's affections. In *Lanval*, Guenevere, much like Meleagant in *La Charrette*, becomes the symbol of harsh reality. She demands love which Lanval is unwilling to give and then punishes him for that rejection. This conflict of interest is one which Lancelot seeks to avoid, owing to the fact that he wants to remain a well-known knight and love the queen. There is, of course, an inherent moral conflict in any affair with a married woman, but with a queen Lanval and Lancelot risk disrupting and undermining the entire fabric of Arthurian society. Marie, unlike Chrétien, confronts this reality in her *lai*:

> "Dame," fet il, "lessiez m'ester!
> Jeo n'ai cure de vus amer.
> Lungement ai servi le rei;
> Ne li voil pas mentir ma fei
> Ja pur vus ne pur vostre amur
> Ne mesferai a mun seignur."
> La reïne s'en curuça. . .
>
> (*Lanval*, 269–75)

> "My lady," he said, "let me be! I have no desire to love you. I've served the king a long time; I don't want to betray my faith to him. Never, for you or for your love, will I do anything to harm my lord." The Queen got angry.[22]

Marie clearly outlines the acceptable boundary between personal fulfilment and obligations to society. She does not however describe a "realistic" way of achieving it. Lanval's solution is to disappear to Avalon. Lancelot's solution in *La Charrette* is more ingenious; he kills Meleagant, the only voice of reality.

The consistent use of the *merveilleux* by Chrétien and Marie as a litmus test of the morality of the characters, bolsters the idea that they deliberately structured their texts to take advantage of certain properties which the use of magic enabled. The function of magic is the key to searching for a deeper purpose in these works.

22 *Lanval*, ed. Rychner, 80; *Lanval*, ed. Hanning and Ferrante, 112.

COMPLEX APPLICATIONS OF MAGIC

Magical encounters force the characters to put to the test the strength of their sense of personal identity, their social status, and their faith in God. When a character requires magical devices – such as Yvain's need to hide with the aid of Lunete's ring – or is at the mercy of magical encounters – such as Lancelot's false encounter with lions at the Sword Bridge – it is clear that the character has not completely matured. The hero or heroine is still struggling to achieve a balance between loyalties: s/he must weigh personal needs and obligations against social duties while observing the rules of faith. To achieve a balance between what are often competing or conflicting ideals or loyalties, Chrétien forces the characters to step outside the norms of Arthurian society so that they can develop their own independent sense of values.

It is clear that the instances of *merveilleux* within the romances were methodically and judiciously organised to develop stories of *bele conjointure* into sophisticated romances. Magic's areas of influence are in the imagination and in the realm of intellectual and political pursuits; this allows the romances to act as a mirror that reflects contemporary concerns back to the medieval audience. This would allow controversial approaches to be used to discuss delicate issues. Hence, a discussion of the morality of adulterous love set in Camelot is less threatening to the community that might have issues concerning its own codes of practice.

In order to argue a clear strategy behind the romance writers' uses of *merveilleux*, it is necessary to examine the context in which magic is used. Chrétien's *Erec et Enide* provides a clear example of natural *merveilleux*, since it is Nature herself who marvels at the exquisite result of her handiwork:

> Molt estoit la pucele gente,
> car tote i ot mise s'antante
> Nature qui fete l'avoit;
> ele meïsmes s'an estoit
> plus de. v^c. foiz mervelliee
> comant une sole foiee
> tant bele chose fere pot;
>
> (*Erec et Enide*, 411–17)

The maiden was extremely attractive; for Nature, who had created her, had put all her care into the work and had herself marvelled times without number that just this once she had contrived to make so lovely a person.[23]

---

[23] *Erec et Enide*, ed. Roques, 13; Owen, *Arthurian Romances*, 6.

This use of '*mervelliee*' clearly indicates nothing more than a phenomenon of nature. Nature is there to state her admiration, and more importantly her responsibility, for her marvellous creation. What is crucial to recognise is that it is only through Enide's beauty that Erec is awarded the sparrow-hawk. Only a worthy man is judged able to find a mistress who is beautiful *and* sensible *and* above reproach (560). Her value is such that her acquisition brings Erec honour, fame, and social standing. This is verified when Chrétien states: "la pucele meïsmes l'arme; / n'i ot fet charaie ne charme" (709-10).[24] At this point in the text Erec knows who he is, and knows his place in the community; it is that of winner and lover. This is reaffirmed when Enide wins for Erec Arthur's contest of the White Stag. A magical test is at this point unnecessary, as Erec's place in society is secure.

This blissful interlude comes to an abrupt end when Enide tells Erec, now her husband, that he will have to fight to establish himself in this new role. The actions of a simple husband, even one married to the wondrous Enide, will not sustain a chivalric reputation or knightly social status. Therefore Erec and Enide begin a journey together in which lovers mature into husband and wife. Equally important, they learn how to manage all their respective roles in society: object of desire and lover, lady and knight, wife and husband, and finally, king and queen. For Erec, this process involves testing his wife's loyalty and successfully facing a catalogue of martial challenges. For Enide, it involves making a series of decisions in which she must risk her husband's life or his hatred for interfering in his affairs.

When Erec finally does establish his identity independently from her status, he is then required to face a situation which seems to involve certain death. Chrétien chose to make this incident one of natural circumstances. Therefore when Erec rises from the "dead" and is accused of being the Devil, there is no mention of *merveilleux*. There is simply no explanation offered as to why it is that he is still alive. Erec does not require the *merveilleux*, hence Chrétien makes it conspicuously absent. Erec tells only Enide a few lines later that he has put her completely 'to the test' and that he loves her. Finally he has made a decision about their relationship. He also establishes his own identity and comes to terms with his role in society. The proof of this arrives in a final *magical* test, the *Joie de la Cort*. The potential for Chrétien's use of magic and otherworldly symbolism here is enormous. Frappier argues that the references to the *Joie de la Cort* and Erec's horn could be taken straight from Celtic source material and/or the Welsh *Gereint Son of Erbin*.[25] Unlike in the Celtic originals, however, Chrétien

---

24 He is armed by the maiden herself – there was no need for magic or charms!
25 Frappier, "Chretien de Troyes" in *Arthurian Literature*, ed. R.S. Loomis (Oxford:

Breaking the Celtic spell

chooses to limit the impact of the magic to emphasis the enormity of Erec's decision to participate in the *Joy*; the mysterious wall of air and the horn of plenty feature, but their function serves to increase Erec's status:

> El vergier n'avoit an viron
> mur ne paliz, se de l'air non;
> mes de l'air est de totes parz
> par nigromance clos li jarz,
> si que riens antrer n'i pooit,
> se par un seul leu n'i antroit,
> ne que s'il fust toz clos de fer.
>
> ... Del cor ne vos dirai je plus,
> fors c'onques soner nel pot nus;
> mes cil qui soner le porra,
> et son pris et s'enor fera
> devant toz ces de ma contree;
>
> (*Erec et Enide*, 5689–95, 5765–9)

> Round the garden there was no wall or fence except of air; yet by magic the garden was enclosed on every side by air so that nothing could enter it any more than if it were ringed about by iron, unless it flew over the top.
>
> ... I shall tell you no more of the horn but that no one has ever been able to sound it. Yet if any man can sound it, his reputation and honour will thereby increase and surpass that of all those in the land.[26]

Chrétien provides a tempting taste of magical encounters so that Erec's choice to undertake the adventure is fully dramatized. His ability to stand firm in the face of what is clearly a dangerous and magical undertaking, serves as evidence of Erec's evolution from a knight who relied on his wife's beauty to bring him status, into a knight whose courage and fearlessness bring him the ultimate honour of kingship.

Clarendon Press, 1959) 169. Loomis, *Chrétien de Troyes*, 172–5. See also Topsfield, *Arthurian Romance*, 45, and Owen, *Arthurian Romances*, 499. Loomis suggests that the horn in Celtic mythology would act as the horn of plenty, one which would provide all the materials for a feast in the Fisher King myths. See also S. Sturm-Maddox, "The 'Joie de la Cort': Thematic Unity in Chrétien's *Erec and Enide*" *Romance* 103 (1982): 313–28. **26** *Erec et Enide*, ed. Roques, 173, 175–6. Owen, *Arthurian Romances*, 76–7.

Loomis suggests that Chrétien selected particular magical motifs from the Celtic arsenal to emphasise certain traits about Erec, the best example being the inexplicable horn, the forefather of which was so crucial in the *Chanson de Roland*.[27] In this, Roland the hero faces death as the result of his poor decision-making powers and his inability to distinguish between when to stay and fight an honourable battle and when to call for help in order not to foolishly waste lives. Roland cannot distinguish the illusion of heroic deeds from the reality of slaughter due to unfair odds. The Horn of Plenty is significant because it represents the hero's last attempt to rectify the enormity of his mistake. In *Erec et Enide*, Erec does rectify his faulty powers of decision-making and thus earns the right to redeem the symbolic horn as his own. It is this ability to make considered decisions which reveals that he is ready to become a king. He has completed his journey of self-discovery and established the correct priorities between his personal and social obligations.

When comparing Erec's experiences with those of Yvain or Fenice, the similarities in Chrétien's treatments of magic become apparent but so too do the differences. In *Yvain*, the hero begins his adventures at the magical fountain. Frappier and Loomis argue that Chrétien borrowed his *Yvain* material from a *conte d'aventure*: the theme of the marvellous fountain and its defender, the setting of the Forest of Broceliande, and the figure of the Monstrous Herdsman all point to Celtic sources.[28] Frappier also argues that this is true for "the love of the hero for a lady who was at an earlier stage a fountain fay".[29] Loomis suggests that the marvels of the Forest of Broceliande were widely known in the twelfth century, "thanks," he says, "to the Breton conteurs".[30] Loomis identifies combat with the Storm Knight to be a tradition going back to the "testing of the Ulster warriors by Curoi in his role as a storm giant".[31] The magical test serves to challenge knights and establish their fitness. Given this information, the modern reader would expect a magical fountain with its wondrous powers to be emphasised in the tale, or at the very least, that Yvain's success at the fountain would establish him as a knight of great renown.[32] Instead, Chrétien

---

27 Loomis, *Chrétien de Troyes*, 168, 172–5; and look to Frappier for a discussion of the connection to Bran's Horn of Plenty; Jean Frappier, "Chrétien de Troyes", *Arthurian Literature*, ed. Loomis, 168. See Loomis, ed., *Arthurian Literature*, 157. 28 Loomis, *Chrétien de Troyes*, 289–93. 29 Frappier does allow that other sources of material may have been brought into play, for example the Grateful Lion episode which is undoubtedly derived through a series of stages from the anecdote of Androcles. Frappier, "Chrétien de Troyes", *Arthurian Literature*, ed. Loomis, 183. See also R.S. Loomis, "The Spoils of Annwn", *PMLA* LVI (1941): 67–76. 30 Loomis, *Chrétien de Troyes*, 292. 31 Ibid., 292–3. 32 For further discussion of the role of the fountain see Erich Köhler, "Le rôle de la coutume dans les romans de Chrétien de Troyes", *Romania* (1960): 386–97.

naturalises the description of the fountain and makes it seem more a part of the forest and the tempests of nature. This puts in perspective Yvain's animalistic qualities, which are revealed in his violent slaughtering of the guardian of the fountain. This incident serves to expose the depth of Yvain's inner conflicts and his lack of self-control.[33] It is really only at the end of the tale that Yvain establishes himself as a glorious knight and a good husband.

In Chrétien's tale, Yvain does not even speak to his opponent when he first discovers the fountain; he simply starts attacking. He is too eager to establish himself as a great knight, an act he justifies with the excuse of revenging the slight done to the honour of his family. Once the knights see each other, they are consumed with the atavistic need to savage one another. Indeed, Yvain's thirst for revenge and desire to shame Keu runs so deep that he risks dishonour by secretly departing Arthur's court to be first to the fountain. Yvain feels passionately that it is his right and duty to avenge his cousin. It is only after putting the woman he loves through complete humiliation that he begins to learn true nobility and see the bitter consequences of impassioned actions.

To develop perspective on the medieval understanding of how magic and passion *without* reason interact in the tales, it is important to appreciate how Chrétien's contemporaries dealt with passion without *mesura*. Again a comparison to the *Lais* of Marie reveals tremendous similarities in the use of *merveilleux* and the applications of it. For example, Chrétien presents two wild men, one who serves Mother Nature and the Forest, and a "wild man" in Yvain, who fundamentally lacks the qualities to function in a chivalric community. Marie also offers a type of "wild man" tale, which is the *lai Bisclavret*. Marie's *lai* depicts a character who while deprived of the trappings of noble life, such as his clothes, is forced to remain in the body of a werewolf. This character is only magically transformed back into his own body when he learns to control his passion and earns the right to justice through his noble actions. It is interesting in this tale that the wolf's "revenge" against the wife – the tearing off of her nose – is considered justice for her behaviour. The werewolf, after the woman is tortured into revealing where the precious clothes are, is

---

[33] See page 95 for the full citation of the Wace quote and further discussion concerning the forest. The linking of emotional reactions, or even psychological revelations, to a visit to the marvellous fountain and the forest of Broceliande has its roots in Wace's *Roman de Rou*; Wace states that he went to seek wonders in the forest, but "A fool I returned, a fool I went". Wace *Roman de Rou*, ed. H. Anderson (Heilbronn, 1879), II, 283 f.

transformed once again into the well-loved knight. The over-arching principle in this tale suggests that when one can control one's actions, even when in the body of a werewolf, it demonstrates true mastery over all passionate emotions.

In the *lai Yonec*, the heroine is given the choice whether or not to use magic. To make the use of magic acceptable, Marie creates a situation where the true love (even if it is adulterous) and the choice to have freedom are made possible by magic, but it is magic sanctified by God. From the very outset of the tale Marie develops an avenue for this character to become aware of her own will-power and to enact her desires. Her request to God for a lover is a necessary prerequisite to his having the magical power to transform himself into a bird (113–15). It is also made clear that his arrival would not have been possible if she had not asked for him:

> "Dam," fet il, "n'eiez poür:
> Gentil oisel ad en ostur!
> Si li segrei vus sunt oscur,
> Gardez ke seiez a seür,
> Si fetes de mei vostre ami!"
> "Pur ceo," fet il, "vinc jeo ici.
> Jeo vus ai lungement amee
> E en mun quor mut desiree;
> Unkes femme fors vus n'amai
> Ne jamés autre n'amerai.
> Mes ne poeie a vus venir
> Ne fors de mun paleis eissir,
> Si vus ne m'eüssez requis."
>
> (*Yonec*, 121–33)

> "Lady," he said, "don't be afraid.
> The Hawk is a noble bird,
> although its secrets are unknown to you.
> Be reassured
> and accept me as your love."
> "That," he said, "is why I came here.
> I have loved you for a long time,
> I've desired you in my heart.
> Never have I loved any woman but you
> nor shall I ever love another,
> yet I couldn't have come to you

>   or left my own land
>   had you not asked for me."[34]

Marie makes it very clear that this character has to give consent for the relationship to proceed and that the lover is only there at her request. Her powers of decision have made this all happen; magic is being used to facilitate the enactment of her desires.

What is especially interesting in this passage is how Marie adroitly links chivalric ideas of love with God, a foretaste of *Perceval*. Marie's characters both feel their love is sanctified by God, and that therefore magic and adultery are acceptable in those circumstances. This emphasises the ability of *merveilleux* to make clear what seems unknowable, and to reveal what *should* be right, regardless of the views of society. It is essential that the heroine has the chance to rectify the wrongs which have been done to her. In the dénouement of *Yonec*, the heroine comes fully into her own power and executes revenge for the loss of her freedom and the murder of her lover.

Without the introduction of magic into this *lai*, the heroine would have been forever trapped by ignorance and by her options. When the heroine jumps out of the window after her lover, hoping to follow him and somehow prevent his death, she also breaks free of all mental and physical restraints. Her leap, as with Fenice's magical "death", frees her from the constraints of all imposed laws and regulations, including those of nature. *Yonec* at this point takes on a surreal quality as the heroine travels through a mysterious underground passage and discovers a beautiful silver city. Breaking free from her prison is a step towards freedom of the heart, mind, and body. The magic ring which she receives from her lover is an important sign of her rebirth; it will make her husband forget everything and treat her as a person, not a slave. It will also erase her past history and provide her with a new identity. The fact that her lover's predictions of her pregnancy and his own revenge come true helps to solidify the impression that their love is sanctioned by God despite its adulterous nature. This is not the stagnant and fruitless passion evident in Lancelot's *aventure*. This is a tale of justice and revenge being acted out through magic.

Magic in *Les Deus Amanz*, as in *Yvain*, serves to reinforce the modern reader's understanding of magic as a tool used to demonstrate or gauge the self-control of a character. In this *lai*, a couple want to marry but the father will only the release the girl if her suitor can carry her up a nearby mountain. Marie tells her audience before the actual test takes place that because the lover has no control over himself he has no chance to succeed. With this

---

34 *Yonec*, ed. Rychner, 106; *Yonec*, ed. Hanning and Ferrante, 140.

information, it is important to analyse why Marie does not have the young hero imbibe the strength-giving potion which is clearly designated as the only option which could save him and fulfill his ambition to marry his true love. The explanation which the boy offers for his behaviour is that he would have become confused if he had stopped in the midst of his struggle. When faced with such a critical situation this excuse rings a bit hollow. This leaves only the explanation which the narrator offers, which is that the boy's lack of moderation in love prevented him from achieving control, through magic or any other means, over his own life: "Mes jo creim que poi ne li vaille, / Kar n'ot en lui point de mesure" (188–9) ("But I'm afraid the potion did him little good, because he was entirely lacking in control.")[35]

The precise directions which Marie offers concerning where one needs to go to get a magical potion places its use in an interesting light: magic is accessible to the average man and clearly controlled by human design. In this format, as in Chrétien's, magic offers a means whereby an individual might exercise power over his or her own fate. Marie uses magic to exemplify free will versus what nature or fate necessitates. In *Les Deus Amanz*, the boy exercises the choice to try to force his body past its human limitations. Death is the only avenue left for one whose passion has pushed him beyond the boundaries of his nature. In Marie's ending, the modern reader can see the sharp differences between the *Lais* and Chrétien's romances: in this *lai*, there is no attempt to teach the boy how to control his passion. *Yvain* offers a similar premise, but in Chrétien's work the hero will firstly be rescued from death, and secondly, be taught how to love with both heart and mind. By employing magic in this way (or not employing it, as is the case in this *lai* owing to the fact that the potion is never used) Marie examines human nature without providing any alternatives to its limitations.

If one compares the ending of *Les Deus Amanz* to the exploits of Yvain, it is possible to see how a hero can discover his weakness and learn how to control the impulses of passion. Yvain requires not only the ingenuity of Lunete to win him Laudine's love, but also their respective rings to keep body and spirit together. Yvain carelessly overstays his St John's Day deadline, but goes mad once he is publicly called to task for it. The formal request for the return of Laudine's magical ring humiliates Yvain in front of his peers.[36] Stripped of his public persona and private sense-of-self (status as a lover), what is left is only a wild man wandering desperately in the woods. It is interesting that the character is so

---

35 *Yonec*, ed. Rychner, 108. *Yonec*, ed. Hanning and Ferrante, 142.   36 A.R. Press, "Chrétien de Troyes's Laudine: A Belle Dame sans Mercy?" *FMLS* 19 (1983): 158–71.

completely destroyed by the public reclaiming of the ring. In and of itself, the action does not seem so dramatic as Yvain has not even taken advantage of Laudine's ring; but symbolically the magic ring has become associated with his social position as Knight of the Fountain and as his role as husband. When the ring is withdrawn publicly, Yvain is stripped of his social status and the sense of his own worth and identity. He is left to roam "wild" or crazed in the wilderness, seeking some sort of solace in that environment. It is, of course, appropriate that he flees to the woods, which is the favoured site of magical quests and adventures.

The importance of the "magical wood" motif does not originate with Chrétien; Wace tells us that he too has searched the woods for marvels and magic. Indeed the design for the story may have had its source in Wace's text, for his disenchantment with the forest of the Bretons is clear:

> Mais jo ne sai par quel raison
> la seut l'en fees veeir,
> se li Breton nos dient veir,
> e altres mer(e)veilles plusors;
> aires i selt aveir *d'ostors*
> e de grant cers mult grant plenté,
> mais vilain ont *tot* deserté.
> La alai jo merveilles querre,
> vi la forest e vi la terre,
> merveilles quis, mais nes trovai,
> fol m'en revinc, fol i alai;
> fol i alai, fol m'en revinc,
> folie quis, pour fol me tinc.
>
> (*Rou*, 6386–98)

I do not know, however, why people were in the habit of seeing fairies there. The Bretons tell of these and other marvels, there were buzzards and lots of huge stags, but the peasants soon left. I went in search of marvels and saw forest and earth but of marvels found none. Mad I came back and mad I went, mad I went and mad I came back. What I was asking was mad and I consider myself mad.[37]

It is impossible to know if Chrétien actually knew this passage, but it is clear that he too was disenchanted with the famous forest and interested in

---

37 *Le Roman de Rou*, ed. A.J. Holder, S.A.T.F. (Paris: Picard, 1970–3) 122. See J. Frappier, *Étude sur* Yvain *ou le Chevalier au lion de Chrétien de Troyes* (Paris: Champion, 1969) 85–6.

breathing new life into old tales and old symbols. It is not surprising that Wace found madness while searching for marvels, as the two seem interwoven in the mythology which surrounds all forests. When a character is in search of an identity s/he often encounters marvels which serve to highlight his or her quest; when a character is completely without identity, s/he is most often found mad, wandering in the forest. Yvain like Wace, was in search of marvels, but when it came time to know his own true self, it would be madness which awaited him on his path to revelation.

Chrétien, unlike Marie in *Bisclavret*, does not allow Yvain the dignity to gather himself and return a new man to society; instead, the knight is cured through an "anti-madness ointment" provided originally by Morgan the Wise. To a twelfth-century audience any concoction linked to Morgan, the original and infamous Fee, would have had magical, and possibly, demonic connotations surrounding it.[38] Owen makes many disparaging claims that Chrétien limited the Celtic influences and the *merveilleux* in his text to attempt to correct problems of "insufficient motivation".[39] It would seem more logical to expect that Chrétien had an overall structure in mind, and an agenda for naturalising some events rather than others. When Yvain does awake, after being doused in Morgan's ointment, he is in a state of amazement and wonder at these new events. Chrétien makes it perfectly plain that Yvain has still not redeemed himself or developed his independent identity. A magical test is not yet required, as the audience knows where Yvain stands, which is lost in the wilderness and far away from civilization.

To achieve a secure place in Arthurian society, Yvain, like Erec, must pass a supreme test. Yvain's place in the community rests upon his decision to fight the goblins and free the damsels in the *Pesme Aventure*. Yvain is warned by the townspeople of the dangers which he faces, and his thoughts on the situation, its pros and cons, etc., are made plain to the audience (5136–57). Despite all this information, Yvain decides to proceed with the dangerous test which awaits him.

This section of the tale bridges the gap between imagination and medieval reality in that Chrétien chooses to depict a "sweatshop" filled with damsels in distress. Their harsh experience of everyday life – for example, poor wages, threadbare clothes, and poor food – crosses the fine line between the world of romance and twelfth-century reality. Chrétien describes the two devil's sons as the offspring of a woman and the goblin, Netun, and states specifically that this is no joke (5265–7). In telling the audience to take the situation seriously, Chrétien forges a connection between

---

[38] Loomis, *Celtic Myth*, 188–96; Loomis, ed., *Arthurian Literature*, 65, 92–3, 109.
[39] Owen, *Arthurian Romances*, xii.

the serious step Yvain is choosing to make, and all the difficulties which must be faced when people make life and death decisions. In other words, Chrétien has Yvain facing a potentially "real" situation that has been cloaked in magic. The addition of demons and goblins creates the tension of expectation which only magical adventures can engender. The presence of magical or mythical demons also generates the feeling of freedom; absolutely anything could happen next. The characters are free to choose a future and fulfill what they deem to be the appropriate course of action. Magic is linked with man's power to design his fate and rebel against the static norms which everyone else has to follow.

Power over the situation and the ability to choose alternatives are the characteristics most often attached to magical encounters within the romances, and regardless of an audience's or a character's lack of belief in magic, its presence still represents a kind of freedom and power which man has sought since the origin of his belief in a god. Whether the character has *really* mastered fate, or whether such a thing is possible, is not the heart of the matter at hand; what is important is that the character has learned to make decisions. It is important to note that there is not a single mention of *merveilleux* in this chapter of the romance. This moment in the text is not about magic, the wonders of nature, or God, but about the reality of man's choices.

Yvain, because he is the best of men, must be challenged by something greater than the average villain. It is also clear, however, from the wrangle which Yvain has to endure over not marrying the beautiful princess, that romance codes of practice no longer fulfill his needs. Normally it is expected that the handsome knight wins as his prize the beautiful lady and all her possessions. Chrétien makes the point, not so very subtly, by orchestrating an encounter with the family reciting a romance aloud in a perfect garden. Chrétien thereby illustrates that romance norms are the rules by which these characters live, and when Yvain refuses to comply with their rules, the father labels him arrogant and improper (5373). This is the culminating moment in Yvain's education; he is finally choosing to sacrifice for, and earn the love and respect of, his wife. Yvain is the pride of the romance world in the beginning of his story, but finds that such accolades are fleeting and shallow. Once brought into the real world, as it were, and taught how to make difficult decisions and painful choices, Yvain becomes both a famous knight and a loyal husband. Topsfield suggests that this ending provokes real emotion; he says: "Yvain suffers more deeply than any other of Chrétien's characters."[40] The ending of *Yvain* could be considered one of

---

40 Topsfield, *Arthurian Romances*, 206.

the most underplayed psychologically realistic moments in the romances. There is no fanfare, only wary lovers hoping for the best. Yvain outgrows the romance and this allows Chrétien to create, not shallow *aventures* which are thrilling but soon forgotten, but rather, a marked analysis of medieval culture and philosophy.

Support for this reading of the conceptual framework behind the organisation of the romances can be further supplied by analysis of *Cligés*, *La Charrette*, and *Perceval*. *Cligés* concerns not only the development and education of a knight, but also the triumph of true love and justice. This is a text which proclaims no certainties in this worldly existence. In *Cligés* "Chrétien is not only offering us a blatant comedy of situation, an essay in literary and social satire, and an Art of Love, but behind all this, he begins to uncover a subtle and intellectually-minded view of the human condition." Topsfield suggests that Chrétien in *Cligés* "praises reason and common sense and mocks them . . . In adopting the twelfth-century view of life as an amalgam of opposites, he begins to reveal doubts which he will amplify in *Perceval*."[41]

The conclusion of *Cligés* provides the key to understanding the romance: Fenice and Thessala devise between them a system to fool all the men in their world; the Emperor, the doctors, and even *Cligés*, are not immune. The power of magic enables the two women to achieve their objectives. It is interesting to note that when this power of self-determination is achieved by Yvain, his greatness is lauded; in women, such power is suspect. The power of magic in this text is not at any point diluted. Fenice knows what she wants from the moment she sees Cligés and, unlike Soredamors, Fenice does not delay, nor do her methods of obtaining him leave much to chance: "Par boene amor, non par losange, / Ses ialz li baille et prant les suens." ("Out of genuine love, not flattery, she lends him her eyes and receives his own") (2768–9).[42] Chrétien alerts the audience to Thessala's magical skill (3002) and the very rational thought processes of Fenice. There is no question that either character is motivated by the kind of passion that drove Lancelot or Yvain to their irrational actions.

In describing Thessala's skills, Chrétien does not try to naturalise or compromise them in any way:

> Sa mestre avoit non Thessala,
> Qui l'avoit norrie en anfance,
> Si savoit molt de nigromance.
> Por ce fu Thessala clamee

---

41 Ibid., 64.   42 *Cligés*, ed. Micha, 85; Owen, *Arthurian Romances*, 130.

> Qu'ele fu de Tessalle nee,
> Ou sont feites les deablies,
> Anseigniees et establies.
> Les fames qui el païs sont
> Et charmes et charaies font.
>
> *(Cligés,* 2962–70)

> Her governess, her childhood nurse, was named Thessala; and she was very skilled in magic. She was called Thessala because she had been born in Thessaly, where devilish enchantments are traditionally taught and practised. The women of that country work charms and spells.[43]

What is especially interesting is that this use of magic, despite being described as devilish, seems to perform positively in the text. Thessala is essentially a witch but there are no evil or sinister connotations attached to the good works she performs for Fenice. In this way her role is very similar to that of Iseut's mother in all of the early extant versions of *Tristan*; the Good Mother is never accused of evil acts. However, the most obvious difference between the two texts is the author's intention for the use of magic.

Fenice believes that achieving her aims through magic is the rational way of obtaining her choice of lover. Chrétien emphasizes that Fenice chooses to love Cligés. Some ideas expressed in Chrétien's earlier poetry also support his views in *Cligés*. In *D'Amor qui m'a tolu a moi* there is little appreciation for overwhelming passion. This poem is cited as Chrétien's response to the earlier *Fin' Amor* poem of Bernart de Ventadorn, *Can vei la lauzeta*, the first lines of which demonstrate how passion steals identity from the lover: "Tout m'a mo cor, e tout m'a me, / e se mezeis e tot lo mon." ("She has stolen my heart from me and has stolen myself from me and that he has lost everything in the whole world".)[44] Chrétien seems to disagree wholeheartedly with these sentiments, as is demonstrated in the following lines which could easily have been spoken by Fenice:

> Onques del bevraje ne bui
> don Tristans fu anpoisonez,
> mes plus me fet amer que lui
> fins cuers et bone volantez.
> Bien an doit estre miens li grez,

---

43 *Cligés*, ed. Micha, 90–1. Owen, *Arthurian Romances*, 133. 44 Chrétien de Troyes, *D'Amòr qui m'a tolu a moi*, ed. K. Bartsch, 28–36 as cited in Topsfield, *Arthurian Romances*, 68.

> qu'ains de rien esforciez n'an fui
> fors de tant, que mes iauz an crui
> par cui sui anla voie antrez,
> don ja n'istrai n'ains n'i recrui.
>
> (*D'Amor*, 28–36)

Never did I drink of that drink with which Tristan was poisoned yet a true heart and a true desire make my love greater than his. The pleasure from this must indeed be mine, for I was never constrained in any way, except in so far as I believed my eyes, through which I have entered the path from which I shall never stray and from which I was never recreant.[45]

The obvious disdain which Fenice feels for the crude morals of Iseut may well reflect Chrétien's opinion of Thomas of Britain's work. Owen writes in the preface to the *Romances* that "Chrétien's attempt to justify Fenice *vis-à-vis* Iseut may reflect a rivalry between him and his contemporary, Thomas of England, whose own *Tristran* appears to antedate *Cligés*."[46] Chrétien makes it clear through Fenice that Iseut and Tristan had abused not only the ideal of true love, but also, the means of achieving it:

> Mialz voldroie estre desmanbree
> Que de nos deus fust remanbree
> L'amors d'Ysolt et de Tristan,
> Don mainte folie dit an,
> Et honte en est a reconter.
> Ja ne m'i porroie acorder
> A la vie qu'Isolz mena.
> Amors en li trop vilena,
> Que ses cuers fu a un entiers,
> Et ses cors fu a deus rentiers.
> Ensi tote sa vie usa
> N'onques les deus ne refusa.
> Ceste amors ne fu pas resnable,
> Mes la moie iert toz jorz estable,
> Car de mon cors et de mon cuer
> N'iert ja fetpartie a nul fuer.
> Ja mes cors n'iert voir garçoniers,

---

[45] Chrétien de Troyes, *D'Amor*, ed. Bartsch, 28–36 as cited in Topsfield, *Arthurian Romances*, 68. [46] Owen, *Arthurian Romances*, 506.

> N'il n'i avra deus parçoniers.
> Qui a le cuer, cil a le cors,
> Toz les autres an met defors.
>
> *(Cligés,* 3105-24).

I would rather be torn limb from limb than have people in referring to us recall the love of Yseut and Tristan, about whom such nonsense is talked about that I'm ashamed to speak of it. I couldn't reconcile myself to the life Iseut led. With her, love was too debased, for her body was made over to two men, whilst her heart belonged entirely to one. In this way she spent her whole life without ever rejecting either one. This was unreasonable, but mine is firm and constant, nor will my body or my heart ever be shared under any circumstances. Never will my body be prostituted between two owners. Let him who has the heart have the body: I reject all others.[47]

Topsfield assesses this passage to signify, not only Chrétien's criticism of Iseut (Thomas), but also Chrétien's attempt to advocate a type of balanced love which comes from mental control and mutual desire. He argues that "Yseut exemplifies life wasted by irrational love which lacks order, moral values and social approval". This is also an attack on the concept of *Fin' Amor*, the songs of Bernart de Ventadorn, and the *De Amore* of Andreas Capellanus.[48]

Owen also supports the argument that Chrétien was opposed to the Thomas *Tristran* by stating in the introduction to Chrétien's *Romances* that in *Cligés* "Chrétien seems to have been very much pre-occupied with the Tristan legend. In *Philomena* he had expressed strong moral views on the evil of an unlawful passion; and the adulterous relationship of Tristan and Iseut, prompted not by the spontaneous attraction of noble hearts and still less by reason, was viewed by him with extreme disfavour."[49]

However, despite the claims of many critics that Chrétien's displeasure at Thomas' *Tristran* was due solely to rivalry between two competing talents, what may have dismayed Chrétien was Thomas' revision of the archetypal versions of Beroul and Eilhart to suit the jaded tastes of the Angevin court, or his exaltation of "love uncontrolled".[50] These older versions of *Tristran* have in common that the powers of the love-drink abate after three or four years.[51] It cannot be argued that Chrétien's

47 *Cligés*, ed. Micha, 95. Owen, *Arthurian Romances*, 135. 48 Topsfield, *Arthurian Romances*, 75. 49 Owen, *Arthurian Romances*, xiv. 50 Frappier, "Chrétien de Troyes", 161. 51 *Tristan*, ed. Hatto, 8. It is unfortunate that Hatto does not reserve his judgment concerning the importance of the three to four year abatement period;

version of the *Tristan* story was a more sophisticated version of these sources, since the tale has been lost; however, it might be safe to say that it could have been in keeping with his views expressed in *Cligés*, a story which discusses the fate of Tristan and Iseut. If Chrétien had written the story to reflect his appreciation of two lovers drawn together by irrational passion, it would seem natural that some hint of those views would have appeared in his works.[52]

Owen in his notes refers to *Cligés* as an anti-*Tristan* or even a "hyper-*Tristan*", but this comment offers little insight into what specifically it is about the Tristan stories that Chrétien wishes to modify.[53] Fenice will not tolerate the wrong kind of magic, which gives the illusion of nobility and honour to what is falsely considered true love. In this regard, Chrétien explains the devastating effect of self-delusion. Jehan, Cligés' faithful servant, becomes the stalwart defender of the differences between illusion and reality. This character and the situation are somewhat reminiscent of the situation of the slave-driven damsels and the events of the *Pesme Aventure* section of *Yvain*. Jehan cannot be frightened or intimidated away from expressing the truth. He knows he has sinned but remains to face the wrath of the king, while Fenice, Cligés, and Thessala flee to Britain. Jehan states that he never lies and that if he has sinned then it will be right for him to be made captive, but that he has only done what he has been told to do (6549–58). Chrétien, as he did in *Yvain*, adds a good dose of reality into his text. Jehan explains what it is like to live in a world without magic, a world where his free will is limited by the wishes of a master. This measure of reality is brought into direct conflict with the illusions which the Emperor tries desperately to maintain. He wants to believe his dreams so that he can deny all the terrible things that he will otherwise have to accept if Jehan actually represents the world of "reality"; this would mean, for example, that the Emperor would have to acknowledge that he never consummated his marriage (6467–6543).[54]

The transition from romance to reality, or illusion to truth, is such that the Emperor is driven mad by the revelations of Jehan and his search for Cligés. The heroes of the story are then free to return to their home. Thus, a "happy ending" seems to be arrived at, not by the magical resources of the romance artillery, but by a shock of reality. There is a high price to be paid,

---

instead, he suggests that the "absurdity of the two-phase love potion" was included purely to facilitate plot function.   52 *La Charrette*, it may be argued, is an attempt to glorify adulterous, passionate love, except that Chrétien tells us that he has been given the theme by his benefactress. See the *La Charrette* commentary in this chapter for fuller discussion of this problematic text.   53 Owen, *Arthurian Romances*, 508. 54 Ibid., 181.

however, in view of the restrictions which are then placed on the generations of empresses who succeed Fenice. Chrétien has rarely been so pessimistic in his conclusions as when he decrees that love will not ensnare any of the succeeding empresses of Constantinople. Chrétien's motivation for ending the story on such a sour note may well be that this romance treads close to a deep source of unease in medieval culture:

> Et chascun jor lor amors crut,
> Onques cil de li ne mescrut,
> Ne querela de nule chose;
> N'onques ne fu tenue anclose,
> Si com ont puis esté tenues
> Celes qu'aprés li sont venues;
> Einz puis n'i ot empereor
> N'eüst de sa fame peor
> Qu'ele nel deüst decevoir,
> Se il oï ramantevoir
> Comant Fenice Alis deçut,
> Primes par la poison qu'il but,
> Et puis par l'autre traïson.
> Por ce einsi com an prison
> Est gardee an Costantinoble,
> Ja n'iert tant haute ne tant noble,
> L'empererriz, quex qu'ele soit:
> L'emperres point ne s'i croit,
> Tant con de celi li remanbre;
> Toz jorz la fet garder en chanbre
> Plus por peor que por le hasle,
> Ne ja avoec li n'avra masle
> Qui ne soit chastrez en anfance.
> De ce n'est criemme ne dotance
> Qu'Amors les lit an son l'ien.
>
> (*Cligés*, 6639–63)

And each day their love grew stronger; and he never doubted her or found fault with her at all. Nor was she ever kept shut away as has since been the case with those ladies who succeeded her; for never again has there been an emperor who was not afraid of being deceived by his wife, once he had heard tell how Fenice deceived Alis, first by the potion he drank and then by that other ruse. For this reason the empress, whoever she might be and however rich and noble, is guarded in Constantinople as in a prison; for the emperor does not trust her so long as he remembers this other lady, but always has her kept in a room, more out of fear than in case of sunburn. And no male will ever accompany her unless he is a eunuch from childhood: with them there is no fear or anxiety that Love will ensnare them in his bonds.[55]

The sheer length and detail of this passage alerts the modern reader to the interest a medieval audience might have had in the consequences of women using magic, particularly in the realm of obtaining new husbands for themselves. Chrétien is not breezily creating closure to this romance; rather he is providing precise information and significant detail as to how all future women will be punished for Fenice's use of magic. She oversteps the boundary of socially acceptable behaviour for women, and perhaps even the delicate line between the perceptions of male and female power in medieval culture.

It is valuable to compare *Cligés* to *Le Conte du Graal* (*Perceval*) as their ideas of love and power seem in direct confrontation. In *Cligés* physical love was of primary importance; in *Le Conte du Graal*, however, love is no longer physical but spiritual. One finds a romance which has been stripped of its silks and satins and reduced to a toughened core. *Le Conte du Graal* is about education and evolution. It portrays the growth of a young ignorant boy into a knight who remains unfulfilled, and then depicts his struggles towards an even higher plane of spiritual and cognitive experience.

Modern critics have often been discouraged by the seeming split personality of this romance, suggesting that perhaps it is comprised of two separate stories brought together by a less-than-brilliant third party.[56] However, it would seem more productive to argue how the existing piece makes sense to the careful reader rather than to discount its value through defining it as a corrupt text. This romance sheds the courtly accoutrements of love and seduction and openly discusses what have been, more covertly, the themes of the other romances: education, identity, and free will. Topsfield argues very effectively that Chrétien employed a Cistercian approach to this revolutionary romance. The Cistercians argued that there were two ways of living life: one governed by the right hand of *caritas*, which represents the search for oneness with God; the other governed by the left hand of *voluntas propria*, which seeks *vaine glorie* in this world.[57]

[55] *Cligés*, ed. Micha, 202; Owen, *Arthurian Romances*, 183–4. [56] Topsfield, *Arthurian Romances*, 15–16, 207–10, 211–301 for general discussion. See also Peter Haidu, *Aesthetic Distance in Chrétien de Troyes* (Geneve: Librairie Droz, 1968) 201–3. See also Maddox, *Arthurian Romances*, 83. [57] Maddox, *Arthurian Romances*, 82; Topsfield, *Arthurian Romances*, 216. See also D.D.R. Owen, *The Evolution of the*

Topfield's argument is based on Chrétien's prologue to *Perceval*, where he states that he is writing for a count who loves righteousness:

> Li quens aime droite justise
> Et loiauté et sainte eglise
> Et toute vilonnie het;
> S'est larges que l'en si ne set,
> Qu'il done selonc l'evangille,
> Sanz ypocrisie et sanz gille,
> Qu'el dist: "Ne sache ta senestre
> Les biens quant les [fera] ta destre."
>
> (*Perceval*, 25–32)

The count loves true justice, loyalty and holy Church and hates all baseness; and he is more beautiful than any man known, since he gives without hypocrisy or deceit, as taught by the Gospels, which state: "Let not your left hand know of the good deed done by your right hand."[58]

Furthermore, Chrétien enlarges on St Matthew (26:23, 3–4) and provides his own gloss of these lines (37–46).[59] In viewing the pains to which Chrétien goes in order to provide a philosophical structure to his text, it is necessary to analyse how this moral code affects the growth of Perceval and Gawain. It is clear from the outset that Gawain's adventure will represent the path of vainglory, as desire for greater honour rules his life. He is the perfect ideal of courtly culture. The figure of Perceval is not quite so clear-cut as his progress proceeds in developmental stages.

It is possible to see the "split personality" of this romance, not only in terms of *caritas* and vainglory, but also in terms of a debate between the spiritual and secular future of noble knights. The dilemma over how to merge, or even find common ground, between these two codes was one which would continuously occupy the romances from this period into the fifteenth century. The English romance *Sir Gawain and the Green Knight*, for example, also sought to resolve the conflict between Church and courtly practices, but, in the end, it too failed to find a satisfactory means of reconciliation. Chrétien may well have anticipated this outcome, as the plot of *Perceval*, in which two quests run parallel and rarely intersect, acts as an apt

---

Grail Legend (Edinburgh: Oliver and Boyd, 1968) 156ff; P.A. Becker, "Von den Erzahlern neben und nach Crestien de Troyes", *Zeitschrift fur romanische Philologie* (1935): 400–16. **58** *Perceval*, ed. Roach, 1–2. See also Owen, *Arthurian Romances*, 374. **59** Topsfield, *Arthurian Romances*, 210–11.

metaphor for the nature of the ideological dilemma which faced the future of knighthood. It is not possible to know how Chrétien would have resolved this ideological problem which his audience faced, as he did not complete the romance. However, it is possible to hypothesize from the events in the text, that Chrétien would have sought to invest love with both human and spiritual qualities. This would serve to enrich the human experience and give virtually mystical importance to the quest of developing self-knowledge.

When Perceval is first introduced, he is completely ignorant of all social and cultural mores. He initially mistakes five visiting knights for devils, then he thinks they are angels, and then he even mistakes one for God (111–86). The only helpful knight of the group tells his fellows that Perceval is ignorant of all their laws, meaning not only civil but also social and religious codes. When asked his name it is clear that Perceval cannot adequately respond, as he has yet to find an identity, or place in the community (340–59). Perceval's poor beleaguered mother tells him that this is because she has tried hard to keep him hidden and apart from the world so that he would never become a knight. The idea of knighthood – formally the epitome of every nobleman's desires – has clearly lost some of its prestige (403–27). Chrétien seems to be preparing the way for some even greater level of status. Perceval, however, is interested in becoming a knight, and he endures through even some rocky moments. He has natural fighting skills, but constant social blunders reinforce the impression of his complete ignorance of every social skill.

It is not until he reaches the castle of Gornemant de Goorz that Perceval is taken in and educated in the social graces of Arthur's court. Once formally knighted and properly indoctrinated, this new knight promptly falls in love. Rescuing damsels and being richly rewarded is clearly a fundamental precept for the Arthurian world. In previous romances, however, love becomes the focal point for the entire subsequent adventure. Love is the linchpin which gives meaning to the preceding and succeeding *aventures*. This is not the case in Perceval's saga; he leaves once he has rescued the fair Blancheflor and her minions. The "love" scene where he is enthralled by the three drops of blood in the snow is there, perhaps, to remind the audience of Lancelot's unhealthy obsession with Guenevere in *La Charrette*. It is an ominous sign that only one knight in all of Arthur's court – Gawain, Lancelot's companion in *La Charrette* – is fluent enough in "true" courtly behaviour to understand Perceval's actions (4194–9). Chrétien expertly manipulates the audience into expecting the worst – a life of unhealthy Lancelot-like obsession – for Perceval's future. This grim prediction is reinforced by his failure to act properly, or to appreciate any spiritual aspects to his encounter at the Fisher King's castle.

Perceval's inappropriate behaviour stems from the one-sided nature of his education. He has only been tutored in the ways of courtly knighthood and this certainly does not prepare him for the spiritual and intellectual demands which are now made upon him. The fact that his courtly accomplishments are in order and respected is proven by the Fisher King's gift of the Great Sword. His inability to employ it successfully is an indication that it is his *soul*, not his social skills, which still needs work.

The cause of his failure at the Castle stems from an inability to think independently. He is too frightened to deviate from the codes of conduct which the good knight Gornemant set out for him. Perceval is obeying courtly procedure in respecting his mentor's instructions. The way the scene is depicted, however, suggests an insecure child obeying his father to the letter of the law, rather than a grown adult making a decision to remain quiet. This image is particularly apt considering the type of advice which Gornemant offers Perceval; he suggests that one should keep quiet, so as not to look foolish, be good to people in need, and to go to Church (1647–56). These suggestions are of course meant to help Perceval; instead, they leave him helpless in the face of his trial at the *Graal* castle.

It is important to observe that courtly accomplishments such as fame and honour are no longer enough to create a well-adjusted knight. Perceval has made a place for himself in courtly society, but clearly this is not enough to gain success in his endeavors at the Fisher King's table. In fact, at this stage in the story, Perceval still does not even know his own name nor has he repented the sin of causing his mother's death. The *Graal* test is not one of martial prowess or ability to resist sexual temptations, but is a test of ingenuity. It is the ability to think and question the surrounding world which has become important.[60] Chrétien is not underplaying the magical overtones of this encounter so much as mystifying the aura surrounding Perceval's adventures at the Fisher King's castle. His encounters with the Lance and *Graal* leave him more mystified about his goal than he was before he began his quest (3220–45, 3290–3).

Topsfield argues convincingly that Chrétien's sources for these items are Celtic myths which attach weighty symbolism to lances and *graals*.[61] The Bleeding Lance was popular in both Welsh and Irish stories concerning the chosen elect whose moral and physical health was intertwined

---

[60] Compare this to *Sir Gawain and the Green Knight* or *Tristan*. In this precedent, we can also see the foundation for Piers Plowman's search for an understanding of Truth. Langland also wrote to convince the reader of the value of knowing the incorrect path before learning the right road to God. [61] Topsfield, *Arthurian Romances*, 210–13.

with the well-being of the land.[62] The mystical *graal* is common in such stories as the Irish tale, *Conn and the Tuatha de Danaan*, in which it symbolises endless plenty.[63] It is important to note that the symbols of chalice and lance also had tremendous value for Christians. The Bleeding Lance was associated with the Blind Centurion who strikes Christ's side at Golgotha.[64] In the medieval gloss, Christ's blood cured his illness and he became a martyr for Christ. The chalice, even today, is significant as the receptacle of divine inspiration passing from Christ to the Church. In spiritual terms, it is the source of man's salvation. All of these important external links imbue the *graal* and Chrétien's text with tremendous resonance. They also focus the audience's attention in a new direction, which is the quest for salvation.

Chrétien, like Marie in her concluding *lai*, *Eliduc*, has begun to consider the concept of sin. This immediately adds to the romance and the figure of the knight another level of complexity. If the knight transgresses against the social codes, he is able to redeem himself through his own actions. He can quest for *aventures* or attempt marvellous tests to prove himself noble and worthy in the eyes of the court. However, once sin becomes involved there is a far more complicated philosophical and theoretical thought process which must be engaged. The penitent must be absolved of sin, which requires acknowledgment of it, repentance of it, and strict atonement. This procedure requires that the sinner analyse both the heart and mind. The conclusion of such an analysis should be some type of awareness of the motivation for sinning and of the need to learn how to resist it.

Perceval is greatly matured by his experience at the *Graal* castle, as evidenced by his ability to *intuit* his name, *Perchevax li Galois*, directly after leaving it. However, it is in this same encounter that Perceval is immediately renamed by the weeping maiden: *Perchevax li chaitis*, Perceval the unfortunate (3582). This maiden identifies herself as his full cousin, and Perceval's place in his community becomes apparent as a series of new family members appear to advise him. It is, however, the death of his mother for which he must now atone. His quest now becomes a pilgrimage in which he can repent his callousness. Perceval's sin must be told to the community and accepted by it, for repentance to be achieved.[65]

The Hideous Damsel arrives at the new gathering of Arthur's court and announces the catalogue of evils which will result from Perceval's

---

62 A.C.L. Brown, "The Bleeding Lance", *PMLA* 25 (1910): 1–59.   63 Topsfield, *Arthurian Romances*, 208, 210–11.   64 John 19:34.   65 See Amelia Rutledge, "Perceval's Sin: Critical Perspectives", *Oeuvres et Critiques* 5: 2 (1980–1): 53–60 for a detailed discussion of Chrétien's use of sin.

Breaking the Celtic spell

inability to act (4638–84). Chrétien emphasizes how different Perceval's response is from that of Gawain, which, of course, points up the dissimilarity for scrutiny:

> Et Perchevax redist tout el:
> Qu'il ne s'aille
> Combatre a lire
> ... et qu'il avra
> Tant que il del graal saura
> Cui l'en en sert,
> La lance qui saine trovee
> Et que la veritez provee
> Li ert dite por qu'ele saine;
> Ja nel laira por nule paine.
>
> (*Perceval*, 4727–9, 4736–40)

Then Perceval spoke quite differently, saying that as long as he lived ... until he discovered who was served from the grail and had found the bleeding lance and been told the certain truth as to why it bleeds. He will not give up, whatever the hardship.[66]

Topsfield interprets this passage as a key step in the knight's development. Perceval ignores the knightly tests which bring worldly fame. Topsfield states: "Free will is added to his predestination as a knight of the *Graal* lineage."[67] Perceval now reflects and chooses; his days of drifting, carefree *aventure* are behind him. Although this is a step in the right direction, Perceval still has not realised that the methods of *vaine gloire* will not help to obtain *caritas*. It is at this halfway point in development that Perceval suffers most. He is no longer part of the Arthurian world and yet he has not passed into a higher community. It is not surprising that he endures madness and loses his path when he struggles to exist without a relationship to society or God (6364–7).

It is important to note that Perceval is the only knight in Chrétien's romances to be concerned with spiritual matters. Donald Maddox in *Arthurian Romances* argues that the very nature of his failure at the *Grail* castle was already indicative of what he now fully realises for the first time: that the essence of his quest is not primarily a tangible object or a special place, but above all a cognitive discovery.[68] Once Perceval recovers

---

[66] *Perceval*, ed. Roach, 139; Owen, *Arthurian Romances*, 436–7. [67] Topsfield, *Arthurian Romances*, 271. [68] Maddox, *Arthurian Romances*, 94–100. See Maddox's 'Remote Locus' argument; this is his term for the tests given to establish supreme heroes.

his spirit, he recovers his direction. The hermit whispers holy secrets in his ear and now Perceval can revitalize his quest for the *graal*. He is defying the predictions of the Hideous Damsel (4638) and demanding to take his fate into his own hands. It is at this portentous moment that Chrétien returns to Gawain's aventures. He establishes the peak moment of interest and then skillfully diverts the audience back into the world of marvels.

There is indeed a stark contrast between the pious devotions of Perceval and the *aventures* of Gawain. Within what seems virtually moments of vowing to find the Bleeding Lance, Gawain's attention is diverted to far more worldly matters. His reputation is under threat: Guigambresil accuses Gawain of foully killing his father. To emphasise that this is once again the world of romance and illusion, Chrétien fits in the neat detail that the judge of this case, King Escavalon, is more handsome than Absalom. Illusion and surface appearances are always important in the world of romance. In terms of physical text it is only fifty lines down the page, and yet the ideology of spiritual quest and devotion is in another dimension. Gawain's path is littered with diversions which range from fighting tournaments for clever and manipulative young girls (5496–612) to seducing the daughter of the man he allegedly killed (5837–69). This world operates under familiar codes and values, which have changed little since the tales of *Erec et Enide* and *La Charrette*. Chrétien's movement from Gawain to Perceval must surely emphasise the link that he is trying to build between these two worlds, despite the myriad differences. It is these differences which need to be resolved so that all of Arthur's knights can follow the highest code of the land, the code of noble conduct *and* spirituality.

In highlighting the link between the two worlds, Chrétien could not offer a starker comparison than presenting Gawain's seductions alongside Perceval's tear-driven penance. It is clear that these two parts of the tale represent two completely different value-systems. When Chrétien returns to Gawain's *aventures*, a host of marvels and fantastic exploits are presented. Gawain's position as the best of courtly knights is not under scrutiny. He survives the Perilous Ford and the Marvellous Bed without a problem, but the reward that accompanies those successes has been devalued. In the case of the Depressed Maiden for example, the maiden in question does nothing but insult Gawain from dawn till dusk. When he successfully passes the magical tests of the Wondrous Castle his reward will be to marry his sister and remain forever locked up in the keep (9043). This is hardly a fruitful or noble future for the Greatest Knight in Arthur's kingdom. The marvellous tests still function as they did in earlier texts; it is just that now the poet does not seem to place a high value on worldly honour or social status. What has become truly important is a spiritual quest, not a

Breaking the Celtic spell

marvellous one. This conclusion is reinforced by the number of magical trials Gawain *successfully* completes without any obvious awards; for example, his success at the magical castle:

> Et la sale est molt bien gaitie
> Par art et par enchantement
> Con vos savois proçainement
> Se il vos plaist que jel vos die.
> Uns clers sages d'astrenomie,
> Que la roïne i amena
> En cel grant palais qui est la
> A fai unes si grans merveilles
> C'onques n'oïstes les pareilles;
> N'ainz mes n'an oistes parler
> Que chevaliers n'i puet ester
> Une liuee vis ne sains
> Qui de coardie soit plains
> Ne qui ait an lui nul mal vice
> De losange ne d'avarice.
>
> (*Perceval*, 7544–58)

The hall there is very well protected by magic and enchantment, as you're about to learn, if you'd like me to tell you. There in the main hall a clerk, expert in astronomy, whom the queen brought with her, established such great marvels that you never heard of their equal; for no knight can enter there and remain alive and well for the time it takes to cover a league if he is full of greed or at all tainted with deceitfulness or avarice.[69]

In the earlier romances this is usually the crowning moment in which the character can exercise free will and adopt a new identity. When a knight successfully completes a magical test, he is normally rewarded in terms of an elevation of social status or worldly fame; in this situation, however, what once were positive accolades, have now been revealed to be of little worth. Gawain's successes at these magical trials begin to look like punishments. It is clear that Gawain is a superior knight, but in comparison to Perceval's spiritual quest, martial accomplishments simply do not match up. Facing magical trials or marvellous adventures is simply not enough to establish spiritual growth. The truth of this reveals itself after

---

69 *Perceval*, ed. F. Lecoy, C.F.M.A. (1972), 44. Owen, *Arthurian Romances*, 473.

Gawain accomplishes three amazing tasks one after another – the Marvellous Castle, the Wondrous Bed, and the Perilous Ford – without gaining anything; he is still going to be trapped in the castle. He is essentially prevented from ever resuming the only quest which is going to allow him any real spiritual growth: the search for the Bleeding Lance. Gawain's paralysis is also evidenced by the "identity" problems which he begins to encounter. It is blatantly clear that neither his sister nor his mother can recognise him. His failure to ask and answer the right questions in his discussion with the queen, particularly at this late point in the tale, reveal how little he has evolved since Perceval's encounter at the *Grail* Castle. It is also telling that Chrétien dredged up a host of significant symbols to reflect with Gawain's failure to mature beyond simple courtly successes. In the case of the Wondrous Bed, the association of Lancelot's experiences with just such a bed are, of course, immediate; in Lancelot's case, his experiences have *seemed* to identify him as successful knight, but his wounds (and the squelching of the Flaming Lance) reveal that his flaws will forever impede him. From the text, it seems that if Gawain remains on his current path, he will be doomed to a sterile and empty life. To encourage this train of thought, Chrétien also reintroduces the test of the lions for the third time in these adventures. In *Yvain*, the hero acquires a new and noble identity by means of befriending the lion. In this tale, the lions are destroyed, leaving no hope for a new identity or place in the community. Indeed, the author is quick to state that not only is Gawain trapped, but that Arthur is made deaf and dumb by grief for him. Arthur's world is slowly disintegrating:

> ... Vos deüssiez estre en effroi
> Et esmaié et esperdu,
> Quant nous celui avons perdu
> Qui toz por Dieu nos sostenoit
> Et dont toz li biens nos venoit
> Par amour et par charité.
>
> (*Perceval*, 9206–11)

... You should be full of alarm and dismay and distress when we've lost the man who sustained us all for God's sake and from whon we received all that bounty out of love and charity.[70]

---

[70] *Perceval*, ed. Roach 271; Owen, *Arthurian Romances*, 495.

Such grim tidings may well spell the end of the traditional courtly value system, but one will never know what Chrétien intended, as this is where the romance ends. However, it might (once again) be helpful to examine Marie de France's *lai*, *Eliduc*, to establish at least a contemporary's view of this new vision of love and spiritual quest.

Eliduc, as with Chrétien's last romance, is designed to compare the follies of romance to the wisdom of love for God. In this *lai* the main characters are all noble paramounts of chivalry. However, Eliduc is maltreated by his king and subsequently forced to search abroad for an income. When he leaves, he promises to remain faithful to his deserving wife. Unfortunately, he becomes overwhelmed with love for Guilliadun and compromises his relationship with his wife. Marie clearly illustrates his human weakness and the familiar preoccupation with love matters:

> Ore est sis quors en grant prisun!
> Sa lëauté voleit garder,
> Mes ne s'en peot nïent jeter
> Que il nen eimt la dameisele ...
>
> (*Eliduc*, 466–9)

> His heart was now in great turmoil. He wanted to keep his faith, but he couldn't keep himself from loving the girl ...[71]

In essence, each character is betrayed by the person he or she trusts. This fact brings home Marie's point that true faith, a belief which encompasses honour and love – what the later English authors would define as *trowth* – can only come from the ultimate relationship with God. All of the characters, even Guilliadun and Eliduc after they achieve their great love, decide to dedicate themselves to the service of God. These characters realise that no matter how great their human love or tragedy may be, nothing is as important as the love of God. Marie's ending certainly makes this interpretation unavoidable:

> Mut se pena chescuns pur sei
> De Deu amer par bone fei
> E mut par firent bele fin,
> La merci Deu, le veir devin!
>
> (*Eliduc*, 1177–80)

---

[71] *Eliduc*, ed. Rychner 169; *Eliduc*, ed. Hanning and Ferrante, 209.

Each one took great pains to love God in good faith and they made a very good end, thanks to God, the divine truth.[72]

This ending to Marie's *lai* provides a plausible solution to Chrétien's story. Gawain, in order to escape his entrapment, could well have devoted his life to a search for God. This would have seemed to be a natural progression in his maturation process, considering Perceval's actions and likely future. However practical such tantalizing theories might be, in leaving the tale unfinished Chrétien captured the imagination of generations to follow.[73] There are reasonable, wild, mystical, romantic, and countless other potential continuations to a tale that is as rich in emotion and drama as it is in philosophy and theology.

Chrétien's final romance critically analyses the structure, craftsmanship, and purpose of the romances which preceded it. Through a discussion of magic, marvels, and free will, Chrétien presents an opportunity not only to arrive at a deeper philosophical understanding of man's place in society, but in *Le Conte du Graal* he goes one step further and reveals the path to a greater understanding of truth and God.

When one analyses the power of magic and marvels in the romances of Chrétien, the *Lais* of Marie, and the tales of Tristan, it becomes apparent that the romance writers of the period displayed a general understanding of, or consensus about, the nature of marvels and magic and their functions within the romances. The inter-textual discussion apparent between *Cligés*, *Le Chevalier de La Charrette*, Marie's *Chevrefoil* and Thomas' *Tristran*, to offer but one viable grouping, sets forth a debate between medieval authors on the moral and appropriate uses of magic.

The concluding romances of both Marie and Chrétien incorporate a new agenda; they demonstrate a concern, not only for love, but for truth and spirituality. This concern will reform the romances in many different ways. What will remain continuous, however, is the way in which magic functions in the romances; it will serve to reflect a character's greatest achievements and in turn symbolise his or her weakest moments. The use of *merveilleux* will evolve into sophisticated illusions, and magic will be acknowledged in later romances as the art of science and the tool of both God and temptresses.

---

[72] Rychner, 191; Hanning and Ferrante, 228-9. [73] See Jean Frappier, *Autour du Graal* (Geneve: Librairie Droz, 1977) for further discussion of Chrétien's intentions.

3

Revising romance

ATTACKING THE HEART OF THE MATTER: INTRODUCTION TO
INSULAR ROMANCE

The *Sir Tristrem*, *Syr Launfal* and *Ywain and Gawain* romances illustrate the complex relationship between twelfth-century French and Anglo-Norman texts and their English thirteenth- and fourteenth-century adaptations. The nature of this relationship is one in which the meanings of the stories have been refined to suit the needs of a new audience and reflect an insular culture, but the methods by which the authors communicate remains largely familiar. The insular adapters have rewritten the French formula of love as supreme inspiration for human advancement, to the point where keeping faith and maintaining honour become the source of motivation for each individual. This represents a recuperation of romance, which even in its English formulation was often characterised as "profane writing often condemned as frivolous".[1] In the *Franklin's Tale*, Chaucer moves one step beyond this agenda and uses magic and the power of *illusioun* to strip away conventional topi of romance and reveal the secular and spiritual concerns of the genre, which are free will, influence and status in the community, and the concerns of men who want to be noble – issues which were as pertinent to a fourteenth-century insular audience as they had been to a twelfth-century continental one.

It has been established that the romances of Chrétien and the *Lais* of Marie de France share a profound interest in the idea of the individual and the power of love. These two themes are at the core of the twelfth-century texts. A sophisticated formula for the use of magic is the technique by which these two authors create access in their texts to such serious issues as the right of every man to free will, the constraints of fate, the nature of justice, and other such morally complex topics. The ties of magic to the twelfth-century world of politics, religion and various intellectual pursuits enable an author to build bridges between the imagination and contemporary debates which are pertinent to the audience. Magic functions to entice

---

[1] David Matthews, "Translation and Ideology: The Case of *Ywain and Gawain*", *Neophilologus* 76 (1992): 456. See also Dieter Mehl, *The Middle English Romances of the Thirteenth and Fourteenth Centuries* (London: Routledge, 1969) 17–18.

the imagination and yet is a concept which carries consequence in the everyday life of everyone from kings to peasants in the medieval world.

It has been a ready temptation for many critics of romance to engage with the medieval world in terms of it being a monolithic structure, in which texts from different countries and different centuries are presumed to represent an essentially homogenous and unified picture of the world. C.S. Lewis is perhaps the most famous proponent of such views, and at times, the lure to work from this presumption is difficult to resist.[2] In this study, it is important to note that the insular authors themselves create the link between the twelfth-century texts of Chrétien and Marie and their own works. In adapting a text from an identifiable source, these re-writers invite analysis of the changes which have, and have not, been made to the source material. This research suggests that the function of magic in the twelfth-century works still applies for the thirteenth- and fourteenth-century insular romances, owing to the fact that the adapters frequently maintain not only the methods of Chrétien and Marie, but in some cases, even their language concerning magic and the marvellous.[3]

With the exception of *Tristran*, however, the majority of critics feel that the insular romances were fairly constrained in their use of marvels, monsters, or signs of the supernatural and it is held that they seem to display "relatively little interest in chivalry, *courtoisie* or passionate love".[4] In fact, the four most famous Anglo-Norman romances – *The Romance of Horn, Folie Tristan, Lai d'Haveloc,* and *Amis e Amilun* – in the opinion of Weiss, seem most absorbed by social issues and represent "socially subversive" ideas.[5]

Finlayson suggests that since "most Middle English romances are of a crude, popular nature, the absence of a full fledged courtly love motif is due to the lack of understanding on the part of the audience and composer".[6] Busby comments that "the general trend, ... toward a faster moving, nononsense sort of romance, in which the subtle interplay between courtesy, chivalry and love plays a subordinate role, might suggest a less aristocratic public".[7] Finlayson seconds Busby in the opinion that "though some critics have seen the omissions as typical of the English dislike of introspection, a more likely explanation is that the English poem was composed for a less sophisticated audience than that for which Chrétien wrote."[8] Dieter Mehl

[2] C.S. Lewis, *Allegory of Love* (Oxford: Oxford University Press, 1936). [3] There are a few different factors which must be taken into account when this formula is applied to Chaucer's *Franklin's Tale*. See the following chapter for a detailed discussion of Chaucer's *Franklin's Tale*. [4] *Birth of Romance*, ed. Weiss, x. [5] Ibid., x. [6] John Finlayson, "Definitions of Middle English Romance", *Chaucer Review* 15: 1 (1980): 59. [7] Keith Busby, "Chrétien de Troyes English'd", *Neophilologus* 71 (1987): 603. [8] John Finlayson, "*Ywain and Gawain* and the Meaning of Adventure", *Anglia* 87 (1969): 313.

suggests that English authors limit the scope of their works as the audience is only "expecting to hear of strange exploits, surprising adventures and many trials."[9]

Reception critics often fall into such traps by building their interpretations of a poem on faulty logic, such as arguing that the poem is less "sophisticated" since it was written for a less sophisticated audience (less sophisticated, it would seem, is defined as a work without emphasis on straightforward psychological analysis). The recent work of William Calin, however, has radicalised such approaches to the Anglo-Norman and English texts, approaches which were often based upon the assumption, demonstrated in the preceding paragraphs, that the character of the insular population was dull and sombre, the audiences simple and unimaginative, and it was assumed, their tastes banal and religious. The research of Calin places insular texts in a different framework, and he suggests instead that the literary flowering of the time period ranged impressively through various modes and genres, and that it marked a "new rise in the vernacular, courtly, personal, and secular literatures in juxtaposition to the Latin, learned, public, and sacred" literatures.[10] This point of view suggests that it would be appropriate for the modern critic to search out new ideas and interpretations for the emendations which the later insular poets made to the works of their predecessors.

It also seems safer to assume, as Bollard does, that "from the outset we are working with an incomplete set of facts about medieval notions of the function of romance and the nature of the (no doubt) varying romance audience".[11] Instead of undermining both the intelligence of the audience and the interpreter, it would seem far more logical to explore what other motivations could have provoked a rewriting and re-evaluation of the parent romances. It might well be the case, as Bollard says, that "the meaning of English romance is carried or expressed in a different vehicle than Chrétien chooses; it may, in other words, have another sort of sophistication."[12] Understanding how the twelfth-century texts function so that one can appreciate the transformations made by their adapters, is the first step to deciphering the new English approaches to romance.

In the twelfth-century texts, magical and marvellous tests gauge the emotional or social status of a character. Chrétien's work demonstrates the influence of such historians as Monmouth and Wace, in that the use of magic allows a separate means, or a secular means, of evaluating characters

---

[9] Mehl, *The Middle English Romances*, 181. [10] Calin, *The French Tradition*, 11. 19–21. [11] John Bollard, "Hende Words: The Theme of Courtesy in *Ywain and Gawain*", *Neophilologus* 78 (1994): 657. [12] Bollard, "Hende Words", 656.

in terms of their social responsibilities and their personal development.[13] When a character is worthy of distinction, he or she receives a magical token, such as the magical sword Excalibur, to publicly honour such an advancement; if a character is vulnerable he or she is put to a magical test which serves to reveal what areas need improvement. This tradition is maintained by the insular authors, as can be seen in the cases of both Aurelius in the *Franklin's Tale* and Gawain in *Sir Gawain and the Green Knight*. There is no question that the tradition of magical swords, rings, bridges etc., is still maintained. In the insular romances, however, the magical tests employed by the author can often be more sophisticated in their conception than these individual instances of magical trials. In *Sir Gawain and the Green Knight*, as well as in the *Franklin's Tale*, for example, the entire plot rests upon the *illusioun* of magic functioning in the text. Magic provides the backbone to the theoretical and conceptual format of the romance.

The twelfth-century parent texts use love as the source of each individual's power, which, once experienced, necessitates the redefining of the relationships one has to God and community, as well as the re-assessment of one's own identity. In the adaptations, it is the ability to maintain *trowth* in the face of illusions and magical encounters, which illustrates and validates the difficult journey of discovery made by the hero or the heroine. *Trowth* is defined by the *MED* as: "(a) Fidelity to one's country, kin, friends, etc. loyalty; allegiance; also, genuine friendship; (b) fidelity and constancy in love, devotion; ... sincerity in love; (c) marital fidelity; ~ of marriage; (d) faithfulness to God, piety."[14] It is apparent, however, that despite this evolution in the treatment of the *Tristan*, *Yvain*, and *Lanval* stories, and the rewriting of elements of Boccaccio's *Filocolo* into a Breton *lai* by Chaucer, magic is still used throughout this period to concentrate the mind on the thoughts and experiences of the characters.[15] The long and complex association of magic with social and religious discussions, not only in twelfth-century France but also in fourteenth-century England, is exploited by romance writers to add a deeper dimension to the texts, thereby encouraging the appreciation of the philosophical and political issues present in the layering of the tales.

The restructuring of the twelfth-century romances by insular poets resulted in the redefinition of the roles of women, and an increase in the symbolic uses of magic, the wilderness, and warfare. Crane argues that the reason for the shift from French tastes to insular tastes lies in the latter's goal for the hero and heroine: "These works present a different model of

---

13 For a discussion of Geoffrey of Monmouth and Wace, see pages 61–73 above. 14 *Trowth*, *MED*, 1996, edn. 15 Robert R. Edwards "Source, Context and Cultural Translation in the *Franklin's Tale*", *Modern Philology* 94 (1996): 141–62.

human existence from that of most Old French romance. Conflict between a hero and his society is not central and problematic. Rather than locating the human drama in self-discovery, the insular romances propose that the human drama is collective, a *communal search for stability* that takes place through the hero's search."[16] Crane suggests that because of the strong link between the "good of the hero" and the "good of the people" the English romances are restricted to resolving situations on the political stage. This would explain what she sees as the English poets' collective loss of interest in the psychological dimensions of the French texts.

However persuasive Crane's argument may be, it does not take into account the role of magic in the romances. The use of magic by individual characters in the English romances, as it did in its predecessors, creates a discussion of the place of the individual in the community. In giving an individual influence over nature or another member of the community which his or her peers do not share, the poet encourages a character's exploration of values which are important, not only to the community, but to the hero or heroine under discussion. This is made possible by the ability of the character, through magic, to step outside the sphere of influence of his or her society. This encourages the hero or heroine to develop his or her own values; for example, when Launfal, much like his predecessor in Marie's *lai Lanval*, is magically given all the goods that make him acceptable to his community, he finds that what he really wants is love.

The phenomenon of English redactors de-emphasising the position of passion in their romances, Crane argues, denotes a lack of concern for the self-discovery of the hero or heroine. However, in examining *Sir Launfal*, *Ywain and Gawain*, and other such popular romances as *Sir Gawain and the Green Knight*, it becomes clear that the hero is still involved in a personal struggle to achieve his place in society. In particular, the emotional and private nature of the experiences of Gawain, Dorigen, Launfal, and Ywain suggest that trials which English heroes undergo serve to represent the same ideas which the French romance writers sought to describe. In each of these romances, it is also true that the emphasis on the reintegration of the hero or heroine into the community is intended to play a provocative or else a non-climactic role in the plot; the experiences of one individual may not automatically benefit the entire community. The painful achievement of self-awareness by Gawain in *Sir Gawain and the Green Knight* through the

---

[16] Susan Crane, *Insular Romances: Politics, Faith and Culture in Anglo-Norman and Middle English Literature* (Berkeley: University of California Press, 1986) 83–4. My italics.

experiences of magical trials, for instance, cannot be learned by the community regardless of their adoption of green girdles.[17] As a result, the romance enthusiast (modern or medieval) may be suspicious of the happy-ever-after ending of the *Franklin's Tale* achieved through Dorigen's abject humiliation, or the inability of Launfal to live in Camelot, or the reunion of Ywain and his wife, which is achieved only through heavy-handed manipulation. These endings certainly do not fulfill what Crane referred to above as the "communal search for stability"; on the contrary, the need for every individual to go through a learning process becomes more pressing in the conclusions of these romances.

It is true that love as Chrétien envisioned it is no longer strictly the focus of the English poets, but magic still remains a crucial element in the romances. Magic is one of the few elements which may be said to unite the body of literature which is considered to be the genre of romance. The interest of the adapter in magic is clear; even in the tales where dialogue or plot structures are severely reduced, detailed references to incidents of magic are retained. The use of magic within the insular tales reveals the inner turmoil which the character is experiencing without forcing the author to indulge in lengthy descriptions. For example, Lancelot in the romances of Chrétien always survives his ordeals but is much the worse for wear; similarly, in the Middle English romance *Sir Gawain and the Green Knight*, Gawain successfully keeps his head but the scars he receives in the process will forever mark his personality. It is also true that the English romance writers take full advantage of the relationship of magic to philosophical and religious issues of the day in order to explore the spiritual growth of a character. For example, Dorigen is confronted with magical encounters which test her faith – *trowth* – not only in herself and her community, but also in "Eterne God".

Understanding the fourteenth-century conception of faith can help to elucidate the medieval conception of *trowth* as a mixture between love, devotion and obligation. The *SOED* defines *faith* as "I. Belief, trust, confidence. 1.a. Confidence, reliance, trust (in the ability, goodness, etc. of a person; in the efficacy or worth of a thing; or in the truth of a statement or doctrine). The *OED* defines *faithfulness* as "good faith, loyalty, honesty, truth; 2. One's faith as pledged or plighted in a solemn agreement or undertaking; one's plighted word; the act of pledging one's faith, a promise a covenant; *spec.*, to engage oneself to marry."[18] To appreciate fully the implications of this word,

---

[17] W.R.J. Barron, *Trawthe and Treason: The Sin of Gawain Reconsidered* (Manchester: Manchester University Press, 1980) 135, 142. See Barron for a detailed analysis of Gawain's homecoming and what it means to the reader.   [18] *Faith*, *SOED*, 1933 edn.; *Faithfulness*, *OED*, 1989 edn.

it must be understood not only in the context of obligations to God, but also to personal vows of marriage and loyalty to state or king. The party to whom *trowth* is pledged gains an enormous amount of control over the loyalties, and therefore the actions, of the individual making the pledge. It is exactly the obligation of the character to meet personal needs within the context of keeping *trowth* and avoiding the possibility of becoming a *traytur* which is at the social and political heart of these English works.

Trowth (as defined in terms of love, loyalty, obligation, and duty), bears a relationship to the sociological role of magic, which has been established both here and in the research of such historians as Thomas, Peters and Goodich.[19] The place of magic in medieval society is related to the need of a person to achieve power, or, in other words, influence over fate, fortune, his/her own actions, and the actions of others. In these romances, magic is intimately linked to this decisive moment when a hero or heroine discovers his or her free will, or lack thereof, in the tales. Its presence heralds the confrontation of the character with his or her status, either as one who maintains one's *trowth*, or a *traytour*. In *Ywain*, the return of Alundyne's magical ring occasions the public humiliation of the character and the acknowledgment of his betrayal of *trowth* to his wife. In *Launfal*, the hero is deprived of social identity by the wicked "*untrewe*" queen (45–48), until a fairy from Avalon agrees to supply him with goods necessary to secure respectability in Arthur's court. In *Syr Tristrem*, the magical love potion forces the characters to see what is of real human value, *luf* and *trowth*, despite social and even religious beliefs to the contrary. In the *Franklin's Tale*, the balance of the story hinges on the ability of a character to maintain *trowth* in the face of magical plots and illusions. In each of the romances, magic is used to test faith, which means that magic holds the key to understanding the growth of the characters and the intentions of the authors.

THE WORLD OF INSULAR ROMANCE

Courtly romances and courtly love originated as literary constructs to help mould and affirm a way of life. George Duby believes that the foundation of romance is in the fertile soil of political ambition.[20]

---

[19] For a discussion of the role of magic in medieval society, see pages 35–45 above. For further information, see Thomas, *Decline of Magic*; Peters, *The Magician*, and Goodich, *Violence and Miracle*; Thomas's work is particularly influential in tracing the evolution of religion's replacement of the needs and functions of magic in society.
[20] Duby, *Love and Marriage*, 58–61.

Romances would have been encouraged to reinforce a set of cultural beliefs and behaviour, which in turn, reinforced a particular idea of government and established order. Crane argues that the literary concept of noble behaviour became the practice of the thirteenth- and fourteenth-century English baronial classes for similar reasons.[21] The need to enact values tried and tested only in literature, however, resulted in a deep-seated anxiety concerning the power structure inherent in the romances of Chrétien, Thomas, and the *Lais* of Marie de France. The insular *bellatores* were not only fighters but landholders, and in the significant movement towards centralisation of the State from the eleventh century to the fifteenth century, the story of the aristocracy is one of loss of power and resistance to the king.

The law of primogeniture, established by the national state, made self-reliance and ingenuity as necessary for success as noble birth, the latter no longer guaranteeing one a position of power in the community. This insecurity and the slow erosion of political and economic power brought with them the need for external sources of justification to maintain the remaining rights of the baronial class. Patterson argues that this struggle manifested itself in "a growing insistence upon the priority of lineage as a definition of nobility, a persistent effort to stratify society as a whole and fix the precedence of its ranks, and a jealous guarding of forms of dress, recreational habits (like hunting), and social rituals (such as tournaments)."[22] These are exactly the elements which comprise the content of virtually every romance – a preoccupation with dress, ceremony, and status – which makes the romance, even in the fourteenth century, the perfect format for discussing the changing face and concerns of nobility. Mary Wack argues that by the fourteenth century courtly love in England was clearly as important as it had been in twelfth-century France. She states that "late medieval art corroborates that the ideals of noble love penetrated the rituals of everyday life among the nobility." Wack further argues that "images on objects of daily use support the claim that 'By 1400 courtly love had become for many not just a way of talking but of feeling or acting' ".[24] Noble ideals, religious and secular orders of knights, and courtly social behaviours found in literature became key institutions and sources of instruction for the implementation of what were once literary ideals.[25]

21 Crane, *Insular Romances*, 176. 22 Lee Patterson, *Chaucer and the Subject of History* (Madison: University of Wisconsin, 1991) 193-4. 23 Mary Wack, *Lovesickness in the Middle Ages* (Philadelphia: University of Pennsylvania Press, 1990) 147. 24 Ibid., 147. For the source of the internal quote, see L. Benson, "Courtly Love and Chivalry in the Later Middle Ages", in *Fifteenth-Century Studies: Recent Essays*, ed. Robert F. Jaeger (Hamden, Conn.: Archon Books, 1984) 249. 25 See May McKisack, *The Fourteenth Century 1307-1399*, Oxford History of England, 5 vols (Oxford: Oxford University Press, 1991) V, 182-209.

The border between fiction and reality began to waver when knighthood in Edward III's time, for example, which was partly shaped by the perceptions of the romances, was revealed to have a hidden core of decay.[26] Matthews argues that "the tournaments and jousts were a blatantly ideological treatment of an institution which fell into greater corruption through the course of the century".[27] Clearly by the fourteenth century the traditional way of noble life, as represented in the twelfth-century romances, could no longer be sustained, as even the concept of nobility and the status it conferred were under intense reassessment.

These arguments allow one to conclude with assurance that English adapters deliberately chose to maintain the romance/*lai* format for their works with the intention of engaging the imagination and intellect of its audiences, and also to challenge the notions about the English way of life and the future of noble society. The history of love and its role in noble life, as well as the traditional focus of the romances on such issues as the relationship between the individual and social authority, and the relationship of man to fate and *aventure*, make it clear that there is no other format which would have suited the turbulent times of a society engaged in the process of self-discovery and revolutionary change.

---

[26] Terry Jones, *Chaucer's Knight: The Portrait of a Medieval Mercenary* (London: Methuen, 1985 rev. edn.) 4–25. [27] Matthews, *Ywain and Gawain*, 460.

4

Magical adaptations

THE SEARCH FOR THE PERFECT WORLD

This chapter will analyse and consider the adapted romances *Sir Tristrem*, *Syr Launfal*, and *Ywain and Gawain*, in order to explore how twelfth-century romances were reconfigured to suit thirteenth- and fourteenth-century insular audiences. It will demonstrate that, despite changes, each adapter paid close attention to the detail of the magical and marvellous elements in the parent text. The English romances shy away from the conception of love which paralyzes and confounds the twelfth-century hero, and instead, focus upon the ability of hero or heroine to maintain *trowth* in the face of difficulties often introduced by magic.[1] A number of critics, such as Crane and Busby, claim that the English translation-romances have in common for the most part, a general reduction of psychological input and concern for love.[2] This would suggest that the literary concept of love, popularised by the twelfth-century French/Anglo-Norman romances, no longer seemed relevant to the succeeding generations. The argument should be that the French means of expressing passion was no longer appropriate for insular audiences, and therefore, a discussion of it was transformed for the English audience into a discussion of *trowth*. *Trowth* by definition encompasses the components of love concerned with commitment, fidelity, and loyalty.[3] One would think that these areas of *amor* might generate less passion, or less drama, but one need only turn to the *Franklin's Tale* to see that that is not the case. Clearly, loyalty and honour are of equal value to passion, and of interest to an insular audience.[4]

The refinements made to the romances by the English redactors consisted of the redefinition of love, the re-evaluation of the main source of strength in a character, and a return to the emphasis on heroic encounters with magic, as opposed to long involved love scenes. Understanding Chrétien's strategy of linking magic, love, and the individual's will, however,

---

1 Geraldine Barnes, *Counsel and Strategy in the Middle English Romance* (Cambridge: D.S. Brewer, 1993) xi, xii, 91–2. 2 Crane, *Insular Romances*, 13–14, 83. See also Busby "Chretien de Troyes English'd", 586–99. 3 See page 118 above for a fuller defintion. 4 See pages 81–2 above for a fuller discussion.

prepares the modern reader for appreciating the re-design of that basic equation by the English adapters. They seek to maintain Chrétien's premise that love and magic are powerful, but most often locate power and desire in one body. The focus is no longer upon two lovers uniting to face the world, as in *Erec et Enide* or *Cligés*, but upon a knight who is establishing his position in society and coming to terms with his own values and beliefs. For the most part this new direction in the romances leaves the hero or heroine isolated from the support which a lover could offer; indeed, most often, trouble is introduced into the life of the hero or heroine in the form of a dangerous magical seducer. This accounts for the focus of English writers on self-reliance in their version of the ideal romantic hero or heroine.

This link between the ingenuity of a hero or heroine and the overcoming of magical obstructions is only one of the many ways English authors expressed their understanding of where power rested within the individual, namely in the intellect, not in the soul or the heart. Chrétien discussed love as the only power universally available to every individual. The English romances, however, reject what they consider to be overwhelming passion in favour of *trowth*, thereby reaffirming the role of magic in the romances as an aid in the interpretation of the relationship of man to the world in which he functions. In the English romances, the role of magic is to demonstrate the complex relationship of man to faith: the will is directed not by want, desire or passion, as in the earlier texts, but by the strength of beliefs. The fundamental role of magic as exemplified in the twelfth-century romances is retained, and in some texts expanded to add interpretive depths to the tale. The presence of magic in the insular works, however, signifies a conflict between the hero or heroine and his/her ascribed role in the community, as well as a conflict with God or Fortune in which the hero or heroine must come to terms with his or her fate.

"SIR TRISTREM"

In *Sir Tristrem*, the Middle English version of Thomas of England's *Tristran*, the modern reader finds a much condensed and often criticized version of the Anglo-Norman text.[5] *Sir Tristrem* is mentioned in connection with the historical Thomas of Erceldoune by Robert Mannyng of

---

[5] *Sir Tristrem*, ed. George P. McNeill (Edinburgh and London: William Blackwood and Sons, 1886) 35. See also Crane, *Insular Romances*, 189. Crane argues that there probably existed an English intermediary.

Brunne in his *English Chronicle* (*c.*1330). The French fragments of the romance of *Tristran* allude to a Thomas as the authority for the facts narrated, and Gottfried von Strassburg refers to a "Thomas of Britanje" as the authority for his source. This text, however, is more than likely a southernised version of an older Northumbrian romance (1260–1300) derived more or less directly from a Norman or Anglo-Norman source. Robert Ackerman has established that the tale of *Tristan* would have been well known in medieval England, despite the small number of extant versions. He states that "English audiences could well have known not only the English *Sir Tristrem*, but also such Anglo-Norman works as the *Tristran* of Thomas, the Oxford *Folie Tristan* and perhaps Marie de France's *Chevrefoil* as well."[6] Barnes describes the work as "lacking any sustained moral dimension," and states that "the narrative manifests little interest in love and none in the ethical problems raised by Thomas in his story of the fateful passion of Tristan". She emphasises that *Sir Tristrem* is only interested in "the process of deception, trick and countertrick, through which the lovers communicate and escape detection".[7]

Crane is equally harsh in her criticism when she argues that "Anglo-Norman romances do not meet the standards of Old French literature, as modern critics and medieval French audiences seem to agree".[8] Crane further suggests that *Sir Tristrem* "does not consistently accommodate the story's central love affair ... Nor can the poet's gestures towards revising Thomas's *fine amor* convince us that the hero's love is natural and untroubled. The Tristan story has lost the significance developed for it by Thomas, and not gained a new one."[9] These criticisms are echoed by Ackerman when he states that "in any case the poem is a crude version of its courtly original. It is full of awkward inversions, and the transitions are frequently disconcerting in their abruptness. If the author felt any sympathy for the tale he was telling it is hard to detect."[10]

However, in the confusion and lack of purpose which the text seems to demonstrate, the modern reader can find elements of a new romance formulation. One is reminded of the confusion and condemnation which Beroul, one of the earliest authors of the Tristan story, engendered as he struggled

---

6 Robert Ackerman, "English Rimed and Prose Romance", in *Arthurian Literature in the Middle Ages*, ed. R.S. Loomis (Oxford: Clarendon, 1959) 514. He also cites artistic representations of the story, such as the pavement tiles dug up at Chertsey Abbey, as evidence of the wide popularity of the legend. See also R.S. and L.H. Loomis, *Arthurian Legends in Medieval Art* (New York: Columbia University Press, 1938) 42–69.   7 Barnes, *Counsel*, 97.   8 Crane, *Insular Romances*, 3. Ramsey, *Chivalric Romance*, 7, 5.   9 Crane, *Insular Romances*, 195.   10 Ackerman, "Rimed", 516.

Magicial adaptations

with his transitional version of the text.[11] His romance, based on a tradition solely interested in the destruction of a great hero, nonetheless contains the seeds of a new story in which love and its power would become of paramount concern. A similar struggle may be reflected in the differences between the English generation of romances and their parent texts. In the English revision, Tristrem's feelings for the second Ysonde, Ysonde of the White Hand, and his confusion concerning the first Ysonde, for example, are reduced from the original eight hundred lines to these few poignant words:

> Þe forward fast he band
> Wiþ ysonde, þat may
> Wiþ the white hand,
> He spoused þat day.
> O niȝt, ich vnder stand,
> To boure wenten þai
> On bedde.
> Tristrem ring fel oway,
> As men to chaumber him ledde.
>
> (*Tristrem*, 2676–84)[12]

The following excerpts from Thomas reveal the very different means of dealing with Tristran's indecision over marrying the second Iseut from that of the English adapter. In this moment he anguishes over his belief that Iseut does not love him anymore:

> Car, s'ele en sur coer plus m'amast,
> D'acune rien me comfortast.
> – Ele, de quei? – D'icest ennui.
>
> (*Tristran*, 138–41)

> For if her heart loved me more,
> she would give me some sort of comfort.
> In what? – In this pain I feel.[13]

---

11 For a discussion of the problematic text of Beroul, see *Tristan*, ed. Fedrick, 9–35.
12 *Sir Tristrem*, ed. G. P. McNeill (Edinburgh and London: Blackwood, 1886). All citations for *Sir Tristrem* will be taken from this edition of the text unless specifically noted otherwise. For a more detailed discussion of this text see Ackerman, "Rimed", 515. 13 Thomas of Britain, *Tristran*, in *Thomas of Britain: Tristran*, ed. Stewart Gregory (London: Garland, 1991) 9. Gregory's text will be used for all subsequent citations and translations of Thomas' *Tristran*.

In the following lines, Tristran debates whether he should marry the second Iseut:

> Se la belté Ysolt n'oüst
> Tristrans amer ne la poüst.
> Pur le nun e pur la belté
> Que Tristans en li ad trové,
> Chiet en desir e en voleir
> Que la meschine volt aveir.
> Oëz merveilluse aventure,
> Cum genz sunt d'estrange nature...
>
> (*Tristran*, 280–87)

> And if she had not had Iseut's beauty, Tristran could not have felt desire for her. Because of her name, and the beauty he saw in her, Tristran conceived a strong desire and a strong urge to have the girl. Here I tell of an extraordinary thing, of how the hearts of men are strange...[14]

The adapter clearly has little interest in the description of Tristran's insecurities; he is far more interested in exploring Tristrem's mistakes. The audiences of all these version of the stories, from Thomas to the English adapter, must have realised that Tristran's act of marrying the second Iseut could only have disastrous results.

The English poet creates a scene concerning the proposed marriage which seems more realistic: the hero finds himself in a situation where he acts without thinking and is then appropriately shocked when it turns out to be the worst decision made in a lifetime of poor decisions. This version of events makes more logical and psychological sense than the sequence in which a character thinks long and hard about all the possible outcomes of a situation and is then surprised when the worst case scenario occurs.

At every step passion has overwhelmed Tristrem's ability to think clearly and he is left without the will to resist inappropriate actions – his marriage to the second Ysonde, for example, is clearly an act of complete folly. In some ways, Tristrem's state is reminiscent of that of Lancelot in *La Charrette* when he gets into the cart or almost falls out of a window due to his bemusement by Guenevere. Tristrem's choice of inaction, his lack of will in letting his ring slip from his finger, or his lack of will in resisting an unsuitable marriage, runs contrary to the behaviour of a romance hero who

---

14 Thomas, *Thomas*, ed. Gregory, 16–17.

is, according to twentieth-century critics, only interested in action. Tristrem seems to leave himself vulnerable, as if no longer in charge of his fate. These passive moments leave every sort of interpretation of his behaviour open to the audience, and his "will-lessness" is more symbolically meaningful than Thomas's efforts to present the emotional confusion of *his* Tristran.

The *Tristrem* poet, unlike his predecessors, seeks to undermine the magically-induced, passionate love from which Thomas's characters are suffering. He mocks this passionate love in two ways: first, he reduces the lovers' trysts to simple physical "playing", and then he allows Tristrem's dog, Hodain, to taste the love drink:

Þe coupe he licked þat tide
Þo doun it sett bringwain;
Þai loued al in lide
And þer of were þai fain ...

Þai loued wiþ al her miȝt,
And hodain dede al so.

(*Tristrem*, 1675–8, 1693–4)

It has been argued that this passage is simply a far-fetched explanation of the faithfulness of Tristrem's dog.[15] In allowing, however, that the author intended a finer design for his plot, it is not difficult to interpret the function of this passage as one which undermines and critiques Thomas's vision of passion. In Thomas's text, this magically-induced passion rages so wildly between the characters that in the end the lovers are consumed by it. Whether they are or are not responsible for their actions, or indeed, whether they had any choice in their fate, is made a secondary issue by the spectacular nature of their deaths.

In the *Tristrem* text, however, the author deals with these issues in a very different way. This ending in which a silly dog is given access to the love philtre, demonstrates primarily, and memorably, the power of the potion itself. Bédier concludes, owing in part to this ending, that the *Tristrem* text offers only "tiny souvenirs of Thomas's monumental conceptions" which are that "*voleir* (will) opposes Tristran to his own love, and that social and even religious fault is an inescapable condition of this *fine amor*".[16] Bédier

---

15 This interpretation of the dog's role is offered by T.C. Rumble, "The Middle English *Sir Tristrem*: Toward a Reappraisal", *Critical Language* 11 (1959): 225.   16 *Le Roman de Tristan par Thomas*, ed. Joseph Bédier, 2 vols S.A.T.F., 46 (Paris, 1902, 1905) as cited in Crane, *Insular Romances*, 190.

further claims that "a discussion of will has no place in an analysis of Tristrem's state of mind". It is not, however, that the *Tristrem* author is not interested in "free will"; he clearly is. It is only that he is not interested in debating the issues surrounding it in his text. Instead, he makes his point of view on passion and free will very clear by adding this memorable final scene to Thomas's original; once passionate love has arrived Tristrem does not have the willpower to resist it, nor does Ysonde; not even the dog has enough willpower to resist the effects of overwhelming passion.

This scene also serves to erase the half-developed claims of the previous authors that love existed between the two characters *before* the aid of the potion.[17] The characters are not responsible for their love, even subconsciously; just as the dog has been given a magical love potion, so too have these lovers. Therefore, the entire interpretative backdrop to Thomas's tale, which concerns the level of responsibility which the characters must shoulder for their adultery and betrayal of the king, is minimised. The *Tristrem* author would argue, it is reasonable to claim, that characters who are consumed by this kind of passion, much like Lancelot and Guenevere, are no longer thinking rationally, hence it is difficult to assign to them the consequences of rational actions.

In somewhat resolving these issues for the audience, the *Tristrem* author does not, however, minimise entirely the complexities of the text. The audience is left with the question of whether or not passion is a good thing, a virtue to be sought, or a catastrophe to be avoided at all costs. The presentation of this quandary is achieved by the repetitive addition of the epithet *"trewe"* to Tristrem's name, particularly in the final moments of the text. This focuses the modern reader's attention upon its importance to an English audience of the time (1728–36).[18] This epithet in many ways ironically encapsulates the heart of Tristrem's difficulties; he is known both for his faithfulness to Ysonde and at the same time for being *untrewe* to everyone and everything else. Magic made him true to love but could not make him have faith in the love of his partner, or be faithful to the oaths and obligations which he owed to his king.

This conclusion serves as an ironic jab at some of the serious issues dealt with by Thomas, such as fate, love, and loyalty. The *Tristrem* poet undermines the concept of fate by linking all who encounter the potion. By creating such a farce as that of the dog drinking the love potion, he undermines both the concept of loyalty, by reducing it to the love which a dog has for its master, and the idea of passionate love, by equating the experience of

---

17 *Ibid.*, 190. See the *Tantris* episode in Gottfried von Strassburg's *Tristan*. 18 Barnes, *Counsel*, 97–8. See also Crane, *Insular Romances*, 190–1.

Ysonde and Tristrem to that of the minor characters of the lady-in-waiting and the household pet. This is not a situation, such as the one discussed in Marie's *Yonec*, where God intervenes through magic to right a clear injustice. In this conception of the tale, the lives of the lovers are irrevocably altered by what might have been a mistake; it is clear that their misery may well be without a higher purpose, which provides the audience of *Tristrem* with serious food for thought. Clearly, passion, or even the cooler and calmer emotion of love, is not the proper means to control or have influence over an individual; it is itself too uncontrollable and all-consuming. Reliance on one's intellect seems by far the more safe and sure road to success in life and love.

"YWAIN AND GAWAIN"

Ywain and Gawain and *Sir Perceval of Galles* are the only two surviving adaptations of Chrétien's work in Middle English. It is clear that the English rewriter of Chrétien de Troyes' *Yvain* intended both to translate Chrétien's story for his insular audience and to revise it in order to develop a stronger focus on the character of Ywain. *Ywain and Gawain* written c.1300–50 in a northern English dialect, maintains Chrétien's story-line while reducing the 6,800 lines of the original text to some 4,000 lines.[19] The *Ywain and Gawain* author is interested, not in the travails of passion, but in the dilemmas concerning the keeping of faith. Ywain is forced at every crucial moment of the text to choose between keeping faith or betraying it, and his choices, along with the magical encounters he faces, illuminate the state of his morals and maturity. The author uses magic in the familiar tradition and therefore it still acts as a test of the development of his characters.[20]

The moral dilemmas faced by the original audience of *Yvain* provide the threads which the English writer uses to weave his interests into his adaptation of Chrétien's text.[21] This is illustrated by the refinements made by the English author to the magic/love combination found in the French version of the romance. The English alterations to Chrétien's "humiliation scene" in *Yvain*, for example, demonstrate a keen interest in a very public announcement of Alundyne's maltreatment and a strong desire for

---

19 *Ywain and Gawain*, ed. Mills, xi.   20 See pages 28–40 above for a discussion of "traditional magic".   21 See Chapter 2 of this study for a fuller discussion of *La Charrette*.

the return of her magic ring. In the adapted version the maiden showers Ywain with accusations of treason and betrayal, which are very different complaints from those of Chrétien's maiden concerning the behavior of Yvain:

> [B]ien a sa guile aparceüe
> qu'il se feisoit verais amerres,
> s'estoit fos, souduianz et lerres;
> sa dame a cil lerres souduite
> qui n'estoit de nus maxestruite,
> ne ne cuidoit pas, a nul fuer;
> qu'il li deüst anbler son cuer;
> cil n'anblent pas les cuers qui ainment,
> si a tex qui larrons les claiment
> qui en amer sont non veant
> et si n'an seventnes neant.
> Li amis prant le cuer s'amie
> einsi, qu'il ne li anble mie,
> einz le garde, et cil qui les anblent,
> li larron qui prodome sanblent,
> icil sont larron ipocrite
> et traïtor, qui metent lite
> en cuers anbler don ax ne chaut;
> mes li amis quel part qu'il aut
> le tient chier, et si le raporte.
>
> (*Yvain*, 2724–43)

She has quite seen through his lying talk, pretending as he did to be a true lover, though he is a false, treacherous thief. This thief has betrayed my lady, who suspected no wrong and had not the slightest idea he would steal her heart. Those who truly love don't steal hearts away, though they are called thieves by some who go about practising deceit in love without knowing anything at all about it. The lover takes his beloved's heart in a way that is not theft: rather he guards it from being stolen from her by thieves in the guise of honest men. These are hypocritical thieves and traitors, competing in the theft of hearts to which they are indifferent; but the lover, wherever he may go, treasures the heart and brings it back again.[22]

---

22 *Yvain*, ed. Rogues 83–4. *Yvain*, Owen, 318.

The idea here of stealing away the heart fits neatly into Chrétien's concept of love.[23] However, in the Middle English text the imagery of the theft of the lady's heart is stripped away and instead the fundamental accusation of treason is emphasised:

> He es ateyned for trayture,
> A fals and lither losenjure;
>   He has bytrayed my lady,
> Bot sho es war with his gilry.
> Sho hopid moght, |> e soth to say,
> |> at he wald so have stollen oway;
> He made to hir ful mekyl boste
> And said of al he lufed hir moste.
> Al was treson and trechery,
> And |> at he sal ful dere haby.
>
>   (*Ywain and Gawain*, 1601–10)

This rewriting of the text denotes a fundamental change in emphasis; Ywain is not the stealer of hearts, but the breaker of promises. This distinction has far-reaching consequences, because if he cannot keep faith with his wife, then his ability to maintain his political or social responsibilities is also brought into question. His disregard for his wife implies that he has not taken into consideration his oath before God, nor has he weighed the social implications of his failure to honour the verbal contract between them. In a society that values the word of a man as his bond, Ywain is a traitor to his community and to himself. This rendering of events, perhaps even more clearly than Chrétien's original, justifies Ywain's complete break with society and sojourn in the wilderness. The magical ring given to him by his wife represents a different type of magic token, one which is meant to symbolise his greatness, much like Excalibur does for Arthur, but Ywain's failure to keep faith demonstrates that he is not worthy of such a magical token. The very public removal of this symbol is indicative of his very public failure to live up to the role of husband, or Knight of the Magical Fountain. This removal of the magical token also explains the need for a magical potion to restore Ywain to his senses. In both instances, magic serves the function of enlightening the audience as to the state of the character's social status and maturity.

---

23 Anne Wilson, *The Magical Quest: The Use of Magic in Arthurian Romance* (Manchester: Manchester University Press, 1988) 78, 50.

After studying the adjustments decided upon by this adapter, it becomes important to examine what was retained and why. The translation of the Monstrous Herdsman incident, for example, is almost verbatim from the text of Chrétien, and the description of Arthur's pouring of the water into the magical spring is only slightly abridged. The adaptation exaggerates the actions of Arthur:

> Et li rois por veoir la pluie
> versa de l'eve plain bacin
> sor le perron, desoz le pin;
> et plut tantost molt fondelmant.
>
> (*Yvain*, 2220–3)

Then, to see the rain, the king poured a basinful of water on to the slab under the pine tree; and at once the rain fell in torrents.[24]

> Þe king kest water on þe stane;
> Þe storme rase ful sone onane
> With wikked weders, kene and calde,
> Als it was byforehand talde.
>
> (*Ywain and Gawain*, 1291–4)

Busby argues that the similarity of these two passages suggests the concern of the English author to depict the original magical incident in detail. Furthermore he argues that the majority of English translators often show a reluctance to abridge any of the magical moments from their sources.[25] The characters themselves best explain the purpose that these magical moments serve in the English context. In Colgrevance's description of his own magical encounter, he tells his audience of the knowledge which he has gained from his quest:

> Þe hende knight and þe fayre may
> Of my come war þai ful glade,
> And nobil semblant þai me made.
> In al thinges þai have þam born,
> Als þai did þe night biforn.
> Sone þai wist whare I had bene,
> And said þat þai had never sene
> Knyght þat ever þeder come,

---

24 *Yvain*, ed. Roques, 68; Owen, 311. 25 Busby "Chrétien de Troyes English'd", 598.

>   Take þe way ogayn home.
>   On þis wise þat tyme I wroght;
>   I fand þe folies þat I soght!
>
> (*Ywain and Gawain*, 446–56)

The adapter expresses his understanding of the purpose of the magical event by adding this mocking line to Chrétien's text: Colgrevance says he has learned better than to risk his life for idle adventures or for "the folies which he [previously] sought!" Magical encounters still serve to teach their participants something about their own motivations and state of being. The English translator maintains the four encounters with the fountain, along with the powerful effects it has on the life of each character that uses it. These magical events serve to demonstrate and reinforce the growth of a character, a technique which the English authors seem to prefer over the continental approach of using magic *and* articulating the changes which characters undergo.[26]

Lunet is the least changed of all the characters in the transition from the parent text to the English work.[27] In the English romances, Ywain is initially desperate with love for Alundyne, but thinks to win his lover by *gyn* [guile]: "I can noght se by nakyn gyn / How þat I hir luf sold wyn" (897–8). This presents a hero very different from Chrétien's Yvain, who acts as the passive recipient of Lunete's magic ring and ingenuity. It should be noted that it is largely Chrétien's lengthy analysis of sentiment and rhetorical expositions of courtly values that have been lost in the redaction, not complete concern for love itself. In initially endeavouring to use *gyn* to woo Alundyne, Ywain's attempts do not meet with much success. He has not developed enough as a character to use his own wit to achieve his goals. Instead, he relies heavily, as in the original, on the magic ring given to him by Lunet. Her ring transforms Ywain physically into another person, demonstrating the radical nature of the changes that Ywain needs to make to his personality. Parent and adapted text both contain careful descriptions of how Lunet's ring works and why she gives it to the hero. The temporary and hollow nature of Ywain's initial transformation via magic is revealed in the servants' and even in Alundyne's suspicions of the Devil at work. The *Ywain* author closely maintains the "mervoille et deablie" tradition of the Chrétien text (*Yvain*, 1203, 1144–53). In *Ywain and Gawain* the people of the keep search for what they are convinced is a bewitched spirit:

---

26 See pages 76–114 above for analysis of how twelfth-century authors employ magic.
27 *Ywain and Gawain*, ed. A. Friedman (Oxford: Oxford University Press, 1964), xxxii.

> ... Whare he myght oway gane.
> Þai said he sold þare be laft,
> Or els he cowth of wechecraft;
> Or he cowth of nygromancy;
> Or he had wenges forto fly!
>
> (*Ywain and Gawain*, 800–4)

The author and the adapter needed to handle the negative aspects of magic very delicately, or the perception of the audience concerning the nature of the hero or heroine could be permanently altered. The English author is careful to maintain the sense of Chrétien's vocabulary: if Ywain had been declared to be a necromancer or to be diabolic rather than a user of *wechcraft*, the story would have taken on a much darker tone. This is a danger which any audience might be assumed to recognise, considering the controversial nature of magic in the political and religious worlds of the fourteenth century.[28]

English adapters were clearly being careful to build upon a tradition already familiar to the audience. The parent texts of these works would have established an acceptable level of magic, one which would not interfere with religious or legal limits already prescribed by the authorities. Neither would the authors have wanted to fundamentally alter the nature of their characters; depicting Tristrem or Ywain as necromancers, for instance, would have prevented the sophisticated treatment of other issues within the stories. Thomas's investigations of English society reveal that there was a fine line between natural or white magic (which was manipulated not only by intellectuals and authors but by the Church itself), and necromancy, the nefarious doings of the devil.[29] This is a line which the romance poets often navigate but had they crossed too far over, their texts would not have been acceptable to the audience or the Church.

Despite transcribing the magical moments of the original text very closely, however, it is also clear that the insular poet has applied them differently to create a new meaning for the text. This is a natural process which the twelfth-century authors would have applied to their use of Celtic magic. In short, it is a formula for maintaining the symbolism and potency of a particular image or event, while applying it in a different manner to achieve a different end result. For example, Chrétien uses the Bleeding Lance encounter to explore Perceval's compromised social status,

---

[28] See pages 28–35 above for a fuller discussion of the vocabulary of magic in the medieval world, and pages 77–9 above for a discussion of magic in *Yvain*. [29] Thomas, *Decline of Magic*, 435–63, 177–253. See Bloch, *Medieval Misogyny*, 176–7, 183–94.

Magicial adaptations

immaturity, and poor faith, not to establish his right to kingship as was its symbolic association in the realm of Celtic myth.[30] The insular adapters likewise use the symbols and techniques of their predecessors, such as plot structures and the function of magic, but apply them to develop in turn a different meaning for their audience. The English text outlines, for example, that Ywain has found happiness and learned to appreciate the rewards of life-long fidelity:

> Now has Sir Ywain ending made
> Of al þe sorrows þat he hade.
> Ful lely lufed he ever hys whyfe
> And sho him, als hyr owin life;
> Þat lasted to þaire lives ende.
>
> (*Ywain and Gawain*, 4009–13)

This ending is very different in tone to the ending of *Yvain*, which does not stress the idea of fidelity. However, despite Ywain having learned to be faithful, the ending of this romance is not a happy-ever-after one. With one master stroke, the entire tale is undermined by this farcical ending; one can only laugh at the prospect of the *liown* living a life of bliss equal to that of the lovers and Lunet:

> And so Sir Ywain and his wive
> In joy and bliss þai led þaire live.
> So did Lunet and þe liown
> Until þat ded haves dreven þam down.
>
> (*Ywain and Gawain*, 4023–6)

This completely ironic twist to a fairytale ending completes the process of disillusionment which began with Lunet tricking her mistress into loving a supposedly new knight, the Knight of the Lion. This subterfuge is only completed after Ywain once again threatens the magical fountain. This happens despite the fact that the author has reached the conclusion of his tale and the audience would expect that the hero has been reformed. The need for magic reveals to the audience that Ywain and his wife must continue to learn about faith and trust.

The use of a provocative ending, or the false fairytale ending, is not a technique limited to the *Tristrem* and *Ywain* authors; the romances *Syr*

---

30 See pages 16–18 above for a more detailed discussion of the relationship between romance and Celtic myths.

Launfal, *Sir Gawain and the Green Knight*, and the *Franklin's Tale* all end with unreal or surreal solutions to the problems of the hero or heroine. It is interesting that humour is inserted into the ending of these tales, whereas their twelfth-century ancestors are often serious and subversive in their conclusions. There are happy endings in the original texts, but the *denouements* are rarely funny. It seems as if, instead of radically altering the plots of their sources, the adapters prefer to shift the tone of their presentations. It requires only a line or two in the conclusion to alter the audience's perception of the text and its content. In having an audience laugh at the fate of a lion or the passionate future of a dog, the English adapters undercut the conclusions of their source texts with irony.

"SYR LAUNFAL"

Syr Launfal and the *Franklin's Tale* both claim to be based on *Breton lais*, but their English authors have done much to alter the nature of their tales. Chestre's *Syr Launfal* (c.1350) exists in a series of five 'short version' fragments, perhaps all originating from the same English translation, now lost. However, in *Sir Landevale* and *Graelent*, two of Chestre's primary sources can be examined. *Sir Landevale* is a close adaptation of Marie de France's *lai*, and the interweaving between the three sources is at times difficult to separate.[31]

One of the striking changes evident in the Chestre text, however, is the reincarnation of the *fee*. Marie's delicate handling of her description creates the impression that the focus of the text is on a sensual woman and the lushness which surrounds her. Her relationship to Avalon is not mentioned until it is clear that she has magical powers. The Chestre adaptation increases both her magical powers and the impact of her physical description in the tale by announcing, before her actual appearance, that she hails from Olyroun and that her father is "Kyng of the fayrye" (276–82).[32]

---

[31] *Launfal* can be found in one manuscript containing *Octavian* and *Libeaus Desconus* (M.A. Cotton Caligula A); see H.L.D. Ward, ed., *Catalogue of Romances* (London, 1883) 180. [32] See *Sir Launfal*, ed. A.J. Bliss, Nelson's Medieval and Renaissance Library (London and Edinburgh: Thomas Nelson and Son, 1960). The Bliss text contains *Sir Landevale*, *Launval*, and Marie de France's *Lanval*; hence it will be used from this point forward for all the citations in the *Syr Launfal* section. See as normal the Hanning and Ferrante edition for a translation of Marie de France's *Lais*. Bliss employs *Sir Launfal* as opposed to the now more generally accepted *Syr Launfal*, so although his text is cited, to avoid confusion, Chestre's text is referred to as *Launfal* throughout the study.

Chestre's description of the fee is very detailed:

> For hete her cloþ es down sche dede
> Almest to her gerdylstede:
> Þan lay sche vncouert.
> Sche was as whyt as lylye yn May,
> Or snow þat sneweþ yn wynterys day-
> He seygh neuer non so pert.
> Þe rede rose, whan sche ys newe,
> Azens her rode nes nauȝt of hewe,
> J dar well say, yn sert.
> Her here schon as gold wyre;
> May noman rede here atyre,
> Ne nauȝt well þ enke yn hert.
>
> (*Launfal*, 289-300)[33]

This sensuous description suggests that the allure of this *fee* is physical.[34] It is equally important that she is the daughter of the Fairy King. Chestre's manipulation of her physical presence seems to prepare the way for a spell of lust and allurement, but this does not happen in the text. This *fee* is important for her magical powers, a conclusion which is demonstrated by Chestre actually increasing the number of gifts that Launfal receives from that in the source texts. Chestre's interest in magic can be monitored through such deliberate changes, and since *Landevale* is very similar to the *lai* of Marie, it can be argued that the differences which appear in Chestre, are reasonably sure to have originated from his own agenda for the text. For example, it is also possible to track the changes which Chestre made to the fairy scenes. In Marie de France's *lai*, the fairy is interested in caring for Lanval:

> Un dun li ad duné aprés:
> Ja cele rien ne vudra mes
> Que il nen ait a sun talent:
> Doinst e despends largement,
> Ele li troverat asez.
> Mut est Lanval bien assenez...

---

[33] *Thomas Chestre*, ed. Bliss, 61. [34] For a discussion of the Fairy's sexual significance to the text see E. Williams, "'A damsell by herself alone': Images of Magic and Feminity from *Lanval* to Sir Lambewell", in *Romance Reading on the Book: Essays on Medieval Narrative Presented to Maldwyn Mills*, ed. J. Fellows (Cardiff: University of Wales Press, 1996), 155-70, 155-6. See also Mary Flowers Braswell "Sin, the Lady and The Law: The English Noblewoman in the Late Middle Ages", *Medievalia et Humanistica* New Series 14 (1986): 81-101.

> Ore est Lanual bien herbergiez!
> Ensemble od li la relevee
> Demurat tresqu'a la vespree,
> E plus i fust, se il poist
> E s'amie li cunsentist.
> "Amis", fet ele, "leuez sus!
> Vus n'i poez demurer plus:
> Alez vus en! Jeo remeindrai."
>
> (Lanval, 135–40, 154–61)

> Afterward, she gave him a gift:
> He would never want anything,
> He would receive as he desired;
> However generously he might give and spend,
> She would provide what he needed.
> Now Lanval is well cared for...
>
> He remained with her
> that afternoon, until evening
> and would have stayed longer, if he could,
> and if his love had consented.
> "Love", she said, "get up.
> You cannot stay any longer.
> Go away now; I shall remain..."[35]

In *Sir Landevale* the situation is much the same:

> "Sir knyght," she said, "curteyse & hend,
> ... J will yeue the grette honoure,
> Gold jnough, and grete tresour.
> Hardley spende largely!
> Yife yeftys blythely!
> Spend and spare not, for my loue!
> Thow shalt jnough to thy behove..."
>
> "Landavale," she said "goo hens now!
> Gold and syluer take with you,
> Spend largely on euery man.
>
> (Sir Landevale, 125, 129–34, 153–5)

---

[35] *Lanval*, ed. Rychner, 77; *Lanval*, ed. Hanning and Ferrante, 109.

Chestre's *Syr Launfal*, however, is quite different in tone:

"Be nauȝt aschamed of me!

Ryche I wyll make þe
J wyll þe ȝeue an alner
Jmad of sylk & of gold cler ...

"Also," sche seyde, "Syr Launfal,
J ȝeue þe Blaunchard, my stede lel,
And Gyfre, my owen knaue ...

And of my armes oo pensel
Wyth þre ermyns, ypeynted well,
Also þou schalt haue.
Jn werre ne yn turnement
Ne schall þe greue no knyhtes dent,
So well y schall þe saue ..."

Sche badd hym aryse anoon.
Hy seyde to hym, 'Syr gantyl knyht,
And þou wylt speke wyth me anywyht,
To a derne stede þou gon."

(*Launfal*, 315, 318–20, 325–33, 351–4)[36]

Chestre at every occasion seeks to increase the impact of the fairies on his tale, which can be seen in the extra time he takes in comparison to the other texts to describe Launfal's interaction with Tryamour.

Chestre also integrates into the text the idea that the power of money would act to smooth over any negative connotations of the use of magic or association with the fairy world. He seems to suggest that all things are acceptable if the acquisition of money is involved; hence, it does not matter that Launfal is getting his money from a fairy. What is of primary importance is that he has access to money once again.

Chestre is also eager to attribute the blame for Launfal's fall from grace to Gwennere. Chestre, diverging again from his sources, depicts Gwennere as crude of character and deserving of harsh punishment for her attempts to ruin Launfal's life. One assumes, under the pressure of Chestre's not-so-subtle persuasion, that Launfal leaves the court for moral reasons, and

---

36 *Launfal*, ed. Bliss, 110–11, 62–3.

because of the snubs offered by the new queen (40–6). It is odd, however, that Chestre did not elucidate a point crucial to the plot, namely Gwennere's past infidelities, the existence of which convinces the nobles to try Launfal rather than instantly mete out the "justice" which Arthur demands when Launfal stands accused by the queen of disloyal behaviour. Perhaps Chestre assumes that it is enough to use the name of Gwennere, as it is already famous in connection with the destruction of Camelot. In Chestre's adaptation, when the hero is faced with the life-changing decision to commit adultery with the queen, his qualms clearly revolve around the issue of "*trowth* or *traytour*". This dilemma has been brought to a head, not by the magical fairy, Tryamour, but through the machinations of the queen, who, it comes as no surprise, is also powerful through her association to magic. Gwennere is chosen by "Marlyn" who is "*Artours counsalere*" (39), for the king to marry. Merlin's name carries with it mixed connotations; he was considered to be the son of a demon and a nun, hence, it is possible for his acts to be considered either positively or negatively by the audience.

It is interesting that each life-altering decision which Launfal is forced to make is related to an encounter with one of these magical characters.[37] These women, both inordinately powerful within the Arthurian world, are shrouded in magical illusions. In a larger sense, they epitomise the anxiety which sexual power generates, an anxiety that was realised in the medieval world by the overwhelming number of women persecuted for magical powers. Proof of this anxiety lies in the path of evolution from Marie's sensuous woman, who also happens to be a fairy, to Chestre's females who operate as doppelgangers of each other. He features the fairy and evil queen as characters who are mutually opposed and yet are also unmistakably alike in that they are equally provocative and derive their power over men and society from forms of sexuality. It is interesting that *Syr Launfal* is the only text in which Gwennere's nose is cut off as justice for her *untrowth*. The destruction of her face acts as a warning to all women who would abuse their sexual power. Reinforcing this reading is Chestre's depiction of Tryamour's entrance to Arthur's court:

Forþ sche wente ynto þe halle
Þer was þe quene & þe ladyes alle,
And also Kyng Artour;

[37] This is demonstrated firstly when Gwennere deprives Launfal of recognition (70); secondly, when she tries to seduce him into betraying his King (683); thirdly, when she seeks to unman him publicly (685); and then, finally, when she accuses him of being a *traytour* to her "naive" king (761).

Magicial adaptations

> Her maydenes come ayens her, ryʒt,
> To take her styrop whan sche lyʒt -
> Of þe lady, Dame Tryamour.
> Sche ded of her mantyll on þe flet
> (Þat men schuld her beholde þe bet)
> Wythoute a more soiour.
>
> (*Launfal*, 973-81)[38]

Williams describes this entrance as the performance of a striptease: Tryamour's cloak slips from her shoulders and all wait with bated breath to discover what other items may be removed so that the men might see her more clearly.[39] The appearance of this luscious woman saves Launfal's life and provides him with the opportunity to depart for the fairy world. His ability to regain his honour and his place at court, and keep his life is completely dependent upon her mercy and pity. In her article "Magic and Femininity from *Lanval* to *Sir Lambewell*", Williams argues that it is possible to compare the scenes featuring the fairy mistresses in the romances discussed and to chart the radical changes of emphasis as the "treatment of the *fee* in particular and the female body in general comes to reflect a whole range of different attitudes towards beauty, sensuality, magic and sheer opulence".[40] These changes, as also charted in the *Lanval lai*, invite the modern reader to reassess the English uses of magic in relation to the female characters of the romances.

Launfal, much like Gawain in *Sir Gawain in the Green Knight*, is unable to survive these courtly intrigues completely unscathed. He compromises himself, not to save his life, but to prove his manhood to the queen and court. His relationship to the fairy clearly acts as a magical encounter, and by betraying her existence, he breaks her trust. He must then suffer the punishment of being stripped of his public status. Launfal knows his situation is dire since he has compromised his *trowth*, not to Arthur and the court, but to the fairy upon whose forgiveness his life now depends. He has to betray either his king or his mistress, and he chooses to betray his mistress. It is only when he realizes what he has given up for so little gain that he takes full advantage of his second chance and leaves with his fairy for mythical Avalon. Ironically, magic is the means by which he effects his return to Arthurian society, while at the same time it enables him to see its flaws. It is an interesting twist to the story that Launfal is allowed to return one day a year to the world which he has abandoned; one might suggest

---

[38] *Launfal*, ed. Bliss, 80. [39] Williams, "A damsell by herself alone", 155. [40] Ibid., 156.

that this is not to reform it but rather to be reminded of how lucky he is to have escaped it:

> Euery er, vpon a certayn day,
> *And hym se wyth sy3t.*
> Me may here Launfales stede nay,
> And hym se wyth sy3t.
> Ho |> at wyll |> er axsy justus,
> To Kepe hys armes fro |> e rustus...
>
> Þer he may fynde justes anoon
> Wyth *Syr Launfal* |> e kny3t.
>
> (*Launfal*, 1024–8, 1031–2)[41]

In many ways this ending grounds the romance in the earthy world of chivalrous romance as opposed to "the evanescent, pychological symbolism of disappearence into a dream world" which marks the ending of Marie's *Lanval*.[42] What becomes apparent is that Launfal is not interested in educating his community, as he has seen that his experiences will not reform the court. He is only interested in his gain and not the improvement of the entire society. In this way this romance seems to be very different from its English siblings, namely *Sir Gawain and the Green Knight*, the works of Gower, or the *Franklin's Tale*, in that it does not attempt to reintegrate the hero back into his community. The lessons learned by the hero or heroine in these other romances *seem* to be shared, with varying degrees of success and acceptance, by the society which welcomes its hero or heroine back into the fold.

Chestre has received a tremendous amount of criticism for this ending, and indeed, the entire text of his romance; Spearing, for example, in an article on Marie de France and her adapters, takes the view that Chestre spoils the romance through redundant phraseology, redundant graphic detail, and redundant romance clichés.[43] Mills claims that Chestre was a "hack-writer", and Spearing comments that Chestre's text is a "disaster" of "extreme and powerful badness".[44] What might be suggested as an alternative reading of Chestre, and the style of his ending in particular, is that Chestre has exposed the "communal" happy ending for the sham it is.

---

[41] *Launfal*, ed. Bliss, 81. [42] W.A. Davenport, *Chaucer and His English Contemporaries* (New York: Macmillan, 1998) 106. [43] A.C. Spearing, "Marie de France and her Middle English Adapters", *SAC* 12 (1990): 117–56. [44] Maldwyn Mills, ed., *Lybeaus Desconus*, EETS 261 (London: 1969) 21; Spearing, "Marie", 148.

Endings, particularly happy ones – as has been demonstrated in these early Middle English romances – are a tricky business. The ways in which humour and magic are called upon to create situations in which happy endings are achieved, demonstrate a quality of magic which has only previously been hinted at: *illusioun*. These happy endings are only an illusion which actually leave much for the audience to resolve. Chestre, perhaps without intending to, presages the last great reformulation of magic in the medieval romance genre – the power of illusion and how disconcerting its presence or absence can be to the expectations of the audience. One expects Launfal to live in the fairy world, not drift back and forth, unable to settle in or become a true member of either society. The absence of a settled ending in Chestre's text is even disconcerting to the modern audience, a conclusion demonstrated by the wealth of negativity which surrounds critical readings of the text. It is, of course, exactly this balance between reality and fantasy which occupies Chaucer so thoroughly in the *Franklin's Tale*. Chaucer's concentration on the power of *illusioun*, astronomy, astrology, and the impact of *magyk natureel* on the imagination, should alert the modern reader to its importance in the medieval world. Chestre does not deal with the forms of "clerical magic" which interest Chaucer, but he does expose the *illusioun* of the happy ending for what it is, a means of unsettling the audience and causing an entire reassessment of the romance which it thought it had just understood.

CONCLUSION

Romance endings

MAGIC IN THE HANDS OF MEN

In choosing one of Chaucer's most intriguing romances, the *Franklin's Tale*, as the last example of magical romances in this study, it is possible to see that regardless of the passage of time and change of environment, the romance form flourished into the fourteenth century. Despite the social and political turbulence, or perhaps because of it, it is this time period in English history which provides some of the most complex of the extant romances, namely, the works of Chaucer, Gower, and the *Gawain* Poet. It is difficult, however, to conclude anything with Chaucer since it seems that rather than resolving old dilemmas, his work opens new doors, explores the use of forms in a new way, and presents the romance reader with new complexities. This is particularly true in the use of *clerical magic* (the use of astronomy, *magyk natureel*, and astrology), which Chaucer employs to achieve his agenda in the *Franklin's Tale*. Chaucer uses this form of magic, as opposed to the perilous fords or magical rings of his predecessors, to demonstrate the power of the *illusioun* of magic. In this way, he speaks to the heart of the romance form by exploring the shades of grey between what is real or right, and what *seems* to be real or right. Chaucer demonstrates how powerful a tool belief can be, particularly in the hands of the unscrupulous. This adaptation of the romance genre although new, still illustrates in many ways what the function of magic has always been: a means of understanding the relationship between reality and fantasy; a revitalisation of the interest in the nature of man's free will in relationship to fate, fortune, and God; and the reframing of the issue of man's place in society.

The view of Chaucer as the writer of complex romances is not one that finds universal favour; Brewer, for example, claims that "English romances are mocked, we may think, not only for their verbal incompetence and general silliness, but because they are *romances*, which to Chaucer means silliness."[1] One can frequently find the view that the *Tale of Sir Thopas*, in particular, exhibits Chaucer's "contempt for the feebler examples of the genre", but, in truth, that story hardly begins to represent

---

[1] Brewer, *Tradition and Innovation*, 140.

the scope with which Chaucer engages with romance in the body of his work.[2] Davenport suggests in a rebuttal to such negative views concerning the importance of romance to Chaucer, that "Chaucer does not complete a single 'strait' romance, shows little interest in some central romance themes, ... but he cannot leave romance alone".[3] This conclusion is supported by the fact that without the power of *illusioun* and *magyk* one of the most popular of Chaucer's tales, the *Franklin's Tale*, much like its magical counterpart, *Sir Gawain and the Green Knight*, could not fulfil its purpose and design.

INFLUENCES ON CHAUCER: WHERE DID CLERICAL MAGIC ORIGINATE?

Brewer wrote some twenty years ago about the idea that Chaucer might have read the romances of Chrétien de Troyes; unfortunately, however, the material which he cites in his argument is not terribly convincing, a conclusion which he himself reaches.[4] It seems impossible to suggest with any certainty that Chaucer would have had access to the original Arthurian romances. It is no more feasible to suggest that he had access to Marie de France's *Lais*. In fact, he may only have been familiar with the *lais* recorded in the Auchinleck manuscript or one comparable to it.[5] The only material that one can comfortably suggest Chaucer drew upon for his "Breton lai", the *Franklin's Tale*, is that of the "ancient histories" of Geoffrey of Monmouth.[6] It is intriguing and tantalising to think that Chaucer could have been influenced in ways similar to those in which Marie and Chrétien were affected by knowing the techniques of Geoffrey and appreciating the goals of his *Historia*. This would explain Chaucer's choice of the antiquated names and selection of geographical sites, and provide one source of Chaucer's affection for stories concerning fate and fortune. It would also bring full circle the interests of romance writers in the intellectual disciplines of magic, theology, philosophy, and history that have been present from the very inception of the romances. Regardless of what influences upon Chaucer can actually be traced, it is enough to say that he creates a tale which is clearly engaged in the exploration of romance motifs. In much the same manner as romance writers and adapters before him, Chaucer

---

2 Davenport, *Chaucer*, 131.   3 Ibid., 132.   4 D.S. Brewer, "Chaucer and Middle English Studies: In honour of Russell Hope Robbins", ed. B. Rowlands (London, 1974): 255–9 as reprinted in Brewer, *Tradition and Innovation*, 137–41.   5 Davenport, *Chaucer*, 124.   6 Ibid., 126. See Chapter 2 for a discussion of Monmouth and his impact upon the texts of Chrétien and Marie.

assessed the most valuable elements of the English, Anglo-Norman, French, and even Italian romance traditions and then created a composite, or a *conjointure*, which best suited his agenda and the interests of his audience.

In claiming that his romance is based upon a Breton *lai*, Chaucer provides his audience with a series of expectations concerning the themes under discussion, namely love and magic.[7] His audience could well have been familiar with the romances previously discussed in this study, or other texts which were equally popular in the period, such as *Sir Orfeo*, *Lai le Freine*, or *Sir Degaré*. These tales, however, would not have prepared an audience for a romance as sophisticated in its construction as that of the Franklin. It is virtually impossible to separate any individual thematic strand from the *Franklin's Tale* and not talk about the importance of *trowth*; so integral is that idea to the conception of the plot that it forms the backbone to the romance itself. Equally vital is the presence of magic in the tale, without which the entire plot could not function. At every juncture in the plot, the use of magic forces the audience to engage with the tale to discover where the meaning in the text resides; is it in the *illusioun* of nobility which the Franklin creates, or is it in the reading of the characters' actual actions?[8]

Despite claims of indebtedness to the *Lai* tradition, Chaucer does not employ the type of magic which was most typical of that form; instead of adopting the idea of several magical or marvellous tests to gauge the hero or heroine's progress on the quest for self-knowledge and security in the community, Chaucer develops his use of magic along different lines. The use of magic in the *lais* usually represents a clear and immediate indication of the hero's or heroine's feelings or vulnerabilities, such as was common also in the romances of Chrétien. Instead of this one-to-one relationship, in which each test reveals something about a particular character, Chaucer employs one magically-induced event which effects the whole community and forces a comprehensive re-analysis of the entire social system. This in effect forces all the characters to react to the same event, a situation that allows the audience to compare and contrast the very revealing actions of characters who are all suffering under a particular set of circumstances.

In looking for comparable models to the use of magic by Chaucer, one can see strong parallels in the *Tristan* texts of Gottfried von Strassburg and Thomas of Britain, in that their use of a magical potion forces not only the

---

[7] See Kathryn Hume's discussion on how the *Lai* tradition influenced Chaucer, in: Kathryn Hume, "Why Chaucer Calls *The Franklin's Tale* a Breton *Lai*", *Philological Quarterly* 52 (1972): 373–9.   [8] See page 156 below for a discussion of the term *illusioun*.

lovers, but all the other characters related to them in any way, to react to a magical incident. The audience then judges the characters based upon how successfully they navigate the circumstances that spring from the magical test. Tristan is often considered to be the character who weathers the situation most adroitly, as Iseut is seen to lie to her husband continuously, endeavour to murder her hand-maiden, and even, to attempt the circumventing of God's justice by making disingenuous oaths.[9]

It is not in any way certain that Chaucer would have had access to either of the *Tristan* texts; one can only argue that the story itself would have been so popular that Chaucer could have had the sense of how magic was employed by these authors. This in and of itself is not much evidence upon which to build an argument for the type of magic which Chaucer employs. What is interesting, however, is that in a genre that mostly leaves the source of its magical tokens and magical events unauthored, Chaucer, as the *Tristan* authors did in their respective texts, clearly assigns an agent to the magical *illusioun* of the *Franklin's Tale*. In *Tristan* there is no question of the power of the potion being illusory, but in the *Franklin's Tale* the question concerning the nature of the clerk's power sparks a fierce debate over the entire issue of the power of man in his world and the relationship of man to the gods. One must question whether a clerk can alter Dorigen's fate through the ability to create the *illusion* of the rocks being moved. In *Tristan*, the characters do indeed suffer from the power of a drink which restricts the freedom of their will, but the fact that the drink is created by Iseut's mother seems to be an issue relegated to the backdrop of the tale, as is the nature of the magic potion itself. Therefore, given some of these fundamental differences in approach, it would be fruitful to search for other influences on the use of magic by Chaucer in the *Franklin's Tale*.

In examining Chaucer's transformation of the heavy-handed use of inspired magic by Boccaccio in the fourth book of the *Filocolo*, into a full-scale discussion of illusion, magic, astrology, and astronomy, one must also wonder at the extent of the influence of the character of Tebano upon the Clerk d'Orliens.[10] Boccaccio stressed the power of the devil-worshipping magician, Tebano; Chaucer focuses, instead, upon the power of the classical gods, the power of astrology or astronomy to effect nature, and the power of the individual clerk orchestrating the magical operation.[11] Sandra McEntire

---

9 See the *Tristan* texts of Thomas and Gottfried for particulars concerning these incidents. 10 For a discussion of Chaucer's familiarity with *Il Filocolo* see David Wallace, *Chaucer and the Early Writings of Boccaccio* (Cambridge: D.S. Brewer, 1985) 6.
11 A.J. Minnis, "Chaucer's Position on Past Gentility", *Proceedings of the British Academy*, LXXII, vol. 1986 (Oxford: Oxford University Press, 1987) 224.

effectively demonstrates evidence of Chaucer's reconfiguration of the magician Tebano, to whom she refers as "a poet, a son of Apollo" as he is the master of "real magic".[12] The Theban magician, for example, does not rely on calculations or the reading of stars, but instead, on what Minnis describes as "ghastly rituals" which include such ingredients as witch's flesh and wolf testicles.[13] Tebano reveals his skills to include "necromancy" and the means of interfering with "the moon's natural course".[14]

This is a very different type of magician from the Clerk d'Orliens portrayed by Chaucer in the *Franklin's Tale*, as indeed, are the majority of magicians which originate from the romance tradition. This discussion illustrates that it is difficult to trace any direct antecedent for the use of "clerical magic" in earlier romances. What one finds instead, is that Chaucer writes with such complexity that it has been seen necessary to argue that *magyk* in his era had taken on a new literary dimension.[15] This is, of course, not true, as the romances have always been intimately connected to various types of scholarly fields, namely, history, philosophy etc. What could be argued, is that because the sophistication of Chaucer is so universally accepted, his application of magic in the *Franklin's Tale* is awarded special status. By incorporating into his text different kinds of clerical magic, for example *astrologye*, *illusioun* and *magyk natureel*, Chaucer brings the romance form to a new level of complexity for his fourteenth-century audience. The cosmological backdrop to the tale makes possible several levels of reading, beginning with the dynamics of power in the universe, and ending with the *trowth* between a husband and wife. This opens the romance to a discussion, not only of the events which transpire in the tale, but also of how the resolution of the tale works in conjunction with existing fourteenth-century conceptions of social order and the science of the stars.[16]

Clerical magic and its sister subjects were the province of the university; thus the ever-increasing number of clerics and well-educated "lay" bureaucrats who comprised the "new bureaucratic English society" in the fourteenth century would have been a ready audience for magic, but not necessarily the other motifs of romance.[17] T.F. Tout explains:

[12] Sandra J. McEntire, "Illusiouns and Interpretation in the *Franklin's Tale*", *Chaucer Review*, 31: 2 (1991): 157.   [13] Minnis, "Chaucer's Position", 226.   [14] Ibid., 224.   [15] See Astell for a comprehensive and provocative discussion of Chaucer's intellectual and "literary" audience. She also addresses in a most interesting fashion, the clerical arts of science, astronomy, etc.; Ann W. Astell, *Chaucer and the Universe of Learning* (Ithaca and London: Cornell University Press, 1997).   [16] See Simpson for an interesting discussion on the relationship of science to medieval literature: James Simpson, *Science and the Self in Medieval Poetry* (Cambridge: Cambridge University Press, 1995).   [17] Astell, *Chaucer and the Universe*, 5.

While at one time we generally accepted that Chaucer wrote for a group of nobles centring around the improvident but artistically sophisticated court of Richard II, now we are more likely to see Chaucer's immediate audience as being more of the 'new men' of his age, an audience more suspicious of the heroic pretences of the immediate past, more alienated from the court and its archaic concerns.[18]

If this were the audience for which Chaucer was writing - and there exists quite a bit of disagreement over this claim – it would illuminate in many ways the use of *clerical magic* by Chaucer.[19] Astrology and astronomy are clearly areas of personal interest, but they nonetheless relate to the main themes of the romances, such as the nature of free will, or the interests in philosophy and society. Their use in this context allows Chaucer the freedom to explore concerns surrounding new boundaries for the social classes. One social class which was under intense reassessment in the fourteenth century, and that would have been of particular interest to Chaucer, is that of the clerics themselves. Astell describes the tension which existed in Chaucer's community between the "lerned" and the "lewed", as well as the struggles between those defined as "gentils" and those categorised as "cherls".[20] The parallel relationship between these two struggles provides some interesting avenues of exploration for the relationship between "lerned" Chaucer and his socially aspirational narrator.

In an environment of political unrest and rapid social change, Chaucer employs magic to explore new ideas of community and society. He is not writing this romance to re-affirm the old courtly ways, but to explain and explore the positions of new characters and political changes. As Duby described the twelfth-century romances, they performed a self-affirming function.[21] Hence, the happy ending created the sense that although the characters had had lessons to learn, their education only served to support the ideas and goals established by the structures of authority already in place in the community.[22] In other words, the values of the community may be questioned, but rarely are they fundamentally undermined. Although this is an over-simplification of what it is that Chrétien and

---

18 Thomas F. Tout, "Literature and Learning in the English Civil Service in the Fourteenth Century", *Speculum* 4 (1929): 367 as cited in Astell, *Chaucer and the Universe*, 5.   19 Strohm, *Social Chaucer*, 9–11, 14, 22, 68–71. Strohm characterizes Chaucer's audience as gentils, a class that was defined by the 1397 Poll Tax.   20 Astell, *Chaucer and the Universe*, 5.   21 See pages 15–16 above for a more in-depth analysis of Duby's research and the functions of the twelfth-century romances.
22 Duby, *Love and Marriage*, 80–3, 58, 60–3.

Marie achieve in their works, as a generalisation about twelfth-century romances, Duby's conclusions provide a useful comparison to gauge how different Chaucer's fourteenth-century romance format has become. In using *magyk* and *illusioun* Chaucer allows a pseudo-happy ending to his romance – a popular technique in the earlier English romances – which allows him to maintain a failsafe key.[23] He demonstrates where the Franklin's ideas of nobility will lead: to a happy ending based on the release of Dorigen, who has been driven to acting half as if she were mad, from a promise she should not technically have had to honour (1511). The audience (internal and external to the *Canterbury Tales*) knows that the argument that the Franklin uses to legitimise this ending has been built on a false premise: "It *semed* that alle the rokkes were awaye" (1296, my italics). The Franklin himself makes it clear that the rocks never actually disappear owing to the fact that the clerk used *illusiouns, jogelrye*, and *japes*, "As hethen folk useden in thilke dayes" (1293). Therefore, the question as to which of the characters was "the moosste fre" is invalidated by the Franklin's own standards; Aurelius and the clerk have not earned to right to be considered noble since neither character has actually moved the rocks (1622). If they have not moved the rocks, then the clerk and the squire cannot be considered noble for releasing their fellow pagans from promises that they themselves have failed to keep.

FOURTEENTH-CENTURY MAGIC AND ITS RELATIONSHIP TO RELIGION, PHILOSOPHY AND SCHOLARSHIP

In the romances examined during the course of this study, the authors have employed the marvellous and magical in ways which were familiar to the audience, thereby insuring that few explanations were needed, and that the controversial aspects of magic, such as its links to necromancy, were minimised. Chaucer takes this one step further in employing the term *magyk natureel*. As discussed in the introduction, the *MED* defines *magyk* as: "(a) The knowledge of natural hidden forces (e.g. magnetism, stellar influence) and the art of using these in calculating future events, curing diseases, etc.; ~ natural; (b) sorcery, enchantment."[24] From these

---

23 For a discussion of the happy ending to the *Franklin's Tale* see Angela and Peter Lucas, "The Presentation of Marriage and Love in Chaucer's *Franklin's Tale*", *English Studies* 72 (1991): 501–12. See for a conflicting point of view, Timothy Flake, "Love, Trouthe, and the Happy Ending of the *Franklin's Tale*," *English Studies* 77 (1996): 209–26.   24 *Magyk, MED*, 1975 edn; *Magician, MED*, 1975 edn. See pages 22–35 above for a fuller discussion of magic.

definitions it is clear that *magyk* overlaps not only sorcery, but also science, the spiritual arena of moral wrongdoing, and the natural world of herbal medicine. In adding *magyk* to *natureel*, Chaucer creates a term that can be read in several new ways. Benson in the *Riverside Chaucer* defines the term as the equivalent to the modern term, "natural science"; Davis in the *Chaucer Glossary* suggests that *magyk natureel* is "magic not involving demonic powers, science".[25] In both cases there is clearly an attempt to move away from the idea of magic as demonically inspired, and an attempt to move towards the belief that man has power over the natural world.

In historical terms, the fourteenth and fifteenth centuries exhibited a rapid progression from magic to science, one which is evidenced by the deep suspicion with which early scientists and doctors were met, and their often elevated but precarious status in the community.[26] The use of the *magyk natureel* by Chaucer simply reflects the shifting parameters between magic, medicine, and science in his own period. The link between these terms is based upon the quest for knowledge concerning how and where things derive the source of their power. So although twelfth-century ideas about magic had changed to incorporate the "science" of astrology, the opposition of the Church remained constant, since magic in all its twelfth- through fourteenth-century forms still represented a questioning of the boundaries between the power of man and God. The works of Aquinas serve to illustrate this point as they are scattered with references to magic and *superstitio*, his term for the crafts of sorcery, divination, and other such practices. In *Quodlibet XI* he deals directly with the problems of sorcerers:

> Concerning sorcerers, it is known that some say sorcery has no existence and that it comes simply from a lack of belief or superstition, since they wish to prove that demons do not exist insofar as they are creatures of man's imagination; insofar as men imagine them to exist, these fantasies afflict the fearful. The Catholic faith, on the other hand, insists that demons do indeed exist...[27]

---

25 Benson, *Riverside*, 183. *Chaucer Glossary*, ed. N. Davis (Oxford: Clarendon Press, 1979) 92. 26 Thorndike, *History of Magic*, vols. I–III. See also: Nancy Siraisi, *Medieval and Early Renaissance Medicine*, (Chicago: University of Chicago Press, 1990). 27 Thomas Aquinas, *Quodlibet, XI Quaestio*, in *Utrum maleficia impediant matrimonium: Opera omnia*, vol. 9 art. 10 (Parma, 1859) 618. cited from and trans. Peters, *The Magician*, 97–8. See also Aquinas, "Superstition and Irreverence", *Summa theologia* (2a 2ae 92–100), ed. and trans. T.F. O'Meara, 60 vols. (London: Blackfriars: Eyre and Spottiswoode, 1968) 65, 2–9, 19, 41, 70–85.

Chaucer plays upon the controversial nature of magic by introducing a series of conflicting images into the *Franklin's Tale*. At various moments, the Franklin uses such terms as *japes*, *meschaunces*, or *jogelrye* to describe the seeming disappearance of the rocks. In introducing terms with mixed spiritual connotations, such as *magyk* and *illusioun*, as well as *myracle* (1299), *japes* (1271), *sighte merverilous* (1206), *supersticious cursednesse* (1272) and several references to fate, Chaucer undermines the scientific/organic element of his use of *magyk natureel* and returns to the older connotations surrounding magic, namely, questions concerning man's influence over nature, a belief in an all-powerful God, and the power of superstition. The science of astrology was already on precarious ground and did not carry much credence in the Church.[28] This is illustrated by Aquinas' discussion of the complex topics of astronomy/astrology and fate:

> So therefore we can admit that fate exists in the sense that everything happening on earth is subject to divine providence in that it is ordained by the latter and, as it were, forespoken. The doctors of the Church, however, avoided using this word fate because of those who twisted the term into meaning a force deriving from the position of the stars. Thus Augustine says: *"If anyone attributes human affairs to fate, meaning by fate the will or power of God, let him keep his view while correcting his terminology"*.[29]

The modern reader, not unlike the confused believer of whom Augustine speaks, wishes Chaucer would redefine his terms. This ambivalence in interpretation is further problematised for the audience by the dichotomy in the thinking of the narrator: the Franklin describes the *illusioun* of the removal of the rocks as both *myracle* (1299) and *meschaunces* (1292). *Miracle* as defined by the *MED* means: "1a. (a) A wondrous phenomenon or event; ... a marvel ... 1b. (a) A miracle performed by God, Christ, angels, saints, the Cross, etc."[30] *Mischaunce* is defined as: "1. (a) A mishap, piece of bad

---

[28] Angela Lucas argues that "astrology and astronomy were largely interchangeable terms in the middle ages" in Lucas, "Astronomy, Astrology and Magic in Chaucer's *Franklin's Tale*", *Maynooth Review* (1991–2): 9.   [29] Aquinas, "The World Order", *Summa theologiae* (1a 110–19), ed. and trans. M.J. Charlesworth, 60 vols (London: Blackfriars: Eyre and Spottiswode, 1970) 111.   [30] Aquinas defines *miracle* as being taken from *admiratio*: "but the word *miracle* connotes something altogether wondrous, i.e. having its cause hidden absolutely and from everyone. The cause is God. Thus the works God does surpassing any cause known to us are called miracles". Aquinas, "Divine Government", *Summa theologiae* (1a 2ae 103–109) ed. T.C. O'Brian, 60 vols (London: Blackfriars: Eyre and Spottiswoode, 1970) 105–8, 85, 84–5.

luck, calamity... 2. Wrongdoing, wicked behaviour, sin; also, a sin, an evil deed; also evil in the abstract; *usen mischaunces* to practise the occult arts."[31]

On the most sophisticated level of interpretation, Chaucer raises an argument over the power of man to effect his or her own fate. The characterisation of the clerk by Chaucer is the best evidence for his interest in the larger philosophical aspects of this situation, and his interest in engaging what Minnis refers to as, the "higher discipline[s]".[32] The Franklin describes the clerk as a *maister* in at least six instances and when the clerk refers to himself he uses the title *clerk* (1611), which suggests that he approves of its significance. Minnis argues that the title *philosophre* – the highest form of praise addressed to a pagan – occurs three times, and that "in sum, the vast majority of terms applied in designating the magician's status and role are honourific."[33] Chaucer is interested in encouraging discussion of free will and fate, not in dismissing the clerk as evil, or suggesting that his works are of no consequence. A clerk who uses magic and is given the title of philosopher can hardly be interpreted in any other way but as a figure who engenders debate over fate and man's connection to it.

Aquinas illustrates the complex relationship between will, fate, and the stars. It is an area of discussion which is clearly of interest to philosophers and theologians:

> It must be observed, however, that the influence of the heavenly bodies can touch the intellect and will indirectly and accidentally in that the intellect as well as the will receives from the lower powers which are bound up with bodily organs ... Consequently, astrologers are able to foretell the truth in the majority of cases, especially in the general sense. However, they cannot do so in particular cases, for nothing stops a man from resisting his passions by free-will. Thus these very astrologers say that the wise man is master of the stars in that he is the master of his own passions.[34]

The relationship discussed here between the will, passion, and astrology is deeply significant to the structure of the *Franklin's Tale*. The parallel

---

[31] *Miracle* and *Mischaunces*, MED, 1977 edn. See pages 28–35 above for fuller definitions and a discussion of these terms. [32] Minnis, "Chaucer's Position", 223. [33] Ibid., 224. The six instances cited for *maister* are lines: 1202, 1209, 1220, 1257, 1302, and 1576. For *philosophre* the three cited instances are lines: 1561, 1585, and 1607. [34] Aquinas, "God's Will and Providence", *Summa theologiae* (1a 19–26), ed. and trans. Thomas Gilbey, 60 vols (London and New York: Blackfriars: Eyre and Spottiswoode, McGraw Hill, 1964) 105–7.

between power within society and power over society is demonstrated by the manner in which the Franklin constructs his version of Divine order: the science of the stars is the study of the workings of the gods and the workings of a society.

In this light, Chaucer's choice to highlight the power of *illusioun* in this magical romance can only be seen as very provocative to his audience, in that one never knows what is real or illusory in the text. *Illusioun* is defined by the MED in two ways: "1. (a) Mockery, scorning, derision; an act of mockery or scorn; (b) a matter for scorn. 2. (a) Deception (usually of the senses or imagination); an act of deception; the fact of being deceived; . . ."[35] The interchangeable manner in which Chaucer employs *illusioun* and *magyk* gives rise to anxiety: is the power of *magyk* nothing more than an *illusioun*? Alternatively, is the *illusioun* in this text that man has any power at all? Could it be that what happens in the story is really the power of the gods being demonstrated through the workings of fate? This would be in line with the teaching of the Church. Chaucer makes it clear that the gods do have a place in the workings of the plot; Aurelius prays to the gods (1030–81), and Dorigen complains to "the Lord" about the placement of the black rocks (865–94). Therefore, one is never quite sure if one is seeing the gods at work, or as the Franklin claims, man-made *magyk* at work. The answer to this question would have implications for the entire outcome of the tale. For if this is really the power of the gods, then one must distrust the ability of the Franklin to judge the inner working of his own tale. If this is the case, then he certainly is not a fit judge for how society should be ordered, and his conclusion at the end of the tale is undermined.

THE SCIENCE OF MAGIC OR FATE

Chaucer has the Franklin recount in detail the prayers of Aurelius and Dorigen, but he does not seem to register them as potentially powerful. For example, the Franklin tell us that Aurelius prays for a miracle to Phebus Apollo, god and planet (1056, 1065, 1299). The fact that Aurelius prays for a miracle but also believes in magic, presents the audience with another mixed message as to who has power in his world.[36] Aurelius hopes Apollo will intercede with his sister Lucina (1046) to bring about such a tide that the rocks will be covered to a depth of five fathoms: "Wherfore, Lord Phebus, this is my requeste- / Do this *miracle*, or do myn herte breste" (my

---

35 *Illusioun*, MED, 1976 edn.   36 J.D. North, *Chaucer's Universe* (Oxford: Clarendon, 1988) 423–33.

Romance endings

italics, 1055–6). If the sister of Apollo will not bring about the tide then she should "synken every rok adoun / Into hir owene dirke regioun / Under the ground, ther Pluto dwelleth inne" (1073–5). These very specific requests would have had the same effect as the *illusioun* of the rocks disappearing.[37] The Franklin, however, does not give any room in the text for this reading, preferring to use the seemingly unanswered demands of the characters to open the door for magic and *illusioun*.

In examining the nature of the magic employed by the Clerk d'Orliens, one can see that magic in this text is required to expand what seems unnatural into something *naturally* possible. The Franklin gives the best part of thirty lines of description to the process through which the *illusioun* of the removal of the rocks is created (1265–99). A scientific process seems to be underway from the Franklin's description of events: "Whan he hadde founde his firste mansioun, / He knew the remenaunt by proporcioun, / And knew the arisyng of his moone weel" (1285–7). The Franklin claims that he does not know anything about astrology, but he is letter-perfect in his description of the astrological terms.[38] It is only when the Clerk "acordant to his operacioun" and his "othere observaunces" actually performs "swiche meschaunces" as the *illusioun* that the boundaries of science are left behind (1291, 1292). The vagueness of this part of the Franklin's description of *magyk* leaves one to speculate on what other knowledge is needed to effect an *illusioun*.[39] North suggests that the Franklin, having earlier given such detail, seems to be holding something back here, and that whatever those other observances are they are "not astrological but in some sense magical."[40] If this is the case then it is odd that the Franklin so emphatically states that we are no longer subject to such *superstitious cursedeness*:

> That longen to the moone, and swich folye
> *As in oure dayes is nat worth a flye* –
> For hooly chirches feith in oure bileve
> Ne suffreth noon illusioun us to greve.
>
> (*Franklin's Tale*, 1131–4, my italics)

The Franklin claims that the Church has rescued humanity from such crude beliefs. By incorporating such a series of mixed messages and confusing terminology, however, Chaucer leaves the audience in the same position as Dorigen, wondering why and how these events are being

---

37 Lucas, "Astronomy, Astrology and Magic", 5–7. 38 North, *Chaucer's Universe*, 252; see also 251, 256–8. 39 Lucas, "Astronomy, Astrology and Magic", 6–7. 40 North, *Chaucer's Universe*, 439.

controlled. This means that it is not only the *hethens* who question the nature of the gods in this tale. The use of clerical magic by Chaucer has stimulated questions concerning *how* the natural world operates, and *who* operates it, for the audience as well.

A WOMAN IN A MAN'S WORLD: MAGIC AND THE INDIVIDUAL

Magic serves in the text as a means of gaining personal control over fate and nature. That would make sense of why it is that Dorigen makes a promise to Aurelius based on his ability to remove the rocks. The parallel between the larger issues underpinning the text and the actions of the characters in the text, is illustrated by Minnis in his argument that Dorigen's dilemma is "why a good God who created and controls the whole non-human world with such apparent wisdom, should leave mankind to the disorderly and arbitrary governance of Fortune".[41] The Franklin indicates to the audience that Dorigen does not believe in magic through her response to the rocks being made to seem to disappear: "For wende I nevere by possibilitee/That switch a monstre or merveille myghte be!/It is agayns the proces of nature" (1343–5). Her circumstances have clearly changed, but initially, she did pray to have the rocks removed regardless of whether or not they were a part of a divine order (865–72, 881–3). Her "pleyful" promise to Aurelius makes clear that she would be happy for anyone to remove those rocks, human or divine (988–98). When Aurelius approaches her, Dorigen is literally given a man-made option to try to control her fate and that is her bargain with Aurelius. For a woman in the romance world there are only two tried and true avenues to power: God and men. The bargain that she makes with Aurelius represents for Dorigen her only access to man-made influence over nature and fate since she does not know about magic. It is her bemoaning of fortune (1355) and questioning of the divine order, however, which puts Dorigen in the path of magic, the only "real" man-made source of influence over nature, to explore her questions and anxieties.

Equally, magic serves as a means for Aurelius to gain influence beyond his "natural" means; he knows that it is not "right" that he should want Dorigen, as she is the property of someone else (1001–5). When the gods do not answer his request to move the rocks, however, he does not have

---

41 Minnis, "Chaucer's Position", 210–11. See also A.J. Minnis, *Chaucer's Boece and the Medieval Tradition of Boethius* (Oxford: D.S. Brewer, 1993) and A.J. Minnis, *Chaucer and Pagan Antiquity* (Cambridge: D.S. Brewer; Totowa, N.J.: Rowman & Littlefield, 1982).

any moral qualms about proceeding to use magic. It seems unimportant to him whether the gods sanction his behaviour or not; at this point in the text, he is not interested in what is morally correct behaviour. This conclusion is reached by noting his initial happiness to pay vast sums of money for a magical means to achieve the conquest of Dorigen.

The question of power in the cosmos is neatly mirrored in the struggle between the characters of the romance for power over each other in terms of sexual control, love, and promises of honour. Minnis succinctly identifies the underlying problem as "the extent and nature of God's control over His creation".[42] Magic makes possible the interplay between not only the characters, but also the critical concepts under debate. This is illustrated when both Dorigen and Aurelius, for example, single out clerks as a source of knowledge concerning issues pertaining to the gods and man. Chaucer decides that it will be from the Clerk d'Orliens that the audience gains insight into who has power in this world and beyond it. Because he has control over magic, this clerk has power over two characters who should be socially superior. Dorigen and Aurelius are made weak and desperate by love, which leaves both vulnerable to poor judgement, not unlike the figures of Lancelot and Erec when deprived of their abilities to think about anything except love. Dorigen and Aurelius both seek to convince the gods to help them, and when that seems to fail, they both attempt "man-made" solutions.

OLD MAGIC AND NEW MAGIC

In the *Franklin's Tate* magic functions to reveal the vulnerabilities of the characters who come into contact with it. This demonstrates that Chaucer did indeed maintain a link with the use of magic as it functioned in the earlier romances. In conjunction with that technique, however, he expands the use of magic to create a new perspective on the issues of honour and society that will be relevant to his audience. Once *magyk* and *illusioun* are used, for example, Dorigen is revealed to be vulnerable; she is unable to sustain both the role of a *powerful* romance heroine, and that of a *powerless*, loving wife. The pilgrims are told that the illusion will last for "a wyke or tweye" (1295), but its temporary nature does not change the reality of its consequences for Dorigen. Dorigen is to be held morally accountable for a promise that she did not believe could ever be naturally realised, demonstrating that ultimately neither her intentions nor her

---

[42] Minnis, "Chaucer's Position", 211.

beliefs have any value in the world of men. For the heroine in this tale, there is no difference between reality and *illusioun*; there are only the laws of men, which demand, in the form of Arveragus' injunction, that she keep her honour and her promises (1595). The end result demonstrates that, regardless of being the character of the highest social class in the tale, as a woman in the role of wife or romance heroine she is powerless, and therefore, placed at the mercy of Aurelius, a mere squire. Magic, or even the illusioun of magic, reveals that her social position as wife and lover, or wife and romance heroine leaves her vulnerable.

In trying to come to terms with the information which the use of magic reveals about Dorigen, it is important to note that the Franklin describes her behaviour in terms of its passion: "She moorneth, waketh, wayleth, fasteth, pleyneth" (819). The anxious reactions of her friends illustrate how out of proportion her passionate grief for Arveragus is: "They prechen hire, they telle hire nyght and day / That causelees she sleeth hirself, alas!"(824-5). Hansen suggests, that

> alone, unguarded by the repression of domestic bliss, Dorigen has dangerous and storyworthy powers. The very devotion to Arveragus that she so passionately expresses in his absence carries with it the possibility of something improper in a wife, as the power that courtly love would impute to the lady. When the narrator says, for instance that, "Desir of his presence hire so destreyneth / That al this wyde world she sette at noght" (820-821), he implies not only excessive but even inappropriate desire, insofar as he suggests that the lady too has a public self, a responsibility to the "this wyde world" which she willfully sets aside for love.[43]

Hansen further argues that the questioning of "God's wisdom" and the order of nature itself by Dorigen in her long protest against "the grisly rokkes blake" suggests the inappropriateness and irrationality of such intense desire in a woman (868, 865-93).[44]

These conclusions are strengthened by the irregular nature of Dorigen's and Arveragus' promises to each other of love without *maistrye*.[45] The Franklin describes a love without constraints as one in which

> ... freendes everych oother moot obeye,
> If they wol longe holden compaignye.
> Love wol nat been constreyned by maistrye.

---

[43] Hansen, *Gender*, 272. [44] Ibid., 272. [45] Block, *Medieval Misogyny*, 1-11.

Romance endings

> Whan maistre comth, the God of Love anon
> Beteth his wynges and farewel, he is gon!
> Love is a thyng as any spirit free.
> Wommen, of kynde, desiren libertee,
> And nat to been constreyned as a thral;
> And so doon men, if I sooth seyen shal.
>
> *(Franklin's Tale, 762–70)*

Lucas and Lucas argue that this type of rhetoric is associated with the *Roman de la Rose*, as well as the works of Ovid and the *Ovide Moralisé*.[46] Since Chaucer claims that his source is from the *lai* tradition, however, it is logical to examine any connections which might exist to that body of material. Traces of love without mastery can be found in Marie's *Yonec*, where the wife is given autonomy but only after securing a magic ring which forces her husband to treat her fairly. There is, however, a more striking example which bears a strong resemblance to the rhetoric of the Franklin in the *lai Equitan*:

> Ne me tenez mie pur rei,
> Mes pur vostre humme e vostre ami.
> Seürement vus jur e di
> Que jeo ferai vostre pleisir.
> Ne me laissiez pur vus murir!
> Vus seiez dame e jeo servanz,
> Vus orguilluse e jeo preianz.
>
> *(Equitan, 170–6)*

> Don't think of me as your king,
> but as your vassal and lover.
> I tell you, I promise you
> I'll do whatever you want.
> Don't let me die on your account!
> You be the lord and I'll be the servant –
> You the proud one and I'll be the begger![47]

Marie does not use this type of rhetoric to discuss the "appropriate" kind of love between husbands and wives as Chaucer did; quite on the contrary, she uses the rhetoric of freedom to lure wives into folly. The seducer in *Equitan*

---

[46] Lucas and Lucas, "Presentation of Marriage", 508–10. [47] *Equitan*, ed. Rychner, 38; *Equitan*, ed. Hanning and Ferrante, 64–5.

uses his "without mastery" speech to inveigle the wife of his loyal vassal into adultery. Hanning and Ferrante describe *Equitan* as an exemplary tale that demonstrates that those "who love irrationally, and excessively, court danger, for love prevents the lover from acting reasonably in the best of circumstances."[48]

When one has examined the literary/historical framework from which love without *maistrye* is derived, the Franklin's words take on a new meaning. What becomes clear is that Chaucer is developing a case for interpreting the passion between Dorigen and Arveragus as one which could be destructive. Fruitful comparisons can be made to the tales of Lancelot and Guenevere or Tristan and Iseut, in that Dorigen is driven to reckless extremes to try and bring Arveragus safely home. It is also useful to compare the relationship between Dorigen and Arveragus to the early love between Erec and Enide; in the *Erect et Enide* text the audience can see that passionate love is not necessarily tamed by the act of marriage, but instead, can be seen as an active cause of the destruction of wedlock.[49] The stress that Arveragus places on keeping their marriage private, as well as the terms upon which their marriage operates, may also find relevance against the backdrop of such twelfth-century texts as Capellanus' *The Art of Courtly Love*. Rule XIII claims that "When made public love rarely endures."[50] The Franklin's rhetoric of love, when examined against this type of source material, suggests that the marriage of Dorigen and Arveragus may be suffering from too much passion.

This conclusion is verified by what the magical test reveals about Dorigen's areas of vulnerability; firstly, she must not reveal the nature of the love which exists between herself and her husband; and secondly, she must try and save her husband from any potential danger. These two needs have placed her in a position in which she must make a promise to Aurelius when he declares his love for her, or she will not be able to maintain her public face and position as a courtly figure. It is her overwhelming passion for Arveragus, however, that ensures that she makes a promise to Aurelius which she thinks could never be realised.[51] This conclusion is supported by the nature of the promise that clearly seeks to keep Arveragus from harm. Chaucer, however, deliberately blurs and problematises the description of this event to complicate the text:

[48] *Lais*, ed. Hanning and Ferrante, 69. [49] "Even more evils than this may be noticed in love, for love wickedly breaks up marriage and without reason turns a husband from his wife, whom God, in the law He gave us, firmly bade not to separate from her husband." A. Capellanus, *The Art of Courtly Love*, ed. and trans. John Jay Perry (New York: Columbia University Press, 1990) 196. [50] Ibid., 185. [51] Duby defines the lady's role as both "judge and prize" in the game of love: "like her husband, she has to be generous. She had to give of herself by degrees. Her largesse seemed as necessary

> But after that *in pley* thus seyde she:
> "Aurelie," quod she, 'by heighe God above,
> Yet wolde I graunte yow to been youre love,
> Syn I yow se so pitously complayne.
> Looke what day that endelong Britayne
> Ye remoeve alle the rokkes, stoon by stoon."
>
> (*Franklin's Tale*, 988–93, my italics)[52]

In problematising Dorigen's delivery of this promise, Chaucer sets the audience the complicated task of trying to decipher the Franklin's motivation for assigning Dorigen this choice of words.

This treatment is in direct contrast to the handling of the plot and the magic by Boccaccio in the *Filocolo*. Boccaccio uses a magical test to force his characters to come to terms with their values, their ideals and the relationships they hold dear, rather than those deemed acceptable by society. Thus one must honour the decision of Gilberto; as he himself says, it is perhaps a choice no other man would make, but he allows his wife honourably to fulfil her promise because she made it with the purest of intentions.[53] The essential difference between Boccaccio and Chaucer is that Boccaccio has his characters explicitly state the intentions which direct their actions. For example, in *Filocolo* Madonna Dianora says to herself: "It is an impossible thing to do, and that is how I shall get free of him."[54] Boccaccio even has the lover admit that these are the probable intentions of his mistress, but he proceeds in spite of her lack of regard.

Aurelius is perhaps the only character who bears any resemblance to his Italian source. He uses magic to obtain Dorigen, despite the clear discouragement which she offers in him in the forms of a verbal warning not to love the property of someone else (1004–5), and an "impossible" quest (995–7). Aurelius should never have had a moral or social claim to Dorigen, but he believed, not unlike Tristan or Lancelot, that love gave him the right to take her anyway. That Chaucer actively tries to limit the negative associations of *magyk* surrounding Aurelius is clear from the alterations he makes to the *Filocolo*; in that text, the lover goes directly to the magician to seek help in capturing his love.[55] In this tale, the squire's brother organises the use of magic, thereby helping to deflect any of the

---

as that of her lord and master." Duby, *Love and Marriage*, 72. **52** Italics have been added to stress how dramatic a difference these two words make to the entire reading of the tale. **53** Boccaccio, *Il Filocolo* in *Chaucer's Boccaccio: Sources of Troilus, The Knight's and The Franklin's Tales*, ed. and trans., Nicholas Havely (Cambridge: D.S. Brewer, 1980) 158. **54** Ibid., 155. **55** Ibid., 155.

immoral associations from Aurelius.[56] *Magyk* and *illusioun* are not, however, the appropriate avenue to love, and it does discredit Aurelius that he takes advantage of them to try to get what he wants. The intention of using an *illusioun* to force Dorigen into adultery serves to reveal far more about his inability to love, and the twisted nature of his passion, than it does about Dorigen's intentions in making her *biheeste*.

What Aurelius' encounter with magic reveals is the very inappropriate nature of his love for Dorigen. The strong association between *illusioun* and the realisation of what he thinks is love for Dorigen immediately makes his love suspect. For the majority of this tale, the Franklin means the word *illusioun* to be understood in terms of its secondary definition "deception (usually of the senses or imagination)"; in this instance, however, the term *illusioun* should be evaluated in terms of its primary meaning as well, which is: "Mockery, scorning derision".[57] This could mean that it is not love from which Aurelius is suffering but *amor heroes*, an excessive or pseudo love, of which death can be the ultimate outcome. The disease is described by Capellanus in these terms: "Love is a certain inborn suffering (*passio*), derived from the sight of and excessive meditation upon the beauty of the opposite sex, which causes each one to wish above all things the embraces of the other and by *common desire* to carry out all of love's precepts in the other's embrace."[58] Dorigen does not consent without duress to the proposition of Aurelius, but this does not seem to be taken into account in the Franklin's moral analysis of him. Gerard of Berry in his glosses on the *Viaticum* writes of *fin' amors*: "This disease (*passio*) ... is very similar to melancholy, because the entire attention and thought, aided by desire, is fixed on the beauty of some form or figure" (2.8.48).[59] These descriptions of lovesickness are very reminiscent of the squire's suffering:

> For wel I woot my servyce is in vayn;
> My gerdon is but brestyng of myn herte.
> Madame, reweth upon my peynes smerte;
> For with a word ye may me sleen or save.
> Heere at youre feet God wolde that I were grave!

---

56 In fact, the criticism for malicious intent is placed squarely on Aurelius' brother when he reveals his motives for finding the clerk: "Thanne were my brother warisshed of his wo;/Thanne moste she nedes holden hire biheste,/Or elles he shal shame hire atte leeste" (1162–4). 57 *Illusioun, MED*, 1975 edn. 58 *Art of Courtly Love*, ed. Parry, 28. My italics. 59 Gerard of Berry, *Glosule on the Viaticum* (Cambridge: St John's College D. 24 (99)) as cited in Wack, *Lovesickness*, 62.

> I ne have as now no leyser moore to seye;
> Have mercy, sweete, or ye wol do me deye!
>
> (*Franklin's Tale*, 972–8)

Lovesickness was certainly something with which Chaucer was familiar, as it was commonly written about in medical texts and romances; he describes it at length in the *Knight's Tale* (1373–5).[60] Ironically, Aurelius' commissioning of the clerk's services suggests that his greatest weakness is the nature of the twisted passion which drives him to pay for a magical way to force Dorigen to comply to his desires. Aurelius believes that magic will give him power over Dorigen, which it does; however, it also makes him vulnerable to one of an even lower social order: the clerk. Aurelius' unnatural desire for Dorigen pushes him to employ unnatural methods to obtain her, which results in him being "unnaturally" subject to one of a lower social class.

It is, of course, the very property of *illusioun* or *magyk* which makes what is unnatural or unreal *seem* real that makes it such an appropriate partner to noble love and its by-product, *amor heroes*. Characters need the power of illusion to make the demands of *amor heroes* or even noble love, for that matter, seem possible. The awkwardness of trying to be simultaneously a courtly romance hero (a standard of perfection and love which is set by literary ideals) and a husband is demonstrated in the two-fold response of Arveragus to the news of the predicament Dorigen faces. The first response is a kind but inappropriately nonchalant reaction:

> This housbande with glad chiere in freendly wyse
> Answerde and seyde as I shal yow devyse:
> "Is ther ought elles, Dorigen, but this?"
>
> "Ye wyf," quod he, "lat slepen that is stille."
>
> (*Franklin's Tale*, 1467–8, 1472)

This response can be contrasted to his tears and then rage which follow shortly after (1480–84). Arveragus demands that Dorigen maintain her honour, as he believes that "Trouthe is the hyeste thyng that man may kepe" (1479). Brewer and Patterson both suggest that this is a moment when Arveragus illustrates that *trouthe* is "an internal condition, a sense of integrity specific to the individual and wholly within his or her keeping".[61]

---

60 Wack, *Lovesickness*, 6.   61 Lee Patterson, *Chaucer and the Subject of History* (Madison: University of Wisconsin Press, 1991) 196. D.S. Brewer, "Honour and Chaucer", *Essays and Studies* 26 (1973): 4, 17–18.

However, the depth of Arveragus' need to keep his cuckolding private suggests the opposite; he is desperate to the point that he forbids Dorigen, "up peyne of deeth", ever to reveal what has happened (1481). It is important to him that he maintain both his private and public sense of honour. The shocking nature of this entire exchange is further enhanced by the apologies of the Franklin to his audience, on behalf of Arveragus:

> Paraventure an heep of yow, ywis,
> Wol holden hym a lewed man in this
> That he wol putte his wyf in jupartie.
> Herkneth the tale er ye upon hire crie.
> She may have bettre fortune than yow semeth;
> And whan that ye han herd the tale, demeth.
>
> (*Franklin's Tale*, 1493–8)

The knight is not given access to magic or the ability to dispel the illusion, so he remains ineffective. However, the use of magic has revealed Arveragus' vulnerabilities, which are that his passion has led him into promises to his wife that have resulted in his being potentially humiliated.

The awkward, contradictory, and even at times inexplicable actions of Arveragus make sense at an emotional level. His intense reactions combined with paralysis are the result of too passionate a love for Dorigen. This is the kind of mesmerising and paralysing emotion which Lancelot suffered when near Guenevere, and it would explain what is at the heart of Arveragus' inaction. His love, it would seem, is as passionate as that of Dorigen, in that he will go to equally extreme lengths to see that she is honourable. This leaves Dorigen to face her enemy while Arveragus stays home, passive, yet fearful that their disgraces will spell the end of his world. This ironic twist to the traditional romance comes at the culminating moment of the tale. It is interesting that normally in the romance tradition, it is through asserting himself at marvellous trials that a hero regains his social position and learns to balance his love with his social obligations. This is not the case in this romance; once Arveragus is faced with a magically-induced trial (an emotional test, as opposed to a physical one) he is forced to rely upon the "goodness" of Aurelius and the word of Dorigen to keep quiet about events which might transpire. Chaucer's use of a magical trial reveals Arveragus to be emotionally and socially vulnerable, but does not give him a means of rectifying that situation. There is no magical ford to be crossed or Excalibur to be found which will assert his position in society; instead, he is at the mercy of Aurelius and Dorigen for his standing in the community. In the "happy ending" his vulnerability is simply ignored; Aurelius sees Dorigen's distress and takes pity, which means he has the power to choose to take her or not. Considering the fact that he did not actually move the rocks, this type of power over Dorigen and Arveragus seems unfair, regardless of whether or not he actually took advantage of it. The fact that he chose to dole out mercy does not make him noble, contrary to the Franklin's opinion, just less manipulative and dishonest. The ramifications of this situation leave the audience wondering about the nature of a happy ending which leaves so many of its characters vulnerable to such injustices.

MAGIC AND SOCIETY

The place of magic in the political sphere of the fourteenth-century world makes necessary the analysis of its function on another level: the serious social and political ramifications of the conclusion in this tale. In a world constructed upon the divisions between social classes, the conclusion of the *Franklin's Tale* has far-reaching implications.

Chaucer uses magic to enable a demonstration of what would happen if a social structure based on noble action, as endorsed by the Franklin, were adopted. Chaucer holds up the Franklin's conclusion for examination by the audience, by choosing to *seem* to support the overly exalted positions of both the clerk and the squire at the end of the tale. In allowing all the male characters to be evaluated in terms of their nobility, Chaucer does something quite different with the romance format. He does not reaffirm the structures of the social and political status quo; instead, he *seems* to be supportive of a new type of society in which men class-climb as a result of their actions.

In the scheme of the Franklin, one can see how through magic Aurelius acquires control over Arveragus and Dorigen, his social superiors. As the story continues, what one finds is that a clerk, the lowliest of all the characters in the social structure and the purveyor of *japes* and man-made magic tricks, acquires a moral hold over the characters in the tale. In building such a conclusion on the power of an *illusioun*, Chaucer invalidates the Franklin's premise, which is that men should be judged by their actions. The rocks, by the Franklin's own admission, were never moved, therefore neither the actions of the squire nor the clerk are morally justified. In this way, Chaucer demonstrates that regardless of how fair and just the social system of the Franklin may sound, beneath the illusion of "fair practice" the entire social structure would be vulnerable to the intemperate aspirations of squires and the magical abilities of clerks. When the *illusioun* is removed, what one finds is that the Franklin asks who is *mooste fre*: Arveragus the conflicted and passionate knight, Aurelius the newly-reformed, would-be adulterer, or the Clerk d'Orliens, the maker of trick and illusions.

Magic in this context evokes a potentially explosive debate concerning social status and the qualifications for entry into the ranks of the political and influential. Chaucer achieves this effect in his text through mixing the use of illusion and magic; since one is never sure of the boundaries between what is real and not real, all options must be explored. However, that Chaucer builds this text upon the power of magic and *illusioun* leads one to suspect that such issues are relevant to an audience beyond that of the pilgrims. Kieckhefer's research explores exactly such possibilities; he argues that the courts were filled with tension and competition between courtiers without formal positions, and therefore in need of seeking favour, and nobles with formal positions who also required royal favour to maintain their status. In such a situation sorcery and magic became a means of seeking royal power. Kieckhefer claims that "courtly society was ridden with magic and the fear of magic".[62] Thus this use of magic in the *Franklin's Tale* would accurately reflect the real misgivings of Chaucer's contemporaries concerning the fact that magic, or the illusion of magic, could be used as a means of achieving influence in politics, or the wider community, where that power was not merited.

Whether the conclusion of the *Franklin's Tale* is based on *magyk* or the *illusioun* of magic, Chaucer creates a romance that reflects the serious nature of political change and social unrest. In this format, the romance form does not validate the establishment as it stands; rather it questions on the most basic of levels the nature of social classes and the institutions which create them. What better preparation for the complexities of the Reformation and the Age of the Renaissance yet to come?

THE FUNCTION OF MAGIC IN ROMANCE

The crucial underpinning of this study is the partial rehabilitation of magic in medieval Europe. Magic was condemned for links to heresy and demonology, while simultaneously being absorbed into Christianity and secular society. Its presence was felt across a wide spectrum of medieval life, from the simplest healers in the smallest of towns to the council chambers

---

[62] Kieckhefer, *Magic*, 96. For further discussion see Peters, *The Magician*, 49, 110–25.

of nobles and kings. Once the reader comprehends that marvels and magic, as Kelly states, "were deemed possible", it places their use and the romances in a different light; a genre which was once considered by critics to be of little value or simply light entertainment takes on a new depth of meaning and interpretative scope.[63]

The important role of magic in medieval society is mirrored by its crucial place in the literature of the period. In understanding and appreciating how romance writers carefully manipulated it, one is exposed not simply to a story of *aventure* but to a political and social analysis of some of the most important facets of medieval culture. The function of magic in society and in literature, is the key to understanding how a story comprised of fairy-tale heroes, martial challenges, and marvellous encounters, is transformed by the willing audience into a commentary upon the meaning of loyalty, love, faith, and honour. Once the modern reader has accepted the importance of magic, the romances may be examined for their contribution not only to how we should understand medieval society, but also, and more importantly, to how it understood itself.

Magic from the twelfth-century world of Chrétien to the fourteenth-century world of Chaucer provided the key to exploring the "real" through the lens of the fantasy of romance. The links of magic to the interests of the intellectual, social, and religious spheres of influence from the twelfth century through to the fourteenth, paved the way for the romances to remain a vibrant and pertinent genre, ever-changing in its details, but always retaining the core formula of characters being evaluated through magical trials and love being the source of endless joy and misery.

Magic as used in the *Historia* of Geoffrey of Monmouth allowed the introduction of a moral but socially-influenced system of evaluation into the romances. This meant that the inflexible and slow-to-change rigours of Catholic dogma could be used in the romances as a form of moral authority, but that it did not have to be the only source of evaluating right or wrong. With the use of magic as a means to evaluate the actions of characters, the door was left open for authors and audiences to engage in changing ideas, new value systems, and the exploration of the human soul.

In beginning this study with Chrétien the "Father of Arthurian Romance", and ending it with Chaucer, the "Father of English Poetry", it is possible to see that the romance form in general, and the function of magic in particular, engaged and intrigued some of the greatest minds of the medieval period.

---

63 Kelly, *Art*, 91.

Bibliography

PRIMARY TEXTS

Abelard, Peter. *Ethics*. Ed. and trans. D.E. Luscombe. Oxford: Clarendon Press, 1971.

Agrippa, H.C. *Three Books of Occult Philosophy*. Trans. J. Freake. London, 1651.

Alanus de Insulis. *De planctu Naturae*. Ed. Nikolaus M. Haring. *Studi medievali* 19 (1978): 797–879.

Alexander (*Le Roman de Toute Chevalerie*) Thomas of Kent. Ed. B. Foster & I. Short, Anglo-Norman Text Society XXIX–XXXI (London 1976 for 1971–3).

Alighieri, Dante. *The Inferno*. Trans. John Ciardi. New York: Mentor Books, 1952.

—— *Il Convivio*. Ed. and trans. Christopher Ryan. Saratoga: Anma Libri, 1989.

—— *The Banquet*. Ed. and trans. Christopher Ryan. Saratoga: Anma Libri, 1990.

Ambrose. *De Officiis*. In *Patrologia Latina*. Vol. 16. Ed. J.P. Migne. Paris, 1878–90. 163–4.

Aquinas, Thomas. *Summa contra gentiles*. Ed. and trans. The Dominican Fathers. The Leonine edn. 3 vols. London: Burns, Oates and Washbourne, 1923–29.

—— "Divine Government". In *Summa theologiae* (1a 2ae 103–109). Ed. and trans. T.C. O'Brian. 60 vols. London: Blackfriars: Eyre and Spottiswoode, 1970.

—— "God's Will and Providence". In *Summa theologiae* (1a 19–26). Ed. and trans. Thomas Gilby, O.P. 60 vols. New York and London: Blackfriars: Eyre and Spottiswoode: McGraw Hill, 1964.

—— "Superstition and Irreverence". In *Summa theologiae* (2a 2ae 92–100). Ed. and trans. T.F. O'Meara. 60 vols. London: Blackfriars: Eyre and Spottiswoode, 1968.

—— "The World Order". In *Summa theologiae* (1a 25 110–119). Ed. and trans. M.J. Charlesworth. 60 vols. London: Blackfriars: Eyre and Spottiswoode, 1970.

Aristotle. *The Nicomachean Ethics*. Trans. David Ross. London: Oxford University Press, 1925.

—— *The Works of Aristotle*. Ed. W.D. Ross. 12 vols. New York: Oxford University Press, 1942.

—— "Rhetorica". Trans. W.R. Roberts. Vol. 11. In *The Works of Aristotle*. Ed. W.D. Ross. 12 vols. Oxford: Oxford University Press, 1912–52.

Augustine. *Against the Academics*. Trans. M.P. Garvey. Milwaukee: Marquette University Press, 1942.

—— *The Heresies*. Trans. L.G. Müller. In Catholic University of America Patristic Studies. Vol. XC. Washington D.C.: Catholic University of America Press, 1956

—— *De civitate Dei*. Ed. and trans. David Wiesen. 3 vols. London: Heinemann, 1968.
—— *The Confessions of St Augustine*. Trans. Sherwood E. Wirt. Grand Rapids: Lion Publishing, 1978.
—— *Concerning the city of God against the pagans*. Trans. Henry Bettenson. London: Penguin, 1984.
Bacon, Roger. *Opus majus*. Trans. R.B. Burke. 2 vols. Philadelphia, 1928.
Bale, John. *Select Works of John Bale*. Ed. H. Christmas. Cambridge: Parker Society, 1849.
Bede. *Historia ecclesiastica gentis Anglorum* (*A History of the English Church and People*). Trans. Leo Sherley-Price. London: Penguin Classics, 1955.
Bernart von Ventadorn. *Seine Lieder*. Ed. C. Apel. Halle: Niemeyer, 1915.
Beroul. *The Romance of Tristran*. Trans. Alan S. Fedrick. London: Penguin Classics, 1970.
The Birth of Romance: An Anthology. Ed. and trans. Judith Weiss. London: Everyman, 1992.
Boccaccio, Giovanni. *Tutte le Opere di Giovanni Boccaccio*. Ed. Antonio Enzo Quagli. Gen. ed. Vittore Braca. Vol. 1. Verona: Mondadori, 1967.
—— *The Decameron*. Trans. G.H. McWilliam. London: Penguin Classics, 1972.
—— *Il Filocolo* Trans. G.H. McWilliam. London: Penguin Classics, 1972.
—— *Il Filocolo*. In *Chaucer's Boccaccio: Sources of Troilus, The Knight's and The Franklin's Tales*. Ed. and trans. Nicholas Havely. Cambridge: D.S. Brewer, 1980.
Boethius. *De consolatione philosophae*. Ed. Adrianvs A. Forti Scvto, S.T.D. London: Burns, Oates & Washbourne, 1925.
—— *Consolation of Philosophy*. Ed. and trans. V.E. Watts. London: Penguin Classics, 1969.
Book of the Knight of the Tower. Trans. W. Caxton. Ed. M.Y. Offerd. Early English Text Society (s.s., 2) 1971.
Book of Vices and Virtues. Ed. W. Francis. Early English Text Society (o.s., 217). London: Oxford University Press, 1942.
Burchard of Worms. *Decretum*. In *Patrologia Latina*. Vol. 140. Ed. J.P. Migne. Paris, 1878–90.
—— *Medieval Handbooks of Penance: A Translation of the Principal Libri Poenitentiales*. Ed. and trans. John McNeill and Helena M. Gamer. New York: Columbia University Press, 1938. 314–45.
Burton, Robert. *Anatomy of Melancholy*. Ed. A.R. Shilleto. London: G. Bell and Sons, 1923.
Capellanus, Andreas. *The Art of Courtly Love*. Ed. and trans. J.J. Parry. New York: Columbia University Press, 1990.
Caradoc of Llancarvan, *Two Lives of Gildas*. Ed. and trans. Hugh Williams. Wales: Llanerch Enterprises, 1990.
Charles de Fresne. *Glossarium ad scriptores mediae et infimae Latinitatis* IV. Early English Text Society. London, 1885.
Chaucer, Geoffrey. *The Franklin's Tale*. In *The Riverside Chaucer*. Gen. ed. L. Benson. Third edn. Boston: Houghton Mifflin, 1987.

Chestre, Thomas. *Sir Launfal.* Ed. A.J. Bliss. London: Thomas Nelson & Sons, 1960.
Chrétien de Troyes. *Christian von Troyes. Sämtliche Werke*, Ed. Wendelin Foerster, 5 vols. Paris: Halle, 1884–99, 1932.
—— *Le Chavalier au Lion:* (*Yvain*). Ed. Wendelin Foerster. *C. von T. Sämtliche Werke.* Vol. II, 1899; and in Romanische Bibliothek V, 2nd Halle, 1912; 3rd edn. Ed. T.B.W. Reid. Manchester: Manchester University Press, 1942; 4rd edn. Ed. Mario Roques. C.F.M.A. 89. Paris: Champion, 1964.
—— *Le Chevalier de la Charrete*: (*Lancelot*). Ed. Wendelin Foerster. *C. von T. Sämtliche Werke.* Vol. IV, 1899; 2nd edn. Ed. Mario Roques. C.F.M.A., 86. Paris: Champion, 1965.
—— *Cligés*: Ed. Wendelin Foerster. *C. von T. Sämtliche Werke.* Vol. I, 1884; and in Romanische Bibliothek I. Halle, 1921; 3rd edn. Ed. Alexandre Micha. C.F.M.A., 84. Paris: Champion, 1970.
—— *Le Conte Du Graal:* (*Perceval*). Ed. Wendelin Foerster. *C. von T. Sämtliche Werke.* Vol. V, 1889; 2nd edn. Ed. Mario Roques. C.F.M.A. Paris: Champion, 1971; 3rd edn. Ed. William Roach. Genève: Librairie Droz, 1959; 4th edn. Ed. Felix Lecoy. 2 vols. C.F.M.A. Paris: Champion, 1972–5.
—— *Erec et Enide.* Ed. Wendelin Foerster. *C. von T. Sämtliche Werke.* Vol. III. 1890; and in Romanische Bibliothek XIII, Halle, 1896; 3rd edn. Ed. Mario Roques. C.F.M.A., 80. Paris: Champion, 1977.
—— *D'Amors qui m'a tolu a moi.* Ed. C. Bartsch. In L.T. Topsfield. *Chrétien de Troyes: A Study of Arthurian Romances.* Cambridge: Cambridge University Press, 1981.
—— *Arthurian Romances.* Ed. and trans. D.D.R. Owen. London: J.M. Dent and Sons, 1987.
Clementine Homilies (V, iii-iv). Ed. and trans. T. Smith. Edinburgh, 1870.
Die nordische und die englische Version der Tristan-Sage. Ed. E. Kölbing. Zweiter Teil. 3 vols. Heilbronn, 1882; 2nd edn. 1985.
Eusebius. *Pamphili. Ecclesiastical History.* Trans. R.J. Deferrari. Vols. XIX and XXIX. Ed. R.J. Deferrari. New York: Fathers of the Church, 1953–5.
Fletcher, J. *The Chances.* Vol. VI. Early English Text Society. London, 1647.
Floriant et Florete. Ed. Harry F. Williams. Ann Arbor: University of Michigan Press, 1947.
Froissart. *Chronicles.* Trans. G. Brereton. London: Penguin Classics, 1978.
Geoffrey of Monmouth. *Gesta regum Anglorum.* Ed. Bishop Stubbs. 2 vols. Rolls Series, 1887–89.
—— *Historia regum Britanniae.* Ed. Acton Griscom. New York: Longmans Green, 1929.
—— *The History of the Kings of England.* Trans. Lewis Thorpe. London: Penguin Classics, 1966.
Gerard of Berry. *Glosule on Viaticum.* Cambridge: St John's College D.24 (99).
Gervase of Tilbury. "Otia imperialia". In *Scriptores rerum brunsvicensium.* Ed. G.W. Leibnitz. Vol. 1. Hanover, 1707.

Gildas. *De excidio et conquestu Britanniae* in Medieval and Renaissance Studies. Trans. T.E. Mommsen. Ed. Eugene F. Rice. Ithaca: Cornell University Press, 1959.

Gottfried von Strassburg. *Tristan und Isolde*. Ed. Herman Kurtz. Stuttgart, 1877.

—— *Tristan und Isolt*. Ed. August Closs. Oxford: Basil Blackwell, 1947.

—— *Tristan with the 'Tristan' of Thomas*. Ed. and trans. A.T. Hatto. London: Penguin Classics, 1960.

—— *Gottfried von Strassburg's Tristan*. Ed. Gottfried Weber. Darmstadt: Wissenschaftliche Buchgesellschaft, 1967.

—— *Tristan*. Ed. Reinhold Bechstein and Peter Ganz. 2 vols. Wiesbaden: F.A. Brockhaus, 1978.

Gower, John. *The English Works of John Gower*. 2 vols. Ed. G.C. Macaulay. Early English Text Society, 81. London: Oxford University Press, 1900.

—— *Confessio Amantis*. Ed. Russell A. Peck. London and Toronto: University of Toronto Press, 1980.

Guillaume de Dole. *Works*. Ed. G. Servois. Paris, 1893.

Guillaume de Lorris and Jean de Meun. *Le Roman de la Rose*. Ed. Felix Lecoy. 3 vols. C.F.M.A. 92, 95, 98. Paris: Champion, 1970.

—— *The Romance of the Rose*. Trans. Charles Dahlberg. Hanover and London: University Press of New England, 1971.

Hale, W.H. "A Series of Precedents and Proceedings in Criminal Cases, extending from the year 1475 to 1640". In *Act-Books of Ecclesiastical Courts in the Diocese of London*. London, 1847.

Havelok the Dane. Ed. G.V. Smithers. Oxford: Clarendon Press, 1987.

Henry of Huntingdon. *Historia Anglorum*. Ed. Thomas Arnold. London: Longman, 1879.

—— *Historia Anglorum*. Trans. Thomas Forester. London: Bohn, 1853.

Hildegard of Bingen. *Scivias*. Trans. Mother Columba Hart and Jane Bishop. New York: Paulist Press, 1990.

Huon de Bordeaux. Ed. Pierre Ruelle. Université Libre de Bruxelles: Travaux de la Faculté de Philosophie et Lettres, 20. Brussels: Presses Universitaires de Bruxelles; Paris: Presses Universitaires de France, 1961.

Joinville and Villehardouin. *Chronicles of the Crusade*. Trans. M.R.B. Shaw. London: Penguin Classics, 1963.

John of Salisbury. *Policratius: The Statesman's Book of John of Salisbury*. Trans. J. Dickinson. New York: Knopf, 1927.

King Horn. Ed. J.B. Hall. Oxford: Oxford University Press, 1901.

Kyng Alisaunder. Ed. G.V. Smithers, Early English Text Society Original Series CCXXVII, CCXXXVII (London, 1952, 1957).

Langland, William. *The Vision of Piers Plowman*. Ed. A.V.C. Schmidt. London: Oxford University Press, 1978. 2nd edn. 1992.

Lay Folk's Catechism. Ed. T.F. Simmons. Early English Text Society. Oxford: Clarendon Press, 1901.

Liber visionum: London, British Library, Additional 18027.

Livy. *History of Rome (ab urbe condita libre)*. Trans. B. Foster. New York: Putnam, 1959.

Bibliography

Lybeaus Desconus. Ed. Maldwyn Mills. Early English Text Society 261. London: 1969.

Maddicott, J.R. "Parliament and the Constituencies." In *English Parliament in the Middle Ages.* Ed. R.G. Davis and J.H. Denton. Manchester: Manchester University Press, 1981.

Mannyng of Brunne, Robert. *Handlyng Synne.* Ed. F.J. Furnivall. Early English Text Society (o.s., 119, 123). London: Eyre and Spottiswoode, 1887. 2nd edn. 1901.

—— *Handlyng Synne.* Ed. Idelle Sullens. Binghamton, New York: Medieval and Renaissance Texts and Studies, 1983.

Marie de France. *The Lais of Marie de France.* Ed. A. Evert. Oxford: Basil Blackwell, 1944.

—— Ed. Jean Rychner. Paris: Champion, 1966.

—— Ed. and trans. Robert Hanning and Joan Ferrante. Durham: The Labyrinth Press, 1978.

—— Ed. Laurence Harf-Lancner. Paris: Livre de Poche, 1990.

Medieval Handbooks of Penance: A Translation of the Principal libri poenitentiales. Ed. and trans. John McNeill and Helena M. Gamer. New York: Columbia University Press, 1938.

Nennius. *History of the Britons.* Ed. and trans. A.W. Wade-Evans. London: Society for the Promotion of Christian Knowledge, 1938.

Ovid. *The Erotic Poems.* Trans. Peter Green. London: Penguin Classics, 1982.

Pliny. *Natural History.* Trans. D.E. Eichholz. 10 vols. Cambridge, Mass.: Harvard University Press, 1962.

Plato. *The Dialogues of Plato.* Ed. and trans. Benjamin Jowett. 4 vols. Oxford: Oxford University Press, 1953.

Polo, Marco. *Mirabilia uniuscuisque provinciase.* Ed. Giorgio Manganelli. Roma: Riuniti, 1981.

—— *The Travels of Marco Polo.* Ed. and trans. Teresa Waugh. London: Sidgwick and Jackson, 1984.

Rabanus. *Poenitentiale ad heribaldum* xxv, xxx. In *Patrologia Latina.* Vol. 110. Ed. J.P. Migne. Paris, 1878-90. 467-94, 1090-110.

The Romance of Horn by Thomas, Ed. MK. Pope, rev. T.B.W. Reid, Anglo-Norman Text Society XII-XIII (Oxford, 1964), vol. II.

Sir Gawain and the Green Knight. Ed. J.R.R. Tolkien & E.V. Gordon. 1925. 2nd edn. Ed. Norman Davis, Oxford: Oxford University Press, 1967.

—— Ed. Sir Frederick Madden. *Sir Gawayne* (1839; rpt.) New York: AMS Press, 1971.

—— Ed. J.A. Burrow. London: Penguin, 1972.

Sir Launfal. Ed. A.J. Bliss. London: Thomas Nelson and Son, 1960.

—— *Middle English Metrical Romances.* Gen. ed. Walter Hoyt French and Charles Brockway Halle. 2 vols. New York: Russell, 1964.

Sir Tristrem. Ed. G.P. McNeill. Scottish Texts Society. Vol. 8. Edinburgh, 1885-86.

—— *Die nordische und die englische Version der Tristan-Sage.* Ed. E. Kölbing, Zweiter Teil. Heilbronn, 1882. 2nd edn., 1985.
Six Middle English Romances. Ed. M. Mills. London: Everyman Publishers, 1973.
Syr Landevale. Ed. A. J. Bliss. London: Thomas Nelson & Sons, 1960.
Thomas. *Les Fragments du Tristan de Thomas.* Ed. Bartina H. Wind. London: Leydon, 1950.
—— *Tristan and the 'Tristan' of Thomas.* Ed. and trans. A.T. Hatto. London: Penguin Classics, 1960.
—— *Die nordische und die englische Version der Tristan-Sage.* Ed. E. Kölbing, Zweiter Teil. Heilbronn, 1882, 2nd edn., 1985.
—— *Thomas of Britain.* Ed. Stewart Gregory. New York: Garland Publishing, 1991.
—— *Le Roman de Tristan par Thomas.* Ed. Joseph Bédier, 2 vols. SATF, 46 (Paris, 1902, 1905).
Thucydides. *History of the Peloponnesian War.* Trans. Rex Warner. Baltimore: Penguin Books, 1954.
Tristan and Isolt. Ed. Basil Blackwell, Blackwell's German Texts. Oxford: Blackwell Press, 1979.
Virgil. *Aeneid.* In *Works.* Trans. H. Rushton Fairclough. 2 vols. Cambridge, Mass.: Harvard University Press, 1950.
Vaughan, W. *The Golden Groove.* London, 1600.
Wace. *Le Roman de Brut de Wace.* Ed. Ivor Arnold. S.A.T.F., 2 vols. Paris: Picard, 1938–40.
—— *Le Roman de Rou.* Ed. A.J. Holder. S.A.T.F. Paris: Picard, 1970–3.
—— *Roman de Brut, A History of the British: Text and Translation.* Ed. and trans. Judith Weiss. London: University of Exeter Press, 1999.
Ward, H.L.D. Ed. *Catalogue of Romances.* London, 1883.
William of Malmesbury. *Chronicles of the Kings of England.* Trans. John Sharpe. Revised J.A. Giles. London: George Bell, 1904.
William of Newburgh. "Writings." In Benoit Lacroix. "*L'historien au moyen âge.*" Conference Albert-le-Grand. Montreal: Institut d'Études Médiévales. Paris: Vrin, 1966.
Ywain and Gawain. Ed. A.B. Friedman and Norman T. Harrington. Oxford: Oxford University Press, 1964.
Ywain and Gawain. Ed. Malywyn Mills. London: Everyman, 1992.

DICTIONARIES

Davis, Norman and Douglas, Gray. Ed. *A Chaucer Glossary.* Oxford: Clarendon Press, 1979.
Drosdowski, Gunther. *Duden Deutsches Wörtebuch.* Mannheim and Wien: Bibliographisches Institut, 1977–81.
Funk and Wagnalls. *Standard Dictionary of Folklore, Mythology & Legend.* Ed. Maria Leach. San Francisco: Harper Collins, 1984.

Godefroy, Frédéric. *Dictionnaire de l'ancienne langue française et de tous les dialectes du IXe au XVe siècle*. Paris: Vieweg, Boullion, 1881–1902.
Grimm and Grimm, ed. *Deutsches Wortebuch*. Leipzig: Verlag von S. Hirzel, 1960–.
Köbler, Gerhard et al. *Worterbuch des Althochdeutschen Sprachschatzes*. Leipzig: Schöningh, 1960.
Kurath, Hans et al. *Middle English Dictionary*. Ann Arbor: University of Michigan Press, 1952–.
Murray, J.H., et al. *Oxford English Dictionary*. Oxford: Clarendon Press, 1933.
Simpson, J.A., et al. *Second Oxford English Dictionary*. Oxford: Clarendon Press, 1989.
Spalding, Keith. *A Historical Dictionary of German Figurative Usage*. 23 vols. Oxford: Basil Blackwell, 1968–.

SECONDARY TEXTS

Ackerman, Robert "English Rimed and Prose Romance". In *Arthurian Literature in the Middle Ages*. Ed. R.S. Loomis. Oxford: Clarendon Press, 1959.
Adolf, Helen. "Althochdeutschen Sprache". *Journal of German and English Philology* 46 (1947): 300–310.
Aers, David. *Community, Gender and Individual Identity in the Middle Ages*. New York & London: Routledge, 1988.
Aijmer, Karin. "The Semantic Development of the Will". In *Historical Semantics, Historical Word Formation*. Ed. Jacek Fisiak. New York: Mouton, 1985. 1–21.
Andreas, James. "'Newe Science' from 'Olde Bokes': A Bakhtinian Approach to *The Summoner's Tale*". *Chaucer Review* 25: 2 (1990): 138–51.
Armstrong, Elizabeth Psakis. "The Patient Woman in Chaucer's *Clerk's Tale* and Marie de France's *Fresne*". *Centennial Review* Summer, 34 (1990): 433–48.
Aspland, A. *A Medieval French Reader*. Oxford: Clarendon Press, 1979.
Astell, Ann W. *The Song of Songs in the Middle Ages*. Ithaca: Cornell University Press, 1990.
—— *Chaucer and the Universe of Learning*. Ithaca and London: Cornell University Press, 1997.
Auerbach, Erec. *Mimesis: The Representation of Reality in Western Literature*. Trans. Willard B. Trask. Princeton: Princeton University Press, 1968.
Bakhtin, Mikhail. *The Dialogic Imagination: Four Essays*. Trans. Carol Emerson. Ed. Michael Holquist. Austin and London: University of Texas Press, 1981.
—— and P.M. Medvedev. *The Formal Method in Literary Scholarship*. Ed. Albert J. Wehrle. Cambridge: Harvard University Press, 1985.
Barnes, Geraldine. *Counsel and Strategy in the Middle English Romance*. Cambridge: D.S. Brewer, 1993.
Barron, W.R.J. *Sir Gawain and the Green Knight*. Manchester University Press, 1974.
—— *Trawthe and Treason, The Sin of Gawain Reconsidered*. Manchester: Manchester University Press, 1980.

—— "The Ambivalance of Adventure: Verbal Ambiguity in *Sir Gawain and the Green Knight* Fitt I". In *The Legend of Arthur in the Middle Ages*. Ed. P.D. Grout. Cambridge: D.S. Brewer, 1983. 28–40.

—— *English Medieval Romances*. London and New York: Longman, 1985.

Barrow, Sarah. *Medieval Social Romances*. New York: Columbia University Press, 1924.

Batts, Michael S. *Gottfried von Strassburg*. New York: Twayne Publishers, 1971.

Bekker, Hugo. *Gottfried von Strassburg's Tristan: A Journey through the Realm of Eros*. Columbia: Camden House, 1987.

Benson, L. *Art and Tradition in Sir Gawain and the Green Knight*. New Brunswick: Rutgers University Press, 1965.

"Courtly Love and Chivalry in the Later Middle Ages". In *Fifteenth-Century Studies: Recent Essays*. Ed. Robert F. Jaeger. Hamden, Conn.: Archon Books, 1984. 237–57.

—— See also Geoffrey Chaucer.

Besserman, Lawrence. "The Idea of the Green Knight". *Journal of English Literary History (ELH)* Summer, 53:2 (1986): 219–39.

de Beauvoir, Simone. *The Second Sex*. Ed. and trans. H.M. Parshley. New York: Knopf, 1953.

Bloch, Howard. R. *Medieval Misogyny and the Invention of Western Romantic Love*. Chicago: University of Chicago Press, 1991.

Bloch, Marc. *La Société Féodale*. 2 vols. Paris, 1939, 1940. Trans. L.A. Manyon. *Feudal Society*. 2 vols. Chicago: Phoenix Books, University of Chicago Press, 1961.

Boitani, Piero and Jill Mann, ed. *The Cambridge Chaucer Companion*. Cambridge: Cambridge University Press, 1986.

—— "The Genius to Improve and Invent: Transformations of the *Knight's Tale*". In *Chaucer Traditions: Studies in Honour of Derek Brewer*. Ed. Ruth Morse. Cambridge: Cambridge University Press, 1990. 185–98.

Bollard, John. "Hende Words: The Theme of Courtesy in *Ywain and Gawain*". *Neophilologus* 78 (1994): 655–70.

Bradstock, E.M. "*Honoure* in *Sir Launfal*". *Paragon* 24 (1979): 9–17.

Braswell, Mary Flowers. "Sin, the Lady and the Law: The English Noblewoman in the Late Middle Ages". *Medievalia et Humanistica New Series* 14 (1986): 81–101.

—— *The Medieval Sinner: Characterization and Confession in the Literature of the English Middle Ages*. Rutherford: Fairleigh Dickinson University Press, 1994.

Brewer, Derek. *Geoffrey Chaucer*. London: Bell and Sons, 1974.

—— *Symbolic Stories: Traditional Narratives of the Family Drama in English Literature*. Cambridge: D.S. Brewer, 1980.

—— *Tradition and Innovation in Chaucer*. London: Macmillian Press, 1982.

Briffault, Robert. Ed. *The Mothers*. Abgd. edn. New York: Allen & Unwin, 1959.

Bromwich, Rachel. "Celtic Elements in Arthurian Romance: A General Survey." In *The Legend of Arthur in the Middle Ages*. Ed. P.D. Grout. Cambridge: D.S. Brewer, 1983. 41–55.

Brook-Rose, Christine. *A Rhetoric of the Unreal.* Cambridge: Cambridge University Press, 1981.

Broughton, Bradford. *The Legends of King Richard I, Coeur de Lion: A Study of Sources and Variations to the Year 1600.* Paris: The Hague, 1966.

Brown, A.C.L. "The Bleeding Lance." *PMLA* XXV (1910): 1–59.

Brown, Peter. *Augustine of Hippo: A Biography.* London: Faber and Faber, 1967.

Brown, J. Wood. *An Enquiry into the Life and Legend of Michael Scot.* Edinburgh: Douglas, 1897.

Brownlee, Martha Scordilis. "Autobiography as Self-(Re)presentation". In *Mimesis from Mirror to Method, Augustine to Descartes.* Ed. John D. Lyons and Stephen Nichols, Jr. Hanover and London: University Press of New England, 1982. 71–82.

Bruce, James Douglas. *The Evolution of the Arthurian Romance from the Beginnings down to the Year 1300.* 2 vols. Gloucester, Mass.: Peter Smith, 1958.

Burlin, Robert B. *Chaucerian Fiction.* Princeton: Princeton University Press, 1977.

Burns, Jane and Roberta, Krueger "Courtly Ideology and the Women's Place in Medieval French Literature." *Romance Notes* Spring, 25: 3 (1985): Introduction.

—— "A Selective Bibliography of Criticism: Women in Medieval French Literature." *Romance Notes* Spring, 25:3 (1985): Bibliography.

Burrow, J.A. *A Reading of Sir Gawain and the Green Knight.* London: Routledge and Kegan Paul, 1965.

—— "*Canterbury Tales*: Romance I." In *The Cambridge Chaucer Companion.* Ed. Piero Boitani and Jill Mann. Cambridge: Cambridge University Press, 1986. 109–124.

—— *The Ages of Man: A Study in Medieval Writing and Thought.* Oxford: Clarendon Paperbacks, 1988.

Bury, J.B. *Ancient Greek Historians.* New York: Dover, 1958.

Busby, Keith. "Chrétien de Troyes English'd". *Neophilologus* 71 (1987): 586–613.

—— Ed. *Courtly Literature: Culture and Context.* Philadelphia: John Benjamin, 1990.

Butler, Judith. *Gender Trouble: Feminism and the Subversion of Identity.* New York and London: Routledge and Kegan Paul, 1990.

Bynum, Caroline Walker. *Jesus As Mother.* Los Angeles: University of California Press, 1982.

—— *Holy Feast, Holy Fast.* Berkeley: University of California Press, 1987.

Cadden, Joan. "Medieval Scientific and Medical Views of Sexuality: Questions of Propriety". *Medievalia et Humanistica* (1986): 151–61

Cagnon, M. "*Chevrefoil* and the Oghamic Tradition". *Romania* 91 (1970): 238–55.

Calin, William. *The French Tradition and the Literature of Medieval England.* Toronto: University of Toronto Press, 1994.

Carasso-Bulow, Lucienne. *The Merveilleux in Chrétien de Troyes' Romances.* Genève: Librairie Droz, 1976.

Cochrance, C.N. *Christianity and the Classical Culture.* London: Oxford University Press, 1940.

Colgrace, B. "Bede's Miracle Stories". In *Bede: His Life, Times and Writings.* Ed. A. Hamilton Thompson. Oxford: Clarendon Press, 1935. 20–35.

Cooper, Helen. "Magic That Does Not Work". *Medievalia et Humanistica* 5 (1976): 131-46.
—— "The Shape Shiftings of the Wife of Bath: 1395-1670". In *Chaucer Traditions: Studies in honour of Derek Brewer*. Ed. Ruth Morse. Cambridge: Cambridge University Press, 1990. 168-84.
Cramer, Patricia. "Lordship, Bondage, and the Erotic: The Psychological Bases of Chaucer's *Clerk's Tale*". *Journal of English and Germanic Philology* 89: 4 (1990): 491-511.
Crane, Susan. *Insular Romance: Politics, Faith, and Culture in Anglo-Norman and Middle English Literature*. Berkeley: University of California Press, 1986.
—— "The Franklin as Dorigen". *Chaucer Review* 24: 3 (1990): 236-52.
—— *Gender and Romance in Chaucer's Canterbury Tales*. Princeton: Princeton University Press, 1994.
Davenport, W.A. *Chaucer and His English Contemporaries*. New York: Macmillan Press, 1998.
David, A. *The Strumpet Muse: Art and Morals in Chaucer's Poetry*. Bloomington: Indiana University Press, 1976.
de Labriolle, P. *The History and Literature of Christianity from Tertullian to Boethius*. Trans. Herbert Wilson. New York: Knopf, 1924.
Delaney, Sheila. *Medieval Literary Politics: Shapes of Ideology*. Manchester: Manchester University Press, 1990.
Dinshaw, Carolyn. *Chaucer's Sexual Poetics*. Madison: University of Wisconsin Press, 1989.
Dronke, Peter. *Women Writers of the Middle Ages*. Cambridge: Cambridge University Press, 1984.
Duby, George. *Love and Marriage in the Middle Ages*. Trans. Jane Dunnett. Chicago: University of Chicago Press, 1988. 2nd edn. Cambridge: Polity, 1994.
Dukes, Eugene D. *Magic and Witchcraft in the Dark Ages*. New York: University Press of America, 1996.
Eckhardt, Caroline D. "Chaucer's Franklin and Others of the Vavasour Family". *Modern Philology* 87: 2 (1990): 239-48.
Edwards, Robert R. "Source, Context and Cultural Translation in the *Franklin's Tale*," *Modern Philology* 94 (1996): 141-62.
Ellis, Deborah S. "The Merchant's Wife's Tale: Language, Sex, and Commerce in Margery Kempe and in Chaucer". *Exemplaria* 2:2 (1990): 595-626.
Erler, Mary and Maryanne Kowaleski. Ed. *Women in Power in the Middle Ages*. Athens: University of Georgia Press, 1988.
Evans, Ruth., and Lesley Johnson. Ed. *Feminist Readings in Medieval Literature* London: Routledge, 1994.
Fanger, Claire. *Conjuring Spirits: Texts and Traditions of Medieval Ritual Magic*. London: Sutton Publishing, 1998.
Faral, C.F. *Les Arts poétiques du XIIe et du XIIIe Siècle*. Paris: Champion, 1962.
Fellows, J. Ed. *Romance Reading on the Book*. Cardiff: University of Wales Press, 1996.

Ferrante, Joan. "Male Fantasy and Female Reality in Courtly Literature". *Women's Studies* 11 (1984): 67–97.
—— *The Conflict of Love and Honour: The Medieval Tristan Legend in France, Germany and Italy*. The Hague: Mouton, 1973.
Fewster, Carol. *Traditionality and Genre in Middle English Romance*. Cambridge: D.S. Brewer, 1987.
Finlayson, J. "*Ywain and Gawain* and the Meaning of Adventure". *Anglia* 87 (1969): 312–327.
—— "The Expectations of Romance in *Sir Gawain and the Green Knight*". *Genre* 12: 1 (1979): 1–24.
—— "Definitions of Middle English Romand I and II". *Chaucer Review* 15:1, 2 1980: 45–61, 172–181.
—— "Marvellous in Middle English Romance". *Chaucer Review* 33:4 1999: 363–407.
Fisher, Sheila. "Leaving Morgan Aside: Women, History and Revisionism in *Sir Gawain and the Green Knight*". In *The Passing of Arthur: New Essays in Arthurian Tradition*. Ed. C. Braswell and William Sharpe. New York: Garland Publishing, 1988. 129–51.
Flake, Timothy. "Love, *Trouthe*, and the Happy Ending of the *Franklin's Tale*". *English Studies* 77 (1996): 209–26.
Fletcher, Alan J. "Lost Hearts: *Troilus and Criseyde*, Book II. Lines 925–31". *Notes and Queries* June, 37 (1990): 235–47.
Fletcher, Robert H. *The Arthurian Material in the Chronicles*. New York: Burt Franklin, 1960.
Flew, R.N. *The Idea of Perfection in Christian Theology*. New York: Humanities Press, 1968.
Flint, Valerie. *The Rise of Magic in Early Medieval Europe*. Princeton: Princeton University Press, 1991.
Foley, Michael. "The Gawain Poet: An Annotated Bibliography, 1978–1985". *The Chaucer Review* 23: 3 (1989): 251–82.
Foucault, Michael. *Discipline and Punish*. Trans. Alan Sheridan. New York: Vintage Books, 1979.
—— *The History of Sexuality. Vol. I. An Introduction*. Trans. Robert Hurley. New York: Random House, 1980.
Fourquet, Jean. "Le Rapport entre l'oeuvre et la source chez Chrétien de Troyes et la problème des sources Bretonnes". *Romance Philology* 9 (1955–56): 298–312.
Fowler, Alastair. *Kinds of Literature: An Introduction to the Theory of Genres and Modes*. Cambridge, Mass.: Harvard University Press, 1982.
Frank, Robert Worth Jr. *Chaucer and the Legend of Good Women*. Cambridge, Mass: Harvard Univ. Press, 1972.
Frappier, Jean. "Chrétien de Troyes". In *Arthurian Literature in the Middle Ages*. Ed. R.S. Loomis. Oxford: Clarendon Press, 1959. 160–75.
—— "Virgile source de Chrétien de Troyes?", *Romance Philology* XIII (1959–60): 50–8.

—— *Étude sur Yvain ou le Chevalier au lion de Chrétien de Troyes*. Paris: Champion, 1969.

—— *Autour du Graal*. Genève: Librairie Droz, 1977.

Friedman, A.B. "Morgan Le Feé in *Sir Gawain and the Green Knight*". *Speculum* 35 (1960): 260–74.

Frye, Northrop. *Anatomy of Criticism*. Princeton: Princeton University Press, 1957.

—— *The Secular Scripture: A Study of the Structure of Romance*. Cambridge, Mass.: Harvard University Press, 1976.

Fyler, John. "Love and Degree in *The Franklin's Tale*". *Chaucer Review* 21 (1987): 321–7.

—— "Domesticating the Exotic in *The Squire's Tale*". *ELH* 55 (1988): 1–26.

Gash, Anthony. "Carnival against Lent: The Ambivalence of Medieval Drama". In *Medieval Literature: Criticism, Ideology and History*. Ed. David Aers. New York: St Martin's Press, 1986. 74–98.

Gaylord, A.T. "Promises in the *Franklin's Tale*". *ELH* 31 (1964): 331–365.

Geil, Gerhild. *Gottfried von Strassburg und Wolfram von Eschenbach*. Wien: Bohlau Verlag. 1973.

Gibson, Margaret. Ed. *Boethius: His Life, Thoughts and Influence*. Oxford: Basil Blackwell, 1981.

Gies, Frances and Joseph. *Women in the Middle Ages*. New York: Thomas Y. Crowell Company, 1978.

Ginzberg, Carlo. "Deciphering the Witches' Sabbath". In *Oedipus and the Devil: Witchcraft, Sexuality and Religion in Early Modern Europe*. Ed. Lyndal Roper. New York and London: Routledge, 1994.

Glasser, Richard. "Abstractum agens und Allegorie im ältern Französisch". *Zeitschrift für romanische Philologie* 69 (1953): 41–57.

Goggin, Sister Thomas Aquinas, S.C.H. *The Fathers of The Church: St John Chrysostom*. New York: Fathers of the Church, 1960.

Gold, Penny Schine. *The Lady and the Virgin*. Chicago: University of Chicago Press, 1985.

Goodich, Michael F. *Violence and Miracle in The Fourteenth Century: Private Grief and Public Salvation*. Chicago: University of Chicago Press, 1995.

Gradon, Pamela. *Form and Style in Early English Literature*. London: Methuen, 1971.

Green, Robert B. "The Fusion of Magic and Realism in Two Lays of Marie De France". *Neophilologus* 59 (1975): 324–36.

Greer, Rowan A. *Origen's Song of Songs Commentary and Translations*. New York: Paulist Press, 1979.

Griffiths, Bill. *Aspects of Anglo-Saxon Magic*. Norfolk: Anglo-Saxon Books, 1996.

Grout, P.D. Ed. *The Legend of Arthur in the Middle Ages*. Cambridge: D.S. Brewer, 1983.

Guyer, F.E. "The Influence of Ovid on Crestien de Troyes". *Romanic Review* XII (1921): 97–134; 216–47.

—— *Chrétien de Troyes: Incentor of the Modern Novel*. London: Vision, 1960.

—— "Some of the Latin Sources of *Yvain*". *Romanic Review* XIV (1923): 286–304.

Haidu, Peter. *Aesthetic Distance in Chrétien de Troyes*. Genève: Librairie Droz, 1968.
Hanna (III), Ralph. "Unlocking What's Locked: Gawain's Green Girdle". *Viator* 14 (1983): 289–302.
Hanning, Robert. *The Vision of History in Early Britain from Gildas to Geoffrey of Monmouth*. New York: Columbia University Press, 1966.
—— *The Individual in the Twelfth Century*. New Haven and London: Yale University Press, 1977.
Hansen, Elaine Tuttle. "Fearing for Chaucer's Good Name". *Exemplaria*, Spring, 2 (1990): 23–36.
—— *Chaucer and the Fictions of Gender*. Berkeley: University of California Press, 1992.
Harding, Carol. *Merlin and Legendary Romance*. New York: Garland Publishing, 1988.
Harward, V.J. *The Dwarfs of Arthurian Legend and Celtic Tradition*. Leiden: N.P. 1958.
Havely, Nicholas. Ed. and trans. *Chaucer's Boccaccio: Sources of Troilus, the Knight's and the Franklin's Tales*. Cambridge: D.S. Brewer, 1980.
Heng, Geraldine G. "Gender Magic: Desire, Romance and the Feminine in *Sir Gawain and the Green Knight*". Dissertation. Dissertation Abstracts (1990). Cornell University.
Hernadi, Paul. *Beyond Genre: New Directions in Literary Classification*. Ithaca: Cornell University Press, 1972.
Holmes, Ronald. *Witchcraft in British History*. London: Frederick Muller, 1974.
Hopkins, A. *The Sinful Knights*. Oxford: Clarendon Press, 1990.
Horgan, A.D. "Gawain's Pure Pentangle and the Virtue of Faith". *Medium Ævum* 56:2 (1987): 310–16.
Howard, Donald R. "Structure and Symmetry in *Sir Gawain and the Green Knight*". *Speculum* 89 (1964): 425–33.
—— *The Three Temptations*. Princeton: Princeton University Press, 1966.
—— *Chaucer and the Medieval World*. London: Weidenfeld and Nicolson, 1987.
Howlett, David. *The English Origins of Old French Literature*. Dublin: Four Courts Press, 1996.
Howlett, J. Ed. *Chronicles of Stephen*. Vols. I and II. Rolls Series, 1884–1885.
Huber, Christopher. *Gottfried von Strassburg: Tristan & Isolde*. Munchen: Artemis Verlag, 1986.
Huizinga, J. *The Waning of the Middle Ages: A Study of the Forms of Life, Thought and Art in France and the Netherlands in the Fourteenth and Fifteenth Centuries*. New York: St Martin's Press, 1924.
Hume, Kathryn. "Why Chaucer Calls the *Franklin's Tale* a Breton *Lai*". *Philological Quarterly* 52 (1972): 373–79.
—— "Romance: A Perdurable Pattern". *College English* October, 36 (1974): 144–50.
—— *Fantasy and Mimesis*. New York and London: Methuen, 1984.
Hunt, Tony. "Chrétien de Troyes: The Lion and Yvain". In *The Legend of Arthur in the Middle Ages*. Ed. P.D. Grout. Cambridge: D.S. Brewer, 1983. 30–42.

—— "Beginnings, Middles and Ends: Some Interpretative Problems in Chrétien's Yvain and its Medieval Adaptations". In *The Craft of Fiction: Essays in Medieval Politics*. Ed. Leigh A. Arrathoon. Rochester: Solaris, 1984. 83–117.
—— *Chrétien de Troyes: Yvain*. London and New York: Longman, 1986.
Jackson, Rosemary. *Fantasy: The Literature of Subversion*. London: Methuen, 1981.
Jackson, W.T.H. "Problems of Communication in the Romances of Chrétien de Troyes". In *Medieval Literature and Folklore Studies: Essays in Honor of F.L. Utley*. Ed. J. Mandel and B. Rosenberg. New Brunswick: Rutgers University Press, 1970. 147–53.
—— *The Anatomy of Love*. New York: Columbia University Press, 1971.
Jacobs, Nicholas and A.V.C. Schmidt. Ed. *Middle English Romances*. 2 vols. London: Hodder & Stoughton, 1977.
Jaeger, Stephan. *Medieval Humanism in Gottfried von Strassburg*. Heidelberg: Carl Winter, 1977.
Jameson, Fredrick. "Magical Narratives: Romance as Genre". *New Literary History* 7 (1975): 135–63.
—— *The Political Unconscious: Narrative as Socially Symbolic Act*. Ithaca: Cornell University Press, 1981.
Jensen, Emily. "Male Competition as a Unifying Motif in Fragment A of *The Canterbury Tales*". *Chaucer Review* 24: 4 (1990): 320–28.
Johnson, Lynn Staley. *The Voice of the Gawain Poet*. Madison: University of Wisconsin Press, 1984.
Johnston R.C. and D.D.R. Owen. *Two Old French Gawain Romances*. New York: Barnes and Noble, 1973.
Jones, Terry. *Chaucer's Knight: The Portrait of a Medieval Mercenary*. London: Methuen, 1985.
Keen, Maurice. *Chivalry*. New Haven: Yale University Press, 1984.
Kelly, Douglas. "Chrétien de Troyes: Narrator and his Art". In *Romances of Chrétien de Troyes Symposium*. Kentucky: French Forum Publishers, 1985. 13–47.
—— *The Art of Medieval French Romance*. Madison: University of Wisconsin Press, 1992.
Kennedy, Elispeth. "Failure in Arthurian Romance". *Medium Ævum* LX:I (1991): 16–32.
Ker, W.P. *Epic and Romance*. New York: Dover Publications, 1957.
Kieckhefer, Richard. *Magic in the Middle Ages*. Cambridge: Cambridge University Press, 1989.
Kittredge, G. L. *A Study of Sir Gawain and the Green Knight*. Cambridge, Mass.: Harvard University Press, 1916.
Klapisch-Zuber, Christiane, ed. *A History of Women: Silences of the Middle Ages*. Cambridge, Mass.: Harvard University Press, 1992.
Knapp, Peggy. *Chaucer and the Social Contest*. New York and London: Routledge, 1990.
Knight, Stephen. "Ideology in *The Franklin's Tale*". *Paregon* 28 (1980): 3–35.

―― "The Social Function of the Middle English Romances". In *Medieval Literature: Criticism, Ideology and History*. Ed. David Aers. New York: St Martin's Press, 1986. 99–122.
Koenigsberger, H.G. *Medieval Europe 400–1500*. London and New York: Longman, 1987.
Köhler, Erich. "Le rôle de la coutume dans les romans de Chrétien de Troyes". *Romania* (1960): 386–97.
―― "Il Sistema sociologico del romanzo francese medievale". *Medioevo romanzo* 3 (1976): 321–44.
Kors, Alan and Edward Peters. Ed. *Witchcraft in Europe 1100–1700: A Documentary History*. Philadelphia: University of Philadelphia Press, 1992.
Kroeber, Karl. *Romantic Fantasy and Science Fiction*. New Haven: Yale University Press, 1986.
Krueger, Roberta L. "Love, Honor and the Exchange of Women in Yvain: Some Remarks on the Female Reader". *Romance Notes* Spring, 25 (1985): 302–17.
―― "Double Jeopardy: The Appreciation of Women in Four Old French Romances of the 'Cycle de la Gageure'". In *Seeking Women in Late Medieval and Renaissance Writings: Essays of Feminist Contextual Criticism*. Ed. Sheila Fisher. Knoxville: University Press of Tennessee, 1989. 21–50.
―― *Women Readers and the Ideology of Gender in Old French Verse Romances*. London: Cambridge University Press, 1993.
Labalme, Patricia. Ed. *Beyond Their Sex*. New York and London: New York University Press, 1980.
Lacan, Jacques. *Language of Self*. Ed. and trans. Anthony Wilden. Baltimore: Johns Hopkins University Press, 1973.
―― *Feminine Sexuality: Jacques Lacan and the "école freudienne"*. Trans. J. Rose. Ed. Juliet Mitchell and Jacqueline Rose. New York: Norton, 1982.
Lacy, Norris J. *The Craft of Chrétien de Troyes: An Essay on Narrative Art*. Berkeley: University of California Press, 1980.
―― Ed. *The Arthurian Encyclopedia*. New York: Peter Bedrick Books, 1986–.
―― Ed. *The Arthurian Handbook*. New York: Garland Press, 1988.
Ladner, L. "*Homo Viator*: Medieval Ideas on Alienation and Order". *Speculum* XLII (1967): 233–259.
Laistner, M.L.W. *The Intellectual Heritage of the Early Middle Ages: Selected Essays*. Ithaca: Cornell University Press, 1957.
―― *The Great Roman Historians*. Berkeley: University of California Press, 1963.
Laskaya, Ann. *Chaucer's Approaches to Gender in the Canterbury Tales*. Cambridge: D.S. Brewer, 1995.
Lea, Henry Charles. *The History of the Inquisition of the Middle Ages*. 3 vols. Philadelphia: Lea Brothers, 1883.
Le Clercq, Jean. *Monks and Love in Twelfth-Century France*. Oxford: Clarendon Press, 1979.
Lee, Ann Thompson. "A Lady True and Fair". *Chaucer Review* 19 (1984): 165–75.
Lees, Clare. Ed. *Medieval Masculinities: Regarding Men in the Middle Ages*. Minneapolis: University of Minnesota, 1994.

Le Gentil, Pierre. "A Propos du Marriage". In *Mélanges de Philologie Romane Offerts à Charles Camproux*. Montpellier: Centre d'Études Occitans, 1978.
Le Goff, Jacques. *The Medieval Imagination*. Trans. A. Goldhammer. Chicago: University of Chicago Press, 1985.
—— *Intellectuals in the Middle Ages*. Trans. Teresa Fagan. London: Blackwell, 1993.
Lehrer, Seth. "Textual Criticism and Literary Theory: Chaucer and His Readers". *Exemplaria*, 2 (1990): 329-45.
—— *Chaucer and His Readers*. Princeton: Princeton University Press, 1993.
Leicester, H. Marshall, Jr. *The General Prologue*: Or, Reading Chaucer as a Prologue to the History of Disenchantment." *Exemplaria Spring*, 2 (1990): 241-61.
Lerner, Robert. *The Heresy of the Free Spirit in the Late Middle Ages*. Notre Dame: University of Notre Dame Press, 1972.
Lewis, C.B. *Classical Mythology and Arthurian Romance: A Study of the Sources of Chretien de Troye's Yvain and Other Arthurian Romances*. Geneve: Slatkine Reprints, 1932.
Lewis, C.S. *Allegory of Love*. Oxford: Oxford University Press, 1936.
Lomperis, L. and Sarah Standbury. Ed. *Feminist Approaches to the Body in Medieval Literature*. Philadelphia: University of Philadelphia Press, 1993.
Loomis, C.G. *White Magic. An Introduction to the Folklore of Christian Legend*. Cambridge, Mass.: Harvard University Press, 1948.
Loomis, Gertrude Schoepperle. *Tristan and Isolt: A Study of the Sources of the Romance*. New York: Burt Franklin, 1970.
—— L.H. Loomis Ed. *Arthurian Legends and Medieval Art*. New York, Columbia, University Press, 1938.
Loomis, R.S. *Celtic Myth and Arthurian Romance*. New York: Columbia University Press, 1926.
—— "The Spoils of Annwn". *PMLA* LVI (1941): 67-76.
—— *Arthurian Tradition and Chrétien de Troyes*. New York: Columbia University Press 1949.
—— *Wales and the Arthurian Legend*. Cardiff: University of Wales Press, 1956.
—— Ed. *Arthurian Literature in the Middle Ages*. Oxford: Clarendon Press, 1959.
—— "The Legend of Arthur's Survival". In *Arthurian Literature in the Middle Ages*. Oxford: Clarendon Press, 1959.
—— *The Grail: from Celtic Myth to Christian Symbol*. New York: Columbia University Press, 1963.
Lucas, Angela. "Chaucer's *Franklin's Tale*: The Case of the Unreliable Narrator". *Maynooth Review* (1977): 3-19.
—— and Peter Lucas. "The Presentation of Marriage and Love in Chaucer's *Franklin's Tale*". *English Studies* 72 (1991): 501-12.
—— "Astronomy, Astrology and Magic in Chaucer's *Franklin's Tale*". *Maynooth Review* (1991-2): 5-16.
Lucas, Peter J. "Chaucer's Franklin's Dorigen: Her Name". *Notes and Queries* December, 37 (1990): 398-400.
Luttrell, Claude. *The Creation of the First Arthurian Romance*. London: Edward Arnold, 1974.

Maas, A.J. "Lollards" and "Translations of the English Bible". In *Catholic Encyclopedia*, vol. XV. Transcribed by Dennis McCarty. Online edition. January 5, 2000 <HYPERLINK http://www.newadvent.org/cathen/ 09333a.htm>.

MacKinnon, Catherine A. "Feminism, Marxism, Method, and the State: An Agenda for Theory." *Signs* 7 (1982): 515-44.

—— "Desire and Power: A Feminist Perspective". In *Marxism and the Interpretation of Culture*. Gen. Ed. Cary Nelson. Urbana: University of Illinois Press, 1988. 300-33.

Maddox, Donald. *The Arthurian Romances of Chrétien de Troyes*. Cambridge: Cambridge University Press, 1991.

Manlove, Colin N. "The Elusiveness of Fantasy". In *The Shape of the Fantastic*. Ed. Olena Saciuk. New York: Greenwood Press. 1986: 53-65.

Mann, Jill. *Chaucer and Medieval Estates Satire: The Literature of the Social Classes and the General Prologue of the Canterbury Tales*. London: Cambridge University Press, 1983.

—— See also Piero Boitani.

Marwick, Max. Ed. *Witchcraft and Sorcery*. London: Penguin, 1970.

Marx, Jean. *Legende*. Paris: Presses Universitaires de France, 1952.

Mathews, David. "Translation and Ideology: The Case of *Ywain and Gawain*". *Neophilologus* 76 (1992): 455-62.

McAlindon, T.A. "Magic and Medieval Narrative in *Sir Gawain and the Green Knight*". *Review of English Studies* 16 (1965): 121-39.

McCash, June Hall. "The Curse of the White Hind and the Cure of the Weasel: Animal Magic in the *Lais* of Marie de France", in *Literary Aspects of Courtly Culture*. Ed. Donald Maddox and Sara Sturm-Maddox. Cambridge, England: D.S. Brewer, 1994

—— "*Amor* in Marie de France's *Equitan* and *Fresne*". In *The Court and Cultural Diversity. Selected Papers from the Eighth Triennial Congress of the International Courtly Literature Society 1995*. London: D.S. Brewer, 1997.

McEntire, Sandra. "Illusions and Interpretations in the *Franklin's Tale*." *Chaucer Review* 31:2 (1996): 145-63.

McFarlane, K.B. *The Nobility of Late Medieval England*. Oxford: Clarendon Press, 1973.

McKisack, May. *The Fourteenth Century 1307-1399*. Vol. 5. Oxford History of England. 5 vols. Oxford: Oxford University Press, 1991.

McKitterick, Rosamund. *The Uses of Literacy in Early Medieval Europe*. London: Cambridge University Press, 1990.

McNamara, Joann and Suzanne Wemple. "The Power of Women through Family". In *Women and Power in the Middle Ages*. Ed. Mary Erler and Mary Kowaleski. Athens: University of Georgia Press, 1988. 83-101.

McNeill, John and Helena M. Gamer. Ed. and trans. *Medieval Handbooks of Penance: A Translation of the Principal Libri Poenitentiales*. New York: Columbia University Press, 1938.

Medcalf, Stephen and Majorie Reeves. "The Ideal, the Real and the Quest for Perfection". In *The Later Middle Ages*. Ed. Stephen Medcalf. New York: Holmes and Meier, 1981.

Mehl, Dieter. *The Middle English Romances of the Thirteenth and Fourteenth Centuries*. London: Routledge and Kegan Paul, 1968.

Michelet, Jules. *Satanism and Witchcraft*. Trans. A.R. Allison. New York: Carol Publishing, 1992.

Miles. Margaret, R. *Carnal Knowing: Female Nakedness and Religious Meaning in the Christian West*. New York: Vintage Books, 1991.

Milhaven, Giles J. "A Medieval Lesson on Bodily Knowing: Women's Experience and Men's Thoughts". *Journal of the American Academy of Religion* LV: 2 (1970): 13–40.

Minnis, A.J. "Aspects of Medieval French and English Traditions of the *De consolatione philosophiae*". In *Boethius: His Life, Thoughts and Influence*. Ed. Margaret Gibson. Oxford: Basil Blackwell, 1981. 312–61.

—— Ed. *The Medieval Boethius: Studies in the Vernacular Traditions*. London, D.S. Brewer, 1987.

—— "Chaucer's Position on Past Gentility". *Proceedings of British Academy* LXXII. Vol. 1986. Oxford: Oxford University Press, 1987: 205–43.

—— *Chaucer and Pagan Antiquity*. Cambridge: D.S. Brewer, Totowa, N.J.: Rowman & Littlefield, 1982.

—— *Chaucer's Boece and the Medieval Tradition of Boethius*. Oxford: D.S.Brewer, 1993.

Morewedge, Rosemarie T. *The Role of Women in the Middle Ages*. Albany: State University of New York Press, 1975.

Morgan, G. "A Defense of Dorigen's Complaint", *Medium Ævum* 46 (1977): 77–97.

—— *Geoffrey Chaucer: The Franklin's Tale*. London: Hodder and Stoughton, 1980.

—— "Boccaccio's *Filocolo* and the Moral Argument of *The Franklin's Tale*". *Chaucer Review* 20 (1985–86): 285–306.

—— *Sir Gawain and the Green Knight and the Idea of Righteousness*. Dublin: Irish Academic Press, 1991.

Muir, Lynette R. *Literature and Society in Medieval France: The Mirror and the Image, 1100–1500*. London: Macmillan, 1985.

Mundy, J.E. *Europe in the High Middle Ages*. New York and London: Longman Group, 1992.

Muscatine, Charles. *Chaucer and the French Tradition*. Berkeley: University of California Press, 1957.

Newstead, Helen. "Arthurian Legends". In *A Manual of the Writings in Middle English 1040–1400*. Ed. Severs J. Burke. 8 vols. New Haven: Connecticut Academy of Arts and Sciences, 1967. Supplements 1–9.

Nolan, Barbara. *Chaucer and the Tradition of the Roman Antique*. Cambridge: Cambridge University Press, 1992.

North, J.D. *Chaucer's Universe*. Oxford: Clarendon Press, 1988.

Novak, John Bullaz. *Magic as a Theme in Sir Gawain and the Green Knight*. Dissertation. New York: University of Syracuse. 1979.

Nykrog, Per. "Rise of Literary Fiction". In *Renaissance and Renewal in the Twelfth Century*. Ed. R. Benson. Oxford: Clarendon Press, 1982.

Nyquist, Mary. "Every (Wo)Man's Friend: A Response to John Fyler and Elaine Tuttle Hansen". *Exemplaria* Spring, 2 (1990): 3747.

O'Brien, Timothy D. " 'Ars Metrik': Science, Satire and Chaucer's Summoner". *Mosaic: A Journal for the Interdisciplinary Study of Literature* Fall, 23 (1990): 122.

Ogrinc, Will H.L. "Western Society and Alchemy from 1200 to 1500". *Journal of Medieval History* March, 6: 1 (1980): 30–58.

Olson, Donald W. "A Note on Planetary Tables and a Planetary Conjunction in *Troilus and Criseyde*". *Chaucer Review* 24: 4 (1990): 309–11.

Opitz, Claudia. "Life in the Late Middle Ages". In *A History of Women: Silences of the Middle Ages*. Ed. Christiane Klapisch-Zuber. Trans. D. Schneider. Cambridge, Mass.: Harvard University Press, 1992.

Owen, D.D.R. *The Evolution of the Grail Legend*. Edinburgh: Oliver and Boyd, 1968.

Partner, Peter. *The Knights Templar and Their Myth*. Vermont: Destiny Books, 1990.

Patch, H.R. *The Goddess Fortuna in Medieval Literature*. Cambridge, Mass.: Harvard University Press, 1927. 2nd edn. London: F. Cass, 1967.

Paterson, Linda M. *The World of the Troubadours*. Cambridge: Cambridge University Press, 1993.

Paton, Lucy Allen. *Studies in the Fairy Mythology of Arthurian Romance*. 2nd edn. New York: Burt Franklin, 1970.

Patterson, Lee. *Chaucer and the Subject of History*. Madison: University of Wisconsin, 1991.

Pearcy, Roy J. "Chaucer's Franklin: A Literary Vavasour". *Chaucer Review* 8 (1973–74): 33–59.

Pelikan, Jaroslav. "The Middle Ages as an Age of Faith". Vol. 3. In *The Christian Tradition: The Growth of Medieval Theology (600–1300)*. 5 vols. Chicago: University of Chicago Press, 1978–.

Peters, Edward. *Witchcraft in Europe 1100–1700: A Documentary History*. Philadelphia: University of Philadelphia Press, 1972.

—— *The Magician, the Witch and the Law*. Philadelphia: University of Pennsylvania Press, 1978.

—— *Heresy and Authority in Medieval Europe*. Philadelphia: University of Pennsylvania Press, 1994.

Pickering, F.P. "Notes on Fate and Fortune". In *Medieval German Studies*. Vol. 36. London: University of London, Germanic Studies, 1965. 1–15.

Pollack, Sir F. and F.W. Maitland. "Statute of Treason". In *The History of English Law before the Time of Edward I*. 2nd Edn., Cambridge: Cambridge University Press, 1968.

Poschl, Viktor. *The Art of Vergil*. Ann Arbor: University of Michigan Press, 1962.

Putter, Ad. *Sir Gawain and the Green Knight and the Influence of the French Romances*. Oxford: Clarendon Press, 1995.

Press, A.R. "Chrétien de Troyes's Laudine: A Belle Dame Sans Mercy?". *FMLS* 19 (1983): 158–71.

Rabkin, Erec S. *The Fantastic in Literature*. Princeton: Princeton University Press, 1976.

Ramsey, Lee. *Chivalric Romance: Popular Literature in Medieval England*. Bloomington: University of Indiana, 1983.

Roberts, W.R. "Rhetorica". In *The Works of Aristotle*. Ed. W.D. Ross. Vol. XI. Oxford: Oxford University Press, 1942.

Robertson, D.W. Ed. *Essays in Medieval Culture*. Princeton: Princeton University Press, 1980.

Rosenhaus, Myra. *Britain Between Myth and Reality*. Dissertation University of Indiana, 1982.

Rosenthal, Joel T. Ed. *Medieval Women and The Sources of Medieval History*. Athens and London: University of Georgia Press, 1990.

Rosmarin, Adena. *The Power of Genre*. Minneapolis: University of Minnesota Press, 1985.

Rumble, T.C. "The Middle English *Sir Tristrem:* Toward a Reappraisal". *Critical Language* 11 (1959): 221–28.

Russell, Jeffrey Burton. *Witchcraft in the Middle Ages*. Ithaca: Cornell University Press, 1972.

Russo, Mary. "Female Grotesques: Carnival and Theory". In *Feminist Studies/ Critical Studies*. Ed. Teresa de Lauretis. Bloomington: Indiana University Press, 1986. 213–226.

Rutledge, Amelia. "Perceval's Sin: Critical Perspectives". *Oeuvres et Critiques* 5: 2 (1980–81): 53–60.

Sawyer, P.H. *From Roman Britain to Norman England*. London: Routledge, 1978, 2nd ed. 1998.

Scattergood, V.J. "Literary Culture of Court Richard II". In *English Court Culture in the Later Middle Ages*. Ed. V.J. Scattergood. New York: St Martin's Press, 1983.

Schlageter, Emil. Reimworterbuch zu Gottfried's Tristan. Müchen: George Callwey, 1926.

Shedd, Gordon M. "Knight in Tarnished Armour: The Meaning of *Sir Gawain and the Green Knight*". *Modern Humanities Research Association* January, 62 (1967): 3–13.

Shippey, T.A. "Uses of Chivalry: 'Erec and Gawain'. *Modern Humanities Research Association* April, 66 (1971): 241–50.

—— "Breton *Lais* and Modern Fantasies". In *Studies in Medieval Romance: New Approaches*. Cambridge: D.S. Brewer, 1988. 69–91.

Shirt, D.J. "Chrétien de Troyes and the Cart". In *Studies in Medieval Literature and Languages in Memory of Frederick Whitehead*. Manchester: Manchester University Press, 1973. 363–99.

Shoaf, R.A. "The 'Syngne of Surfet' and 'the Surfet of Signs' in *Sir Gawain and the Green Knight*". In *The Passing of Arthur*. Ed. C. Braswell and W. Sharpe. London and New York: Garland Publishing, 1988. 152–69.

Shotwell, James. *The Story of Ancient History*. 2nd edn. New York: Columbia University Press, 1961.

Siebers, Tobin. "The Uses of Fantasy". *The Michigan Quarterly Review* 21: 3 (1981–82): 520–24.
—— *The Romantic Fantastic.* Ithaca: Cornell University Press, 1984.
Simpson, James. *Science and the Self in Medieval Poetry.* Cambridge: Cambridge University Press, 1995.
Siraisi, Nancy. *Medieval and Early Renaissance Medicine.* Chicago: University of Chicago Press, 1990.
Southerland, Ronald. *The Romaun of the Rose and Le Roman de la Rose.* Oxford: Basil Blackwell, 1967.
Southern, R.W. *The Making of the Middle Ages.* New Haven: Yale University Press, 1953.
Spearing, A.C. *Medieval English Poetry: The Non-Chaucerian Tradition.* London: Faber and Faber, 1957.
—— *The Gawain Poet: A Critical Study.* Cambridge: Cambridge University Press, 1970.
—— *Criticism and Medieval Poetry.* New York: Barnes and Noble, 1972.
—— *Medieval to Renaissance in English Poetry.* Cambridge: Cambridge University Press, 1985.
—— *Readings in Medieval Poetry.* Cambridge: Cambridge University Press, 1987.
—— "Marie de France and her Middle English Adaptors". *Studies in the Age of Chaucer* 12 (1990): 117–56.
Staines, David. *The Complete Romances of Chrétien de Troyes.* Bloomington: Indiana University Press, 1993.
Stevens, J.E. *Medieval Romance: Themes and Approaches.* London: Hutchinson University Library, 1973.
Stewart, Gregory. *Thomas of Britain's Tristran.* New York: Garland Press, 1991.
Stock, Brian. *The Implications of Literacy.* Princeton: Princeton University Press, 1983.
Strohm, Paul. "The Origin and Meaning of Middle English Romaunce". *Genre* 10 (1977): 1–28.
—— *Social Chaucer.* Cambridge: Harvard University Press, 1989.
Sturm-Maddox, S. "The 'Joie de la Cort': Thematic Unity in Chrétien's *Erec and Enide*". *Romance* 103 (1982): 313–28.
Tatlock, J.S.P. *The Legendary History of Britain.* Berkeley: University of California Press, 1950.
Taylor, Charles. *Sources of Self: The Making of the Modern Identity.* Cambridge: Cambridge University Press, 1989.
Thomas, Keith. *Religion and the Decline of Magic.* New York: Charles Scribner's Sons, 1971.
Thompson, Lee Ann. "A Lady True and Fair – Chaucer's Portrayal of Dorigen in The Franklin's Tale". *Chaucer Review* 19: 2 (1984): 169–78.
Thompson, Rodney. *William of Malmesbury.* London: Boydell Press, 1987.
Thorndike, L. *The Place of Magic in the Intellectual History of Europe.* New York: Columbia University Press, 1905.

Thorndike, L. *The Place of Magic in the Intellectual History of Europe*. New York: Columbia University Press, 1905.
—— *Michael Scott*. New York: Columbia University Press, 1910.
—— *A History of Magic and Experimental Sciences*. 2 vols. New York: Macmillan, 1923.
Todorov, Tzvetan. *The Fantastic*. Trans. Richard Howard. Cleveland and London: The Press Case of Western Reserve University, 1973.
Tolstoy, Nikolai. *The Quest for Merlin*. Boston: The Little Brown Book Company, 1985.
Topsfield, L.T. *Chrétien de Troyes: A Study of Arthurian Romances*. Cambridge: Cambridge University Press, 1981.
Turville-Petre, T. *The Alliterative Revival*. Cambridge: Cambridge University Press, 1977.
Vance, Eugene. *Mervelous Signals: Poetic and Sign Theory in the Middle Ages*. Lincoln and London: University of Nebraska Press, 1986.
Vinaver, Eugene. *The Rise of Romance*. Oxford: Clarendon Press, 1971.
—— "The Love Potion in the Primitive Tristan Romance". In *Medieval Studies in Memory of G. Schoepperle Loomis*. Ed. Collette Renie. Genève: Slatkine Reprints, 1974.
Voloshinov, V.N. *Marxism and the Philosophy of Language*. Trans. L. Matejka. New York: Seminar Press, 1973.
Wack, Mary Frances. *Lovesickness In the Middle Ages*. Philadelphia: University of Pennsylvania Press, 1990.
Wailes, Stephen L. *Medieval Allegories of Jesus' Parables*. Berkeley: University of California Press, 1987.
Wallace, David. *Chaucer and the Early Writings of Boccaccio*. Cambridge: D.S. Brewer, 1985.
Wallace-Hadrill, D.S. *Eusebius of Caesarea*. London: A.R. Mowbray, 1960.
Walton, Kendall L. *Mimesis as Make-Believe*. Cambridge, Mass.: Harvard University Press, 1990.
Warner, Marina. *Alone of All Her Sex: The Myth and the Cult of the Virgin Mary*. New York: Knopf, 1976.
Weston, Jessie. *From Ritual to Romance*. New York: Doubleday Books, 1920.
Wilhelm, James J. *The Romance of Arthur*. New York: Garland, 1984.
Williams, Elizabeth. "*A damsell by herselfe alone*: Images of Magic and Femininity from Lanval to Sir Lambewell". In *Romance Reading on the Book: Essays on Medieval Narrative Presented. to Maldwyn Mills*. Ed. J. Fellows. Cardiff: University of Wales Press, 1996. 155–170.
Wilson, Anne. *The Magical Quest: The Use of Magic in the Arthurian Romances*. Manchester: Manchester University Press, 1988.
Wimsatt, James. *Chaucer and his French Contemporaries: Natural Music in the Fourteenth Century*. London and Toronto: University of Toronto Press, 1991.
Zum Brunn, Emile. *Women Mystics In Medieval Europe*. Trans. Sheila Hughes. New York: Paragon House, 1989.

Index

Abano, Peter, 50
Ackerman, Robert, 126, 127n
Aelfric (*Lives of Saints*), 44
Aeneid (*see Virgil*), 56n, 67
Aesop, 56n, 58
Aijmer, Karin, 50
Alanus de Insulis (*De planctu Naturae*), 65n, 74
Alban the Martyr (St), 68
Albertus, 44
Alcuin of York, 38–9
Amis e Amilun, 116
Amor heroes, 164–5
Anglo-Saxon Chronicle, 61
Anselm (St), 49
Aquinas, 13, 28, 30, 34, 44, 50, 153; *Quaestio* III, 30n; *Quodlibet* XI, 153; *Summa theologiae*, 153n, 154n, 155n
Arnold of Villa Nova, 44
Ars notoria, 34, 35n
Arthur, 19, 21, 24, 52, 55, 57–8, 60–4, 68–71, 79, 82–4, 86, 87, 91, 96, 106, 108, 109, 110, 112, 121, 133–4, 142, 143
Arts of Rhetoric, 74
Astell, Ann, 150n, 151
Auerbach, Erec, 22
Augustine, 13, 24, 28, 36–7, 66n, 154
Avalon, 47, 70, 86, 121, 138, 143

Bacon, Roger, 28, 34
Bakhtin, M., 20

Barron, W.R.J., 21n, 120n
Bede, 38n, 66, 68
Bédier, Joseph, 129
Bekker, Hugo, 50n, 51
Benson, Larry, 25n, 61n, 122n, 153
Beowulf, 31, 60
Bernard (St), 49
Bernart von Ventadorn, 83, 99–101
Bliss, A.J., 138n, 139n, 141n, 143n, 144n
Bloch, Howard, 27n, 136n
Bloch, Marc, 63n
Boccaccio, 118, 149, 163; *Il Filocolo*, 118, 149, 163; *Tebano*, 149–50
Boethius, 50–5, 67
Boitani, P., 25n
Bolingbroke, Roger, 40
Bollard, J., 117
Braswell, Mary Flowers, 52, 139n
Breton Lai, 12, 58, 38, 147–8,
Brewer, Derek, 22, 25, 146–7, 165
Brown, A.C.L., 108n
Brown, Peter, 36n
Broughton, Bradford, 39n
Brut (Laʒamon's), 61
Burchard, Bishop of Worms (*Decretum*), 44
Bury, J.B., 67
Busby, Keith, 116, 124, 134
Butler, Judith, 28
Burrow, J.A., 25

Caesarius (St), 44
Calin, William, 21, 117

Cambrensis, 34, 39
Canute, 39
Capellanus, Andreas (*De Amore*), 101, 162, 164
Caradoc of Llancarvan (see *Vita*), 57, 61
Caritas, 104–5, 109
Chanson de Roland, 49, 57, 90
Charlemagne, 39
Charles IV, 40
Chaucer, 9, 11, 12, 20, 21, 24, 25, 47, 48, 52, 115, 118, 145, 162, 163, 169; romances: *Franklin's Tale*, 12, 19, 27, 47–9, 51, 78, 115, 118, 120, 121, 124, 138, 144–68; Arveragus, 27, 160–168; Aurelius, 19, 48, 49, 51, 118, 152, 156, 158–60, 162, 164n, 165, 166–8; Clerk d'Orliens, 49, 78, 149, 150, 152, 155, 157, 159, 165–8; Dorigen, 19, 27, 48, 49, 51, 52, 119–20, 149, 152, 156–67; Phebus Apollo, 156; *Knight's Tale*, 51, 165; Arcite, 51; Palamon, 51; *Miller's Tale*, 20; *Reeve's Tale*, 20; *Sir Thopas*, 146
Chestre, 20, 138–45
Chrétien, 11, 21–2, 24, 54–6, 60–3, 73–5, 117, 120, 122, 124, 148; *Arthurian Romances*: *Cligés*, 11, 21, 46–8, 57, 71, 71–3, 76, 82, 98–104, 114, 125; Emperor, 48, 72, 82, 98, 102, 103–4; Fenice, 21, 27, 48, 57, 71, 72, 76, 84, 90, 93, 98–104; Jehan, 102; Soredamors, 98; Thessala, 98, 99, 102; *Erec et Enide*, 31, 52, 64–6, 82, 84, 87–90, 110, 125, 159, 162; Erec, 31, 52, 65, 84, 88, 90, 96, 159, 162; Enide, 88, 162; *La Charrette*, 17, 19, 22, 49, 57, 76, 79–86, 93, 98, 102n, 106, 110, 114, 120, 128, 131, 159, 163; Gawain, 82, 83, 106, 115; Guenevere, 18, 80–6, 106, 128, 130, 162, 166; Lancelot, 15, 17–19, 18, 24, 49, 79, 80, 82, 93, 98, 112, 120, 128, 130, 159, 162, 163, 166, 106, 130; *Le Conte du Graal* (*Perceval*), 46, 52, 56–7, 82, 93, 98, 104–12, 136; Fisher King, 56, 106–7; Gawain, 46, 105, 109–14; Gornemant de Goorz, 106; Guigambresil, 110; Hideous Damsel (Hag), 108, 110; Perceval, 46, 52, 56, 105, 110, 114, 136; Perchevax li Galois (Perchevax li chaitus), 108; *Philomena*, 101; *Yvain*, 17, 19, 26–7, 31, 52, 57, 72–3, 76, 78, 82–4, 90–1, 93–7, 102, 112, 118, 131, 132, 134, 135, 136n, 137; Laudine, 26, 76, 84, 94, 95; Lunete, 17, 26, 76, 84, 87, 94, 135; Yvain, 19, 31, 46, 52, 83, 84, 87, 90–1, 94–8, 132, 135; vocabulary, *Conjointure*, def. of: 14–15, 76; 17, 60, 63, 65, 76, 87, 148; *Matière*, 14, 76; *Romanz*, 14; *San*, 14n, 76
Christmas, H., 53
Cistercians, 104–5
Cobham, Eleanor (duchess of Gloucester), 40
Cochrane, C.N., 67n
Colgrace, B, 38
Confessions of Egbert, 44
Conn and the Tuatha de Danaan, 108
Corrector (Bishop of Worms), 44
Crane, Susan, 21, 28, 45, 46n, 118, 119, 120, 122, 124, 125n, 126, 129n, 130n

Dante, A., 51
Davenport, W.A., 144n, 147n
Dinshaw, Carolyn, 28
Duby, George, 15–16, 121, 151–2, 162n
Dukes, Eugene, 36n, 37n

Index

Edgar, 38
Edward II, 40
Edward III, 123
Edward the Confessor, 38, 63
Edwards, Robert, 118
Egbert (*Confessions*), 39, 44
Eleanor of Aquitaine, 60
Éneas, 58
Erler, Mary, 27n
Ethelstan, 38
Eusebius, 66
Evans, Ruth, 27n
Excalibur (*see* magic)

Fagan, Theresa, 14n
Faith, 120
Fanger, Claire, 33, 50n
Faral, C.F., 74n
Fedrick, Alan, 16n, 25, 127n
Ferrante, Joan, 28, 162
Fin' Amor, 73, 82, 99–101, 126, 129, 164; Terms of: *Conoissena*, 73; *Cortesia*, 73; *Jois*, 73; *Jovens*, 73; *Valors*, 73; Finlayson, John, 30, 34n, 116
Fisher King (see Chrétien), 56, 89n, 106, 107
Flake, Timothy, 152n
Fletcher, J., 44
Fletcher, Robert, 61n
Flint, Valerie, 29, 35, 37n, 38n, 43n, 44n, 66n, 78n
Foerster, Wendelin, 57n
da Fotana, Giovanni, 50
Fourquet, Jean, 76n
Frank, Robert W., 25n
Frappier, J., 57, 88, 90, 95n, 101n, 104n
Funk and Wagnells, 32

Gaetani, Francesco, 40
Gaimar, Geoffrey, 61
Geoffrey of Monmouth, 13, 54–5, 58, 65, 117; *Historia*, 18, 24, 55, 60–3,
66–72, 147, 169; Gorlois, 72; Maximianus, 68; Merlin (*see also* magic/ magicians), 68–71; Uther, 68–9, 71–2; Vortigern, 68; Ygerna, 68, 72
Gerard of Berry (Viaticum), 164
Gereint Son of Erbin, 57, 88
Germanus (St), 68
Gervase of Tilbury, 32, 34
Gesta regum Anglorum, 62
Gildas, 61, 66, 68
Glasser, R, 77n
Golden Groove, 44
Goodich, M., 121
Gospel of Nicodemus, 57
Gower, 52n, 146
Gradon, Pamela, 21n
Graelant, 138
Gratian (*Causa 33* in *Decretum*), 43, 44
Gregory, Stewart, 127n, 128
Gregory of Tours, 66n
Griscom, Acton, 55n
Grosseteste, 44
Guthrum, 38
Guyer, F.E., 57n

Hale, W.H., 43n
Haidu, Peter, 104
Hanning, Robert, 13n, 55, 56n, 58n, 63–9, 71, 86n, 92n, 94n, 113n, 138n, 140n, 161n, 162n
Hansen, Elaine Tuttle, 28, 160
Harding, Carol, 66n
Harrowing of Hell, 57
Hatto, A.T., 16n, 25, 60, 101n
Havely, Nicholas, 163n
Henry II, 39, 57, 63
Henry VI, 40
Henry Huntington, 61
Herodotus, 67
Hincmar of Reim (*De divortio lotharii*), 43
Holmes, Ronald, 38n, 40n

Hopkins, A., 52n
Howard, Donald, 14, 15
Howlett, David, 59n
Hume, Kathryn, 148n
Hundred Years War, 60

Innocent III (pope), 40
Inquisition, 40, 41
Ivo, 43

Jackson, Rosemary, 23
James the Carthusian, 50
Jameson, F., 20n, 45
Jesus, 36
John (King), 39
John of Salisbury, 14, 33, 39
Johnson, Lesley, 27n
Jones, A.H.M., 36
Jones, Terry, 123n

Kelly, Douglas, 14n, 23, 32, 76, 169
Kieckhefer, R., 26, 29, 33n, 36n, 45, 49n, 66n, 67n, 168, 178n
Klapisch-Zuber, C., 27n
Köhler, Erich, 77
Krueger, Roberta, 28
Kyng Alisaunder, 59

de Labriolle, 66n
Lacroix, Benoit, 32n
Lai d'Haveloc, 58, 116
Lai le Freine, 148
Laistner, M.L.W., 67n
Langland, William (*Piers Plowman*), 107
Langtoft, Peter, 58
Laskaya, Anne, 28n
de Latilly, Pierre, 40
Lazarus, 36
Lay of Haveloc the Dane, 58
Lea, Henry Charles, 40
Le Goff, J., 14n, 23, 32n, 39n, 77
Lewis, C.B., 57
Lewis, C.S., 116

Libeaus Desconus, 138n
Liber juratus, 44–5
Liber visionum Marie, 34, 35
Livy, 61, 67
Loomis, C.G., 36n, 52n
Loomis, L.H., 126n
Loomis, R.S., 16, 17, 54, 79, 80n, 82n88, 90, 96n, 126n
Louis VII, 60
Louis X, 40
Lucas, Angela, 152n, 154n, 157n, 161,
Lucas, Peter, 152n, 161
Lucifer, 42
Luttrell, Claude, 16n

Maas, A.J., 42
Mabinogion, 56
MacCulloch, J.A., 34
Maddox, Donald, 71n, 104n, 109
magic, criticism, 22–26; definition of, 13, 28–35; *Fantasie*, definition of, 23–4; *Fee*, 138–9; Folklore, 32; function of, 18–20, 45–7, 74; gendered magic, 26–8; *Magic and the Everyman*, 42–5; *Magic as a Literary Tool*, 70–3; magic vocabulary: English vocabulary for magic: astronomy, 35, 48, 111, 145, 146, 149, 150n, 151, 154; *Astrologye* (astrology), 35, 48, 145, 146, 149, 150, 151, 153, 154, 155, 157; clerical magic, 145, 146, 150–6, 158; *Illusioun*, definition of, 148n, 156; 115, 118, 142, 145, 146, 147–68; *Japes*, 152, 154, 167; *Jogelrye*,152, 154; *Magyk* (M.E.), definition of, 152–4; 28, 29n, 146, 147, 156, 157, 159, 163, 164, 165; *Magyk natureel*, definition of, 152–3; 145, 146, 150, 154; *Wechcraft*, 136; French vocabulary for magic: *Charme*, 78; *Magicus*, 77;

Index

magic (*continued*):
  Merveilleux (see terms), definition of, 31; 23, 28, 76–8, 86–8, 91, 93, 96–7, 110, 114; *Mirabilis*, definition of, 31, 32; 77; *Miraculus*, definition of, 30; 34n, 77–8, 121n, 154n, 156; *Nigromance*, definition of, 31; 78; *Poisonez bevraje*, 78; magicians: Merlin, 66n, 68–9, 70, 71, 78, 142; Morgan le Fay, 27, 47, 49, 52; 78, 96; terms used in discussion: *Maleficia*, 43; *Marvellous*, 31; *Merveille*, 28, 158; *Merveilleux*, 23, 28, 31, 76–9, 86, 87–8, 91, 93, 96, 97, 110, 114; *Meschaunces* (*mischaucnce*), definition of, 154–5; 157; *Miracles* (*Myracle*), definition of, 30; 31, 36, 37, 52, 53, 69, 78, 154, 156; *Necromancy*, definition of, 30–1; 48, 78, 136, 150, 152; *Philosophre*, 155; *Sighte merverilous*, 154; *Superscticious cursednesse*, 154, 157; types of: *Aventures*, 47, 50, 63, 73, 98, 106, 108, 109, 110, 169; Bleeding Lance, 80n, 107–110, 112, 136; Excalibur, 118, 133, 166; *Graal* (*aventures*, castles, cups, and tests), 107–12; Horn, 88–9, 90; *Joie de la Cort*, 88, 89n; lances, 78, 80, 107, 112; Marvellous Bed, 110; Perilous Ford, 110, 112, 146; *Pesme Aventure*, 84, 96, 102; rings, 18, 47, 48, 76, 78, 79, 94, 118, 121, 135, 146; Sword Bridge, 19, 79, 83, 87; Water Bridge, 83; Weeping Lance, 80; Wondrous Bed, 112; Wondrous Castle, 110
Malleus maleficarum, 41
Mann, Jill, 25
Manlove, C., 24

Marcabru, 73
Marie de France, 11–13, 21, 24, 46–8, 54, 56–8, 76, 79, 85–6, 91–6, 108, 113–17, 119, 120, 122, 126, 127, 131, 132, 138–9, 142–5, 147, 149, 151, 153, 161, 163; *Lais*: *Bisclavret*, 91, 96; *Eliduc*, 108, 113; *Equitan*, 161–2; *Chevrefoil*, 48, 58, 114, 126, 146; *Lanval*, 12, 85–6, 118, 119, 138–141, 143, 144; *Les Deus Amanz*, 93–4; *Yonec*, 48, 79, 92–3, 94n, 131, 161; *L'Espurgatoire Seint Patriz*, 58
de Marigny, Enguerrand, 40
Mark (Apostle), 36
Marx, Jean, 80n
Matière de Bretagne, 60, 61
Matilda of Artois, 40
Matthew (Apostle), 36
Matthews, David, 115, 123
McAlindon, T.A., 25
McEntire, Sandra, 150
McKisack, May, 122n
McKitterick, Rosamund, 63n, 69n
McNamara, Joann & Susan Wemple, 27n
Mehl, Dieter, 115n, 116–7
Mesura, 81–2, 91
Mills, Maldwyn, 11n, 131n, 144
Minnis, A., 149n, 150, 155, 158, 159
Morgan, Gerald, 46–7n
Muir, Lynette, 17

Nennius, 61, 68
North, J.D., 156–7n
Novak, John Ballaz, 38n
Nykrog, Per, 61, 64n, 65n, 79, 80n

Octavian, 138n
Opitz, Claudia, 27n
Oresme, Nichole, 50
Orosius, 66
Ovid, 56n, 57n, 58, 161

Owen, D.D.R., 57, 65n, 73n, 80,
    81n, 84n, 85n, 87n, 88n, 89n, 96,
    98n, 99n, 100, 101, 102, 104n,
    105n, 109n, 111n, 112n, 132n

Patch, H.R., 51
Patterson, Lee, 122, 165
Peters, Edward, 43
Pettersson, Olof, 36
Philip IV, 40
Picatrix, 44–5
Pickering, E.P., 51n
Piramus and Tisbé, 56n, 58
Pliny the Elder, 35
Polybius, 67
Prouder, 57

Rabanus (*Poenitentiale ad Deribaldum*), 44
Rabkin, Erec, 23
Ramsey, Lee, 20, 74, 126n
Richard II, 151, 188n
Robert Mannyng of Brunne (*Principal Libri Poenitentiales/Handbooks of Penance*), 44, 58, 125–6
Robertson, D.W., 64n, 65n
Romance of Horn, 59, 116
Roman de la Rose, 161
Roman de Renard, 56n, 58
Roman de Toute Chevalrie, 59
Roman Empire, 36
Romances: Beyond Celtic, 16–18;
    Celtic sources, 16–18, 45, 54,
    74–5, 77, 79–81, 88–9, 95–6,
    107–8, 136; Chaucer and rom.,
    146–7; Definition of, 15; New
    form of 14–16, 73–5; use magic,
    18–20; *Romance of Horn*, 59, 116
Rumble, T.C., 129n
Rychner, Jean, 13n, 86n, 92n, 94n,
    113n, 140n, 161n

Salisbury, J., 39
Sawyer, P.H., 39n

Scot, Michael, 33, 48n
Seneca, 35
Shotwell, James, 67n
Siebers, Tobin, 23n
Simpson, Jane, 150n
Sir Degaré, 148
Sir Gawain and the Green Knight,
    25, 38n, 46n, 48–9, 105, 107n,
    118, 119, 120, 138, 143, 144,
    146, 147
Sir Landevale, 138–40
Sir Launfal, 119, 138n, 144; Launfal,
    119, 120, 138, 139, 141–5
Sir Perceval of Galles, 131
Sir Orfeo, 148
Smithers, G.V., 58n
Southern, R.W., 14n, 49, 63
Southwell, Thomas (Canon of St
    Peter's Chapel, Westminster), 40
Spearing, A.C., 25, 144
Staines, David, 56n.
Standbury, Sarah, 27n
Stevens, J.E., 48, 78, 79n
Strohm, Paul, 20, 21n, 151n
Sturm-Maddox, S., 89n
Summis desiderates, 41, 42
Sworn Book of Honorius, 34
Sylvester II (Pope), 62
Syr Launfal, 11, 12, 46–7, 115, 121,
    124, 137–45, 141; Artour, 142;
    Gwennere, 141–2; Launfal, 119,
    120, 139, 141–5; Marlyn, 142;
    Olyroun, 138; Tryamour, 141–3

Templars, 40–1
Theodore of Canterbury, 38
Thomas of Erceldoune, 125
Thomas, Keith, 37, 43n, 44n, 53,
    66, 121, 136n
Thomas of Kent, 59
Thorndike, Lynn, 29, 30n, 33n,
    34n, 40, 48n, 66, 153n
Thucydides, 67
Tilbury, 32, 34

Index

Topsfield, L.T., 73n, 74n, 80, 83n, 89n, 97, 98, 99n, 100n, 101, 104–8, 109n
Tout, T.F., 150–1
Traytour, 121, 142
Tristan texts, 58, 83, 114, 118, 126, 149, 163; King Mark, 50, 60; Tristan (Tantris), 21, 50, 83, 99, 100–2, 126, 128, 148, 162, 163; Ysolt, 60, 100; Beroul, 16n, 25, 101, 126; 127n; Eilhart, 101; *Folie Tristan*, 116, 126; Gottfried von Strassburg, 16n, 21, 25, 46, 50, 76, 126, 130n, 148; Thomas of Britain, 11, 46, 57–60, 100–2, 114, 122, 125–9, 148; Tristran, 127–9; Iseut, 21, 83, 99, 100, 101, 102, 127, 128, 149, 162; Thomas of England, 100, 125–6; *Sir Tristrem*, 11, 46–7, 115, 124, 125–31, 136–7; Hodain, 129–30; Tristrem, 127–31, 136; Ysonde, 127, 128, 130, 131; Ysonde of the White Hands, 127; *Syr Tristrem*, 121; *Tristran*, 11, 16n, 46, 100, 101, 114, 116, 125ñ9; *Trowth (trouthe)*, definition of, 118; 47, 113, 114, 120–1, 124, 125, 142, 143, 148, 150, 152n, 165
Tryamour, 141–3

Vaughan, W., 44n
Victor (St), 44
Vinaver, Eugene, 14, 17
Virgil, 56n, 57, 61, 67
Vita Sancti Gildae (Caradoc of Llancarvan), 57, 61
Vogel, C., 44n

Wace, 13, 18, 55, 62–5, 70–2, 95–6, 117; *Roman de Brut*, 18, 55–8, 61, 63–4, 70–2; *Roman de Rou*, 91n, 95
Wack, Mary, 122, 164n, 165n
Wallace, David, 149n
Ward, H.L.D., 138n
Weiss, Judith, 58n, 59n, 64n, 70n, 116
William of Auvergne, 44
William the Conqueror, 39
William of Malmesbury, 62, 61
William of Newburgh, 62
Williams, Elizabeth, 139, 143
Wilson, Anne, 133n
Wimsatt, James, 12
Wycliffe (Lollards), 41–2

Ywain and Gawain, 11, 20, 47, 78, 115, 121, 124, 131–8; Alundyne, 121, 131, 135; Colgrevance, 134, 135; Lunet, 135, 137; Ywain, 96, 119, 120, 131–8

ALSO FROM FOUR COURTS PRESS

The Lost Tradition
Essays on Middle English Alliterative Poetry

JOHN SCATTERGOOD

Four stresses, a line broken in two by a caesura, and a pattern of alliteration linking the two half-lines were features of the staple manner of Anglo-Saxon verse. And this tradition of writing continued into post-Conquest England, sometimes providing a distinctive alternative to rhymed or stanzaic verse, sometimes coexisting with it, occasionally a little uneasily. The late efflorescence of alliterative writing in fourteenth-century and early fifteenth-century England is remarkable for its range and quality, and this is the focus of this collection of essays, five of which have not been published before.

There are four essays on some of the lyrics preserved in London, British Library MS Harley 2253, two on *Winner and Waster* and *The Parlement of the Thre Ages*, both of which are preserved in London, British Library MS Additional 31042, and two on poems from London, British Library MS Cotton Nero A. x – one on *Sir Gawain and the Green Knight* and contemporary knighthood, and one on *Patience* and the question of obedience to authority. One essay focuses on an incident in *Piers Plowman* dealing with the lawlessness of the gentry. Another looks at *Pierce the Ploughman's Crede* and Lollard attitudes to written texts. And another considers the clerical agenda of *St Erkenwald* and the writing of history. Two related texts – *Richard the Redeles* and *Mum and the Sothsegger* – are analysed, along with Gower's *Cronica Tripartita*, as verdicts on the reign of Richard II and as expressions of the determination of poets to comment on political affairs in contexts which sought to silence them. Finally, what may have been the last great English alliterative poem, *Scotish Ffeilde*, is considered in relation to other contemporary poems on the Battle of Flodden of 1513.

John Scattergood is Professor of English at Trinity College, Dublin.

ISBN 1-85182-565-7 hbk

ALSO FROM FOUR COURTS PRESS

Nation, Court and Culture
New Essays on Fifteenth-century English Poetry

HELEN COONEY EDITOR

The fifteenth century in England saw a radical shift in the idea of England as a nation and the nature of 'Englishness' itself, a sometimes discomfiting re-definition of the concept of the 'court', and an efflorescence of some literary genres and modes together with a crisis in others. This collection of essays seeks to focus on concepts of nation, court and culture as these were treated in English poetry of the period, and the studies included are variously political, cartological, textual, and thematic in orientation. The volume is driven by a desire to examine the literature of what has until recently been a neglected period but with reference to political and cultural issues which are prominent in much current literary scholarship. It includes contributions from several of the leading international scholars in the field of late-medieval English literature.

Contents: The idea of Englishness in the fifteenth century: *Derek Pearsall (Harvard U.)*; The Libelle of Englyshe Polycye: the nation and its place: *John Scattergood (TCD)*; Writing for the nation? Fifteenth-century literary miscellanies: *Phillipa Hardman (U. Reading)*; Hoccleve and the 'Court': *J.A. Burrow (Bristol U.)*; Thomas Hoccleve and manuscript culture: *John Thompson (QUB)*; 'Forto compleyne she had gret desire': the grievances of fifteenth-century dream-visions: *Julia Boffey (U. London)*; Fifteenth-century complaints and Duke Humphrey's Wives: *Tony Davenport (U. London)*; A reassessment of the courtly poems of John Lydgate: *Sue Bianco (U. York)*; Skelton's *Bowge of Court* and the crisis of allegory in late-medieval England: *Helen Cooney (U. Nottingham)*; English lyrics and carols of the fifteenth century: *Douglas Gray (Oxford U.)*.

ISBN 1-85182-566-5 hbk

ALSO FROM FOUR COURTS PRESS

The Siege of Jerusalem *in its Physical, Literary and Historical Contexts*

BONNIE MILLAR

The *Siege of Jerusalem* is a late fourteenth-century poem probably of 'extreme West Yorkshire provenance'. Scholars here tended to marginalize it, dismissing it as derivative, decadent, unnecessarily violent, precious, anti-Semitic. In this first full-length study of the poem Dr Millar challenges traditional interpretations. Not a history, not a religious narrative, more a romance than anything else, the *Siege* encourages the audience to reconsider the nature of Christian-Jewish relations, the validity of chivalric ideals, the justification for war, etc. It is a beautifully written poem, deserving of a better scholarly press.

Bonnie Millar is a graduate of Trinity College, Dublin and of the University of Nottingham, where she completed PhD research in 1999.

ISBN 1-85182-506-1 hbk

ALSO FROM FOUR COURTS PRESS

Wisdom and the Grail
The Image of the Vessel in the Queste del Saint Graal *and Malory's* Tale of the Sankgreal

ANNE MARIE D'ARCY

Dr D'Arcy investigates the symbol of the Holy Grail in the *Queste del Saint Graal,* a branch of the Vulgate prose cycle of Arthurian romances, and Thomas Malory's redaction of this Old French text, *The Tale of the Sankgreal.* While most previous studies of the *Sankgreal* have concentrated on the question of language and meaning as regards to Malory and his relationship with his source, this study concentrates on that of image and meaning. It analyzes the iconographic divergences between the treatment of the Holy Grail in the haunting thirteenth-century clerical narrative and its vibrant fifteenth-century lay offspring.

ISBN 1-85182-496-0 hbk